GRAPHIC ARTISTS GUILD HANDBOOK
PRICING & ETHICAL
GUIDELINES
5TH EDITION

Editorial

Project directors:
Volker E. H. Antoni
Dean Ellis
D. K. Holland
Jerry McConnell
Jeff Seaver
Simms Taback

Project coordinator:
D. K. Holland

Consultants:
Volker E. H. Antoni
Tad Crawford
Joel L. Hecker
Arie Kopelman
Hank De Leo

Copy editor:
Hank De Leo

Design

Design:
Peter Ross
Ross Design Associates

Design Production:
Laurel Daunis
Ross Design Associates
Nancy Ng

Cover illustration:
Gerard Huerta

Design consultation:
Seymour Chwast
Pushpin Lubalin Peckolick

Editorial Production:
Rachel Bird
Caroline Ginesi
Margi Trapani
Peggy Ann White

Typography:
Aire Graphics
I, Claudia

Printing:
Zarett Graphics

*Distributors to the trade in
the United States:*
Robert Silver Associates
95 Madison Avenue
New York, NY 10016

*Distributors to the trade in
Canada:*
General Publishing Co. Ltd.
30 Lesmill Road
Don Mills, Ontario, Canada M3B 2T6

GRAPHIC ARTISTS GUILD HANDBOOK
PRICING & ETHICAL
GUIDELINES

CONTENTS

Standard Contracts

Business Management

Reference

We wish to thank the following members and consultants for their assistance in the preparation of the *Guidelines:*

Volker E. H. Antoni
artist business management consultant, writer

Rick Anwyl
graphic designer

David Archambault
illustrator

Laura Ausubel
textile designer

Brent Baylor
comp illustrator

Noel Becker
representative

Shelley Beckler
graphic designer

Ed Benguiat
hand letterer

Ben Benson
hand letterer

Irving Bogen
graphic designer

Charles Boyter
medical illustrator

Lynn Braswell
book designer

Alice Brickner
illustrator

Ellen Brief
textile designer

Ginger Brown
illustrator

Tom Carnase
hand letterer

Marsha Camera
graphic designer

Seymour Chwast
graphic designer

Elizabeth Çook
textile designer

Gil Cowley
art director

Doug Cramer
medical illustrator

Tad Crawford
attorney

Ray Cruz
hand letterer

Roland Dacombs
comp illustrator

Zelda Dana
needleart designer

Stewart David
calligrapher

Hank De Leo
illustrator

Sherry DeLeon
needleart designer

Joe DelGaudio
graphic designer

Diane Dillon
child's book illustrator

Susan Dooha
organizer of professional graphic artists

Michael Doret
hand letterer

Dean Ellis
illustrator

Stephanie Farago
illustrator

David Gatti
calligrapher

Dick Gill
comp illustrator

Jan Giolito
textile designer

Susan Gray
illustrator

Sam Gross
cartoonist

Joann Grossman
needleart designer

Jacquie Hann
child's book illustrator

Joel Hecker
attorney

Jim Heimann
illustrator

Jacqui Henderson
needleart designer

Lynn Hertzman
textile designer

Robert Heindel
illustrator

D. K. Holland
organizer of professional graphic artists

Walter Hortens
cartographer/illustrator

Gerald Huerta
hand letterer

Zuelia Ann Hurt
needleart designer

Brooks Jones
graphic designer

Ruth J. Katz
needleart designer

Deborah Kaufman
director, Good Works

Peggy Keating
fashion illustrator

Gregory King
illustrator

Jim Kingston
illustrator

Alice Koeth
calligrapher

Arie Kopelman
attorney

Kitty Krupat
organizer, District 65, UAW

Jane Lander
Joint Ethics Committee

Cecily Lang
illustrator

Gail Litvak
needleart designer

Shelley Lowell
graphic designer

Richard Lyons
graphic designer

Linda Mancini
graphic designer

Susan Mayer
graphic designer

Kathy McCarthy
illustrator

Jerry McConnell
illustrator

Carol Michelson
needlearts designer

Rohit Modi
graphic designer

Paula Monroe
calligrapher

Carol Morley
scientific/medical illustrator

Barbara Muccio
needleart designer

Barbara Nessim
illustrator

Tom Nikosey
hand letterer

Linwood B. Peale
comp illustrator

Scott Pike
comp illustrator

Peter Ross
graphic designer

Craig Russell
graphic designer

Gerard Salvio
organizer of professional animators

Dan Schuder
technical illustrator

Kitty Stavros
employment expert

Jeff Seaver
illustrator

Ed Seltzer
textile designer

Chas B. Slackman
illustrator

Carol Spier
needleart designer

Simms Taback
illustrator

Marvin Tannenberg
cartoonist

Frank Truglio
retoucher

Sam Viviano
illustrator

Karen Watson
illustrator

Anne Weinbrenner
textile designer

Ricci Weinstein
graphic designer

Gregory Wier-Quiton
fashion illustrator

Bob Winkler
graphic illustrator

Harry Winters
hand letterer

Ron Wolin
organizer of
professional cartoonists

Jeahyee Wong
calligrapher

Doyald Young
hand letterer

Mary Galaty
administrative assistant

Judith Yourman
graphic designer

and the thousand
anonymous Guild
members and
nonmembers who
aided us by com-
pleting the pricing
survey that was
the basis for most
of our pricing data.

This book is dedicated to Debbie Holland,
whose energy and vision made it possible.

PREFACE

This fifth edition of the *Graphic Artists Guild Handbook: Pricing & Ethical Guidelines* summarizes the best thinking by leading graphic arts practitioners on how to arrive at fair prices and maintain fair business conditions.

All prices and trade customs were determined through the most thorough and widely distributed national survey of professional artists ever attempted in the graphics communications field. The material included in this book is intended to provide a framework for competent, publishable work delivered under mutually understood terms. Weighted against all the variables of an assignment, the *Guidelines* should provide a point of departure for buyer and seller to arrive at just compensation for the work at hand.

It is not the intent of this document to suggest minimum or maximum prices. The Guild is mindful of the newcomer struggling to establish financial security and of the fledgling company seeking to survive against stronger competition. It is also aware of the established professional whose reputation enables him or her to command fees commensurate with the demands on his or her time and talent.

The *Guidelines* is continuously updated to include the latest information on our constantly changing industry. You are encouraged to send your ideas for the book to: Pricing and Ethical Guidelines Committee, c/o Graphic Artists Guild, 30 East 20th Street, New York, New York 10003.

Our fifth edition includes new sections on computer graphics, salaried artists and negotiation, plus updates on pricing for our regular sections.

Beyond the goal of establishing equitable pricing structures, the Guild is committed to raising the ethical standards of the profession. Abuses of industry standards sometimes stem from ignorance of established criteria, but many stem from attempts to take advantage of the unwary, the inexperienced and the unorganized. It is the Guild's aim to change these conditions.

Jeff Seaver
President
National Graphic Artists Guild

How to Use the Guidelines

This book provides both graphic artists and their clients with a current compilation of the going rates and professional business practices applied throughout the industry. The growing complexity of uses, fee arrangements, and business and financial considerations now makes information of this type essential for all participants in the field.

Part 1: How Artwork Is Priced provides an overview of the many factors that must be taken into account by all parties pricing works of design or illustration. The discussion shows how to weigh such diverse elements as usage and reuses, per diem fees, royalties on merchandise for sale, billable expenses, special time demands arising out of unique style or deadline requirements, and overall size of project or print order. The use of advertising page rates as a basis for compensation in advertising or editorial work is also evaluated.

Part 2: How Artwork Is Commissioned examines the role of representatives, studios, and brokers. Details are provided on how these intermediaries secure assignments for their graphic artists and what kinds of contractual arrangements are most common between graphic artist and agent in many crucial matters, including payment for and the protection of artwork.

Part 3: Business and Legal Practices when Artwork Is Commissioned is a concise summary of virtually all current practices in the field. It focuses on the enhanced status of graphic artists under the Copyright Revision Act of 1976 and the bundle of rights to be negotiated on every assignment. It then covers the eleven specific issues to be resolved in every purchase order or contract covering an assignment, and the eight issues to be resolved in every royalty agreement (which are becoming commonplace in merchandising fields such as posters, greeting cards, and the like). Other matters carefully reviewed include evaluation of trade practices that now call for return of original art to the artist, payment for all time expended in the form of rejection and cancellation fees, and liabilities for lost art or portfolios. Evolving practices in the area of credit lines for all graphic artists are considered, and the discussion concludes with a guide to collecting money when difficulties arise.

Part 4: Pricing is in many respects the heart of the book. It covers the going rates in virtually all design and illustration specialties. Both art buyers and graphic artists should note that there has been a substantial increase in rates since publication of the prior editions of this book. Two factors are at work here: (1) the rates in the current edition are based on a survey that covered many more thousands of professionals than in the past; and (2) the elapsed time of more than two years between the two editions witnessed a total inflation throughout the nation's economy which exceeded 25 percent.

Illustration prices cover comparative fees for all media in Advertising Illustration (including magazine, newspaper, brochure, catalogue, mailer, point of purchase, packaging, transit-car, film, audiovisual, and motion picture and theater posters); Comps, Animatics, and TV Storyboards; Institutional and Corporate Illustration (including in-house organs, calendars, annual reports, and company magazines); Book Jacket Illustration; Book Illustration (including adult, juvenile, childrens books, and textbooks); Editorial Illustration (including national, regional, and trade magazines and newspapers) Fashion Illustration; Record Album Cover Illustration; Medical Illustration; Technical Illustration; Novelty and Miscellaneous Products Illustration; and Limited Edition Prints.

A highlight of most of the specialty sections above is that the work functions and trade practices unique to that field of illustration are spelled out in detail. In this manner both art buyers and graphic artists will better comprehend the demands on time and talent necessitating the range of fees being paid in each area.

Design prices cover the following areas in like manner: General Graphic Design (including corporate reports and brochures, magazine and newspaper advertising, logos, record album covers, posters, and point of purchase); Book Design (including text, trade, and juvenile books); Book Jacket Design (including hardcover, trade paperback, and mass market); Letterforms (including corporate, type houses, and publications); Textile Design (including apparel, decorative and home furnishing, wovens and knits, rugs, and special orders); and Needleart Design. Freelance Cartooning; Animation; Production; Retouching; terms and prices and Staff Salaries in advertising, corporate, studio, publishing, broadcast, textile, and animation are also covered.

As with illustration, a unique element of the Design Prices section is the detail provided on the precise functions and trade practices of virtually all of the specialists listed above. Again, this should render more understandable the time and talent demands underlying the fee and compensation structures found throughout the industry and presented here.

Part 5: Ethical Guidelines explains aspects of the Graphic Artists Guild's work in support of the professional and economic needs of graphic artists throughout the nation. Included are: the Joint Ethics Committee Code of Fair Practice (subscribed to by leading organizations of both graphic artists and art buyers); the Guild's Grievance Committee (an entity members may call on for assistance on business and collection matters); the Guild's Art Contest Guidelines (to assure participation within the limits of fairness to all parties); the Guild's Position Paper on Work for Hire (the practical reasons why such contract provisions are not acceptable to graphic artists), and the Guild's Position Paper on Cancellation Fees (to assure reasonable compensation for all work efforts of graphic artists).

Part 6: Standard Contract Forms is the most complete set of forms ever assembled for all work specialties in the industry. The forms are designed to handle most of the *basic* contract issues that arise between graphic artists and client, although special situations (such as when royalties are involved) may require amplification or modification. These twelve forms include model contracts for both graphic artists and art buyers.

First, there is an artist-agent model agreement form. Then, for art buyers, there is an all-purpose order form and a special purchase order form for magazine illustration.

For illustrators there is a general confirmation of assignment form (which can be made applicable to any commissioned work) and an invoice that assures that the terms agreed to on the assignment confirmation form are reinforced. For graphic designers there is a single form that covers the estimate, assignment confirmation, and invoice. For textile designers three separate forms cover confirmation of commissioned work, the invoice for work sold, and agreements with agents. Finally, for needlepoint designers there is a form for confirming commissioned work and an invoice to reinforce the agreed terms.

In addtion to a useful glossary of terms, the final sections of the book provide more information about the Guild and how its work serves the interests of graphic artists and art buyers everywhere. Continuing improvement in professional practices is promoted by the Guild as it provides all participants in the industry with such vital data as can be found in this book.

How Artwork Is Priced

Graphic art is commissioned in highly competitive and specialized markets—there are *no* standard prices. Prices depend upon several factors: the type of work required; the complexity of the art; the use to which it will be put; the artist's reputation and "track record"; etc. Actual prices are the result of negotiations between the artist and the buyer, taking into consideration all the relevant factors. The guidelines for pricing vary from discipline to discipline, so the discussion that follows should be amplified by reading the appropriate sections on pricing for each discipline.

Accordingly, although the prices listed in our *Guidelines* are based on extensive nationwide surveys, they are not meant to be taken literally as standard prices. The nature of the art market makes this impossible—nor do we think it necessarily desirable. Our figures are *benchmarks* which individuals may use as beginning points in establishing prices according to the particular relevant factors.

These figures reflect market conditions and do not necessarily represent what the Guild considers proper compensation to the artist. Some art markets may be depressed or overcrowded and therefore provide inadequate compensation and substandard employment conditions to artists. For example, the Guild is making special efforts in the textile design and children's book illustration fields to improve the conditions that have previously existed.

Price determined by use

The most general principle for determining the price of artwork is that the price should be related to the value of the intended *use* the buyer will make of the art. This means the more extensive the use, the greater the compensation to the artist. Some inexperienced art buyers are shocked by such a concept. They assume that they are buying a *product* at one flat price, with which they can do whatever they wish upon payment. But artists normally sell only certain *rights* to the use of their creative work. *The more rights sold, the greater the compensation required.*

Artists should take their basic standard to be that of licensing "first reproduction rights" or "one time reproduction rights" for such and such specific use. Reuses, extended uses, differing uses, etc., should receive additional compensation. "Exclusive" rights should command yet higher compensation. Greater compensation is due for "unlimited rights," "foreign rights," etc. "All rights" must command the highest compensation.

In many cases, such as corporate logos, advertising, product identity, etc., the buyer may genuinely need to acquire most, or all, rights. Buyers should be aware that artists must be adequately compensated for such extensive grants of rights to the use of their work. In other cases the buyer has no need for such extensive rights. If the buyer is asking for excessive rights, the artist should point out that all additional rights require additional compensation and then negotiate only those rights which the buyer specifically needs and is willing to pay for.

If buyers are asking for "all rights" or "work for hire" to protect themselves from competitive or embarrassing uses of the work, a limited rights contract can be worked out that prohibits the artist from making uses that are in fact competitive or embarrassing.

The chart of Media Usage demonstrates how usage can be narrowed or broadened. The implication of the chart is, again, that greater usage commands greater compensation. Any usage category can be given restrictions as to duration of use or number of uses and the geographic area in which usage is permitted. Also, the usage should be specifically limited to one title or product. And within each category, there are frequently subcategories too numerous to list here. The grant of usage rights might very well refer to the specific category or sub-category of intended use.

Media Usage

Advertising
Animation
Billboards
Brochures
Catalogs
Consumer magazines
Newspapers
Product packaging
Point of purchase
Trade magazines
Television
Other

Editorial or Journalism
Anthology
Book jackets
Consumer magazines
Encyclopedias
Film strips
Newspapers
Newspaper supplements
Television
Textbooks
Trade books
Trade magazines
Other

Industrial
Album covers
Annual reports
Brochures
Film strips
House organs
Trade slide shows
Other

Manufacturing
Apparel
Domestics
Home furnishings
Jewelry
Novelty items
Paper products
Other

Promotion
Booklets
Brochures
Calendars
Cards
Posters
Press kits
Other

Royalties

A good way of establishing price in relation to use is by a royalty arrangement. This is the accepted method of payment in the book publishing industry. A royalty is actually a percentage paid to the artist based on the total of the buyer's sales. Royalty arrangements must always include a basic "up-front" payment to the artist as an advance against royalties, otherwise the artist is working on speculation with no monetary commitment from the buyer. Royalties are not applicable in cases where the use of the art does not involve any resale or where a resale is difficult to determine.

Licensing

When a design or illustration is developed for resale and marketing as a product, it is usually done under a licensing agreement. B. Kliban's cats, Peanuts, the Muppets and Strawberry Shortcake are examples of products that have been licensed successfully.

Peanuts and the Muppets were already famous cartoon characters and were licensed very easily. Strawberry Shortcake was a character that was carefully developed by a major company and was marketed with a strategic and well-financed advertising campaign specifically for the purposes of licensing. These characters were sold to decorate all kinds of novelty items, clothing, dishes, calendars and posters; all of which are very common forms of licensing.

In the fashion and textile industries, name designers like Ralph Lauren, Gloria Vanderbilt and Jack Prince market their special design collections (usually called "marketing concepts") to mass markets under a licensing agreement. It is difficult for lesser name designers to market their designs in a similar manner, but it is becoming a more common practice.

Recently new companies have formed to specialize in representing licensed properties. They plan marketing support for these products through animated movies, TV series, publishing ventures, records and other forms of promotion.

A license is an agreement whereby the artist, designer or developer who owns the rights to the art permits another party, usually the client, to use the art for a limited specific purpose, for a specified time, in return for a fee or royalty. At the expiration of the license, the right to use the property reverts to the owner.

Payment under licensing agreements normally take the form of royalties. Where the product or artwork is to be sold commercially, royalties are usually a percentage of the profit or retail price.

To provide for sufficient payment, the license should be subject to certain sales or production requirements that insure the artist or owner the royalty payment agreed to by both parties. If these requirements are not met, the license should terminate. In the event that this happens, the artist or owner is free to license the work to others for the same or similar uses.

Artists and owners should insist upon proper quality control of the product to prevent inferior goods and to maximize sales potential. It is up to the artist, in consideration of client needs, to set those standards. In the event that the client or manufacturer fails to meet these standards, the license should terminate.

The duration of a license must be clearly spelled out. Many licenses are for relatively short, fixed terms with renewal clauses based upon successful performance. This type of agreement is fair to both parties since it provides for continued license of the art only when the artist is assured of obtaining payment and the client is satisfied with the product.

It is important to differentiate between rights granted and those retained, since there are usually multiple markets available and more than one license agreement for a particular piece of artwork.

The artist or owner is entitled to periodic accounting statements with details of sales made and royalties due. And, the artist should have the right to audit the appropriate books and records to verify the statements and to insure that payment is forthcoming.

Proper copyright notice must accompany the distributed art and, where possible, name credit should be given to the artist. This can be written into the licensing agreement.

Licensing can be a very lucrative source of revenue because it is on-going with all rights ultimately returning to the artist. The terms of the licensing agreement should be carefully set forth in writing and the performance of the license should be monitored. It is advisable to retain an attorney before signing a licensing agreement.

Per diem rates

Often artists are hired on a per diem or daily-rate basis. The Guild feels this is a perfectly acceptable method of employment provided the day rate is adequate and just compensation for the work involved and is agreed on beforehand by both artist and buyer.

The artist should always have in mind a basic per-day rate for his or her work. This, together with an estimate of the number of days needed to complete the work, art direction, consultation, travel, etc., can also give one a rough estimate for pricing. *A word of caution:* some jobs look deceptively simple and even the most experienced artists sometimes encounter greater expenditures of time than first anticipated. Questions concerning delivery time, degree of finish, complexity, expenses and responsibilities in general ought to be generously estimated and it should be made clear that an estimate is merely that and is not binding.

Hourly rate formula

The hourly rate formula is a method used to figure pricing, as opposed to "the going rate" or the guesswork of supply and demand.

The hourly rate takes into consideration factors that make up an artist's overhead such as rent, utilities, salaries, benefits, promotion, outside professional services, equipment, transportation, office and art supplies, business taxes and entertainment. In order to come up with an hourly rate, divide yearly overhead costs by 900 hours or whatever total billable hours you feel you will work in a year (based on a 35 hour week, 50 week year). The number used by many accountants for a year's total work hours is 1800. However, for self-employed artists, a great deal of time is spent on work activities that can't be billed to a client, like writing proposals, working on self-promotion, billing clients, etc. For example, dividing an overhead figure of $100,000 by 1000 billable hours would produce a billing of $100 an hour to break even.

When estimating an hourly rate, a quick multiplication of the minimum number of hours a project will verify whether the project will make money, lose money or break even. At that point, the artist has the option, if necessary, of negotiating for more money or paring down the project to meet a realistic time projection.

Design studios usually have two hourly rates: the principals' and the employees'. The difference is the salary level. For example, in the graphic design sections, the Principal hourly rate is an average of $50-100 and the studio staff hourly rate is $25-50.

Page-rate pricing

Page-rate pricing is a method of pricing determined by a percentage of the advertising page rate of a given publication. Therefore, it is directly plugged into the same pricing system used by the publication and its advertisers and uses a vocabulary already familiar to the client. The fee is automatically tied into inflationary rises due to the spiraling costs of paper, printing, and mailing (as the page rate rises, so will the fee).

It is clear that page rates vary according to the nature and circulation of a magazine. These rates provide a good barometer of the magazine's resources. *Reader's Digest*, for example, charges $90,500 (Jan.1, 1984) for a one-page black-and-white advertisement. Obviously, the *Digest* delivers a potential market to the advertisers that make this cost worthwhile. A page in *Forbes* costs $20,280. A page in *Business Week* goes for $24,120. Page-rate pricing means that fees paid for artwork ought to reflect these different costs.

This method of pricing is best suited to the so-called *higher priced markets* when a higher fee is more appropriate than otherwise recommended in the *Guidelines*. However, it should always be used in conjunction with the appropriate guideline figures *(see Note in chart below)*. Suggested percentages for page-rate pricing:

Page Rate pricing

Editorial		Advertising	
B&W page	PR* × .10	B&W page	PR × .125
B&W spread	PR × .125	B&W spread	PR × .135
Color cover	PR × .15	Color page	PR × .1675
Color page	PR × .13	Color spread	PR × .175
Color spread	PR × .14	*PR = Page Rate.	

	Business Week	Inc.	New York
Circulation	770,000	402,000	422,819
Non-bleed B&W page rate	$23,330.00	$17,220.00	$10,860.00
Editorial			
B&W page × .1	$2,333.00	$1,722.00	$1,086.00
B&W spread × .125	2,916.25	2,152.50	1,357.50
Color cover × .15	3,499.50	2,583.00	1,629.00
Color page × .13	3,032.90	2,238.50	1,411.80
Color spread × .175	4,082.75	3,013.50	1,900.50

Page-rate pricing formula applied to 1983 rates for *Business Week, Inc.* and *New York* magazines for a one-page, single insertion, black & white non-bleed page.

Reuse and extended use of artwork

Artwork purchased for a specific use should not be reused or adapted for purposes other than originally planned without additional compensation to the artist. If this possibility exists at the time of purchase, it should be so stated and the price adjusted accordingly. If reuse or adaptation occurs after purchase, the buyer should negotiate reasonable additional compensation with the artist. Whenever adaptation requires the services of an artist, and the creator has performed to the buyer's satisfaction, the artist should be given the opportunity to revise his or her own work.

Complexity of style

Consideration should be given by the artist and buyer to the diversity of style involved. Some styles and techniques require considerable time to execute even though they appear simple.

Print orders

Consideration should be given to the contemplated print order in the case of publishing or, in the case of advertising, to the contemplated space orders, quality and circulation of media. Large print orders require commitments by publishers for paper, printing, binding, and distribution, while large space usage in widely circulated quality media requires substantial outlays by advertisers. The price of artwork to be used should reflect these considerations.

Inflation

During periods of sharp inflationary rises the Guild recommends that the government price index on cost of living increases, for the date of publication of this edition, be added to the figures contained herein. For example, on Jan. 1, 1979, the rate for a one-page black-and-white advertisement in *Reader's Digest* was $62,000, in *Forbes* $10,210 and in *Business Week* it was $18,500. When compared to the Jan. 1, 1981 rates given on page 15, we can see how advertising page rates have increased 20 to 40 percent in two years to at least keep pace with inflation. It might be worthwhile to review whether your prices have been increasing at least as fast as inflation.

Unusual time demands

Deadlines requiring the artist to work unreasonable hours over weekends, nights and holidays should be taken into consideration when negotiating fees. Whatever the reasons for unusual time demands, the artist should not be expected to produce acceptable work at regular rates when the buyer fully expects to pay overtime rates for typography, printing, and all other services produced outside normal working hours.

Inordinate costs

Inordinate but necessary costs of producing a job—such as model fees, prop rental, consultation, research time and travel expenses—should be recognized as negotiable items in pricing. Reimbursement for these elements has been recognized accepted in photographic assignments. Assemblage, for example, may require substantial outlays for rental or purchase of elements, plus photographic fees, to achieve the desired result. In cases where the artist and/ or designer is required to make substantial commitments of large sums for type, photostats, model fees, etc., it is customary to charge a markup in the range of 15 to 25 percent on such commitments to cover overhead and provide adequate cash flow.

Consultation

Consultation must be adequately compensated. The artist can estimate the hourly or daily rate at his or her price level and propose a consultation fee comparable to time away from productive work. It is not uncommon, especially for a brief consultation to solve a particular problem, for the consultation fee to be substantially in excess of what an hourly rate would total.

The nature of the project, proposed usage, unusual time demands, travel requirements and similar factors govern the setting of the consultation fee. Both artist and client should require a written contract covering compensation, the scope of the work, fees for consultation beyond the initial assignment, ownership of artwork created in the consultation process, credit, and any other issues likely to arise.

Large projects

L arge and substantial orders may carry lower per-unit prices than single or smaller orders. The reason for this is that large projects sometimes allow for efficiency and time saving. In such cases, lower prices are in keeping with standard business practices.

Buyer's budget

B udgets break down into different categories depending on the *bottomline* method of determining value: quality or price.

Most artists can tell from the budget, if revealed, which the client has chosen, although the client may not have chosen wittingly. Clients (graphic designers as well as art directors and corporate clients) either refer to the going rate by using this book, or the *ASMP Business Practices Guide* for photography to budget for quality. Clients also use the budget for the last similar project, or ask a colleague for pricing ranges.

The problem with any project budget is projection: exactly what is needed for the project and how much it will cost. Previous budgets only show what the last person hired charged for a similar project. Items such as inflation, new concepts, new talent and new expenses create too many variables to budget accurately.

Another method of budgeting is a yearly projected arts budget which places a value on the entire year's graphics activity. This system, while it allows for flexibility in the short run, can produce some stark graphic pieces towards the end of a fiscal year.

In any art, mechanical or printing budget, the client must consider what is generally billable. The contract section of the *Guidelines* offers a listing of practically every billable item (refer to pages 133-160).

Freight and sales tax are often excluded from budget estimates since they are subject to complicated sales tax law. These charges must be estimated, if appropriate, in order to realize the full expenses that may be incurred.

Research and development

A fter a project is commissioned, the next step is often research. Research may be as simple as opening one's files to locate clippings or reference material (photographs, magazines, illustrations) that relate to the project. Or it may be a lengthy, complicated process such as a corporate identity search to verify the originality of a logo design. In some cases, the client and artist may collaborate on the research phase, depending on the resources available to both.

After the research is completed, the development stage generally begins. In the simplest cases, development is the refinement of an idea. Using the corporate identity example again, development may mean considering several ideas, exploring the applications and visual impact of those ideas and developing a presentation.

Research and development, therefore, for a corporate identity program is a substantial portion of the entire project in terms of cost and time. Yet the custom of preparing a thorough proposal has not been as widely accepted in disciplines outside the design area, such as illustration or textile design.

Billable expenses for computer-assisted graphics and illustration

I llustrators or graphic designers who do not own computer equipment but are able to arrange access to equipment should maintain strict records of expenses in order to bill the client. In the current market, billable expense related to the use of outside computer equipment include: rental fees; transportation to and from the equipment (especially if rental time is off peak hours when travel may be hazardous); any costs incurred in recording work on hardcopy, including 35mm film and processing or video tape. Also to be billed are such items as fees paid for technical assistants if they are required or included in the equipment rental fee, research and reference costs and expenses for preparing raw art (photos, stats, line art, etc.) to be used with digitizing camera input.

There are other expenses that should be negotiated; for example, equipment or technology purchases or expenses to meet unrealistic deadline requirements (i.e. purchase of a telecommunications program to transmit a digital image to another region or city in time for an unreasonably short print deadline).

Artists should also follow basic markup considerations in instances where time is spent negotiating for rental time, purchasing supplies and services. These items should be factored in as regular overhead, or charged as consulting fees.

The going billable rate for computer animation/paint systems is $250-$350 per hour, and rental fees range from $100-$200 per hour.

Any artist working in this area should be aware that the newness of this technology and the speed with which the technology changes requires a continual review of expenses and charges.

PROFESSIONAL
PRACTICES

The Professional Relationship

The communications field is increasingly reliant on sophisticated graphics, as the print and broadcast media shower the consumer with new styles and looks, creating a "graphics conscious" public.

The client

Clients have tremendous choice now in terms of professionals they may go to for graphic services. And with more choice comes the dilemma of deciding which is the correct choice. You may wish to refer to *Sources of Talent* on page 25 to understand further the agencies and directories available to clients and artists. For sake of this discussion, we may state that clients fall into two categories: those who buy art on a regular basis and those who do not.

The client that buys art regularly, more often than not, has staff with expertise in that area: art directors, art buyers and stylists who are well versed in the procedures, rights, pricing and trade customs of the professions contained in this book.

The client who only buys art occasionally relies on free-lance art directors, stylists, graphic designers, design firms, studios or agencies for this knowledge and the ability to coordinate many talents.

The first problem the client with no art staff faces is, of course, which free-lance professional to hire. It is wisest for the client to consider hiring a professional who is able to coordinate the entire project: a free-lance art director would be able to produce a magazine; a free-lance stylist would coordinate a textile collection; a design studio would handle brochures, catalogs and a design firm would produce annual reports and corporate identity programs, to name a few examples. (Each pricing section of this book begins with detailed descriptions of the various graphic disciplines.)

The client who has no art staff does not need to have a full understanding of the graphics business. In fact, the client plays a very specific role no matter which professional relationship may be appropriate—as expert in his/her own field. The client must communicate to the professional graphic artist what his/her company's needs and problems are in an abstract yet practical way, *not* in terms of the graphics needed, but the client's own knowledge of the product, the field, the competition. In other words, the client has *precisely* the expertise the graphic artist lacks to solve the problem and client and artist become perfect complements. It is through their communication that the client injects the company's personality, philosophy and strategy into the graphic artist's visual solution.

The graphic artist's role is, conversely, to restate what the client has addressed as the issues, priorities, goals of the project. This is how the client begins to understand, aided by the artist's portfolio, whether there is apt to be a meeting of the minds. It is at this point that the client decides whether to proceed or go elsewhere.

The art director

Practically all businesses these days hire graphic artists at one point or another, so there is an ever increasing community of professional artists emerging to fill those needs.

With the director as focus of the project, the roles of other artists needed to complete the assignment, such as illustrator, mechanical artist, photographer, etc., come under the director's supervision.

The designer, art director, or stylist generally selects the talent necessary to complete a project. Portfolios may be presented to the client for review, but generally the director is viewed as the expert and the client most often defers to his/her judgment.

All projects start with a proposal of costs, time schedules, description of the type of solution that would be pursued, and, of course, rights transferred, terms and conditions for all art and photography.

When the client and director agree to proceed, the director is the authorized art buyer for the project. The director suggests several steps so that the client may assess how the project is progressing. The director also subcontracts the illustration, photography, design, production or typography on behalf of the client.

The subcontractor

The illustrator, mechanical artist, photographer, printer or designer becomes a subcontractor when working for a director. The subcontractor negotiates rights, terms, fees with the director and, although client contact may be appropriate and necessary, all graphic direction generally comes from the director. It is trade custom, for instance, for the printer to refuse to make changes on press when requested by the client; it is also trade custom for printers to refuse to release mechanicals to the client unless the director authorizes it.

The director, on the other hand, understands the nuances of style and technique. When art directing a graphic artist, the director and artist are keenly aware of the look they hope to achieve. Portfolio viewing is essential in this respect, since artists can only be expected to create work in styles and quality represented in their books.

In no case should a director or subcontractor be expected to create work on speculation (see Code of Fair Practice, page 36). It is the purpose of the portfolio viewing to determine if the work can be done by the artist; if the portfolio does not give the director confidence, other portfolios should be reviewed.

The subcontractor relates to the director just as any staff director. The only difference is that the staff art director may have a more permanent involvement with the company and, therefore, more in-depth knowledge and experience. At any rate, the illustrator, designer or photographer goes through much the same sort of probing process that the director would with the client only in shorthand and using professional jargon. It is necessary to arrive at a description of the purpose of the piece, limitations, audience, deadline, intended impact, place-

ment, and any one of a dozen or more aspects of the job. It is through this discussion that the director decides whether there has been a meeting of the minds and, matching the talent shown in the portfolio, whether to proceed with the project with a particular artist.

At all points, when the client or authorized art buyer agrees to proceed, a commitment of money and effort is implicit. If a project is curtailed, agreements must be honored to that point (see cancellation, page 48). If art work has not gone to the point of completion, then no rights have been transferred and the copyright remains with the artist.

The professional relationship between the client, director and artist always focuses on the needs of the project and the desired results. The final creation ideally reflects the purity of the collaboration.

How artwork is commissioned

Aside from directly commissioning the free-lance artist, artwork is secured through negotiations with various intermediaries, such as agents. It is of utmost importance that the ground rules for the relationship between the artist and the person ordering the work be established clearly before beginning the work. Also, it should be kept in mind that trade practices differ from discipline to discipline. For a standard guide to ethical practices, the Code of Fair Practice on pages 36 should be consulted.

Advertising agencies

Artwork for advertising agencies is usually purchased by the art buyer or the art director (if there is no art buyer). Artists are selected based on the style of illustration needed and the portfolio submitted. At the time of assignment, most agencies provide the artist with a purchase order that details: rights purchased, ownership of art, delivery dates for pencil and finish, prices for completed assignment, cancellation fee at pencil and finish stages and any additional expenses (such as delivery charges, or shipping).

Rights purchased may be in any or all of the following categories, which should be spelled out in the purchase order. However, uses of a color illustration in various ad sizes or in black and white are not usually considered causes for additional payment.

Complete buyout: includes the purchase of all rights and ownership of the original art.

Limited buyout: includes the purchase of all rights, but the ownership of the original remains with the artist.

Publication use: includes use in newspapers, magazines, Sunday supplements, internal publications and any material included as part of a publication such as free standing inserts, etc.

Point of sale (Collateral use): includes all point of sale materials such as signs, leaflets, shopping cart posters, catalogs, brochures, direct mail, etc.

Out of home: all posters that are not point of sale, such as painted bulletins, 30-sheet posters, transit posters, bus shelters, etc.

TV use

Presentation and research use: purchased at the lowest possible rates since the material will not be used in commissionable media (the artist's order should cover an agreement for an additional fee if used extensively).

Test market use: purchased at lower rates for use in a limited number of markets. As in *presentation and research use,* an artist's agreement should cover additional fees if use is expanded.

Representatives

S ome representatives work under contract and the Guild has its own standard Artist/Agent Agreement which is reproduced on pages 138-139,, as well as a standard Textile Designer/Agent Agreement which appears on pages 154-158. The agent has the legal right to act on behalf of his or her artists. The agent can legally obligate the artist, but only in ways agreed to in the agent-artist contract. Thus, the artist should have a lawyer read any contract and make certain the terms are clearly understood before signing. If a more casual relationship is undertaken, the Guild recommends that both parties sign a memo that spells out their various responsibilities. Exclusivity or nonexclusivity is a crucial issue in any contract, since the artist must feel that *all* of his or her work will be marketed in the best manner. If the representative asks for exclusive representation, the artist should be entitled to know who else is being carried by the representative who should not be free to broker unlisted talent, unless so stated. Some items to be considered follow.

Mounting of portfolio pieces and presentations, laminations, etc.: A clear understanding should be reached as to who pays the cost of these items and the fact that the artist ultimately owns them.

Mailing of promotion pieces, shipping of artwork, insurance, etc.: Many representatives will split or absorb these costs with the artist. The arrangement should be understood by both parties.

Billing: Whether it is wisest for agent or artist to handle the billing will depend on the circumstances. Any reputable party will supply copies of the purchase order and a copy of the invoice to the other party. If a purchase order does not exist, then a copy of the check should be supplied to the other party. One practical aspect of this procedure is that should the person handling the billing die, go into bankruptcy or reorganize, the other party has proof of what is owed.

Commissions: The conventional artist-representative arrangement calls for a 25 percent commission to the representative. In the textile design field, the range for commissions is 25 to 40 percent. The rate of commission reflects the degree of responsibility assumed by the representative. See, in particular, the section covering business practices in textile design on page 87. For this the representative provides most client contact and art sales, promotion of the artist, delivery, billing and other services in an effort to keep the artist in full production. These commisssions should be based only on the fee paid to the artist, not on expenses normally billed to the client; the expenses should be subtracted from a flat fee before the commission is computed. Also, accounts that an artist has prior to retaining a representative (i.e., *house accounts*) are usually serviced by the agent at a lower commission rate (if the agent is given these accounts).

Termination: This is a sensitive area for both agent and artist. Each party should be able to terminate on thirty days written notice, but the agent may demand a continuing right to receive commissions after the termination date. This right should not apply to house accounts. With respect to active accounts obtained by the agent, the agent might reasonably request the right to a commission on any assignments received by the artist from such active accounts for a period of three months after the termination date. If the agent has represented the artist for more than six months, the right to receive commissions after termination might be increased by one month for each additional six months of representation (so that after two years of representation, the agent would receive commissions for six months after termination). The circumstances in each case will differ, but the artist should rarely agree to give the agent commissions on assignments obtained more than six months after the effective date of termination. Of course, if an agent is entitled to receive a commission, it doesn't matter *when* payment is actually received.

Studios

Many studios delve into the freelance market for styles of work they cannot create. Studios may act as buyers in purchasing artwork directly or act as intermediaries in obtaining assignments for the artist on a commission basis. The problem can be complicated for the artist who may work on a project involving several other talents. In most cases, the artist is a subcontractor, and the artist's fee for his or her contribution should be established in very clear terms. Some of the considerations on billing mentioned with respect to representatives should apply. However, since studios frequently handle complete packages involving layout, illustrations, lettering, type, retouching, etc., it may not be practical to supply individual copies of invoices. For this reason the working conditions should be established clearly at the outset. (Studio staff see section on Salaried staff on page 125.)

Brokers

Most brokers do not represent talent on an exclusive basis; relying instead on their contacts among clients and their knowledge of various talents to put together a deal. Some of these, as with studios, can be quite complex complete packages. Most of the points raised in the sections on representatives and studios would apply. Perhaps it cannot be emphasized too strongly that it is imperative to establish price, relative responsibilities, and working conditions before accepting the assignment. In the absence of a formalized working relationship, *the artist should establish a price that the artist considers adequate for the work,* leaving the broker free to negotiate above that price and keep the excess as a commission.

Sources of talent

There are several resources available to clients and artists to find and/or promote talent. Among the most widely known and used are the advertising directories. These directories generally showcase a specific type of work, such as illustration or graphic design. Normally artists purchase space in a directory that displays representative work chosen by the artist and gives a contact address for either the artist or the artist's representative. Other directories are compilations of juried shows. Directories also serve the industry as references for the types and styles of work being done in each field.

Among the best known directories nationally are: For illustration: American Showcase (published in NY), Art Directors Annual* (NY), Creative Blackbook (NY), Chicago Talent (IL), Graphic Artists Guild Directory (NY), Society of Illustrators Annual* (NY), RSVP (Brooklyn), and the L.A. Workbook (CA). For design: AIGA Annual* (NY), American Illustration (NY), Creative Blackbook (NY), The Graphic Artists Guild Corporate Design Directory (NY). And for photography: ASMP Book (NY), Creative Blackbook (NY), and the L.A.Workbook (CA).

Employment agencies and "freelance" referral agencies in various cities around the country refer artists to clients for a fee. They operate in the same way that most employment agencies do, they simply specialize in the arts markets. Often these agencies are listed in trade magazines and the Yellow Pages.

Good Works is the Graphic Artists Guild New York Chapter's job referral service. The service refers artists active in illustration, graphic design, textile design, needleart design, computer graphics and production. Good Works is a free service to clients. For further information on the Guild's job referral service, please see page 181.

If none of these services is accessible in a particular area, it is recommended that a client or artist contact the local professional organization that services the graphic arts industry for referrals.

*These directories are compilations of juried shows.

Business and Legal Practices for Commissioned Artwork

This section is designed to give both artist and buyer an overview of the business and legal issues that constantly arise in the commercial arts. Since the rights of copyright are what the artist sells to the buyer by contract, the information on copyright is essential to a full understanding of the contractual practices prevailing in the field. More detailed information on copyright can be found in *The Visual Artist's Guide to the New Copyright Law* by Tad Crawford, while more extensive advice on contracts and other business issues is available in *Selling Your Graphic Design and Illustration: The Complete Business, Marketing and Legal Guide* by Tad Crawford and Arie Kopelman.

Negotiation

If the buyer's standard contract or purchase order contains unacceptable provisions, the artist or agent should negotiate to have these stricken out or changed to the artist's satisfaction. Negotiation is an art in which each party seeks to accommodate the needs of the other party while satisfying his or her own needs. The relative degrees of need determine whether one has a weak or strong bargaining position. The artist must have self-confidence in order to negotiate successfully. By the Guild's efforts to clarify trade practices and survey pricing structures (based on usage, etc.), the parties have a common frame of reference from which to negotiate.

Both artist and art buyer must also have goals by which to judge a negotiation. The buyer must stay within the budget and obtain satisfactory art. The artist must earn enough to pay for overhead and leave a profit. The more information each party has about the other, the more effectively he or she will be able to negotiate. An artist who knows the budget for a given job and knows what other artists have been paid for similar work by the same agency or publisher will have a very good idea of what he or she can command. Similarly, a number of buyers have different contract forms or are willing to change certain provisions on request. A little research, for example, by calling other artists, can yield substantial benefits to an artist who has negotiating strength and wishes to make use of it. At the same time, the artist must keep in mind the negotiating goals of the buyer and seek to satisfy these goals as fully as possible. One common bit of advice is that both parties should have at least one demand that they are willing to relinquish. This encourages the process of compromise that leads to agreement. Of course, if either artist or buyer find that the other party will not permit them to achieve their essential goals, then the negotiation will break down and the parties will seek to fulfill their needs elsewhere. The Guild makes available to its members, and to buyers, standard contract forms outlining the general provisions which should govern artist-buyer agreements. Many of these forms, including a purchase order, confirmation form, and invoice, appear on pages 133-160. We urge artists and buyers to use these model forms as the basis for standard contracts or purchase orders. Of course, all contracts should conform to standards of the Code of Fair Practice.

Business Forms

Under the new copyright law, in order for a buyer to obtain any exclusive rights to the use of the artist's work, the buyer must have written and signed authorization from the artist. It is in the artist's interest to make sure that any agreement with a buyer specifies clearly only those rights which the artist is willing to transfer. Many buyers have standard purchase orders or contracts. The Guild is opposed to the use by buyers of standard purchase orders or contracts that specify as a matter of course the transfer of all rights. Artists can always present a contract to a client even if they have already received one from a client. Also, if the word "contract" may intimidate an art buyer, an artist can always refer to his or her contract as a "letter of agreement." Such a contract—whether called a confirmation or a letter of agreement—should be signed by both parties prior to the commencement of work. Contract or purchase order terms must be a matter of negotiation between the artist and buyer.

Contracts and purchase orders must contain provisions covering at least the following points:

1. The names of the artist and client, including the name of the client's authorized art buyer.

2. A complete description of the assignment.

3. The basic fee.

4. Special usage or other fees (e.g., travel time, consultations, alterations, cancellations, kills).

5. Expense reimbursements.

6. Advance and/or payment schedule.

7. Usage by: A. Category (such as advertising, promotional, corporate, editorial); B. Medium of use (such as brochure, magazine, hardcover book); and C. Title of publication or product name.

8. Return of originals– When and how.

9. Credit line and copyright notice requirements.

10. Releases. The use of people's names or images for advertising or trade purposes can cause an invasion of privacy. If a release is needed, artist and client should agree as to who will obtain the release and who will pay damages if the release is not obtained or proves inadequate.

11. Arbitration. The submission of a dispute to a neutral third party for resolution can be quicker and less expensive than going to court. In New York City the Joint Ethics Committee will arbitrate disputes, while in parts of the country without such a group any neutral party or the American Arbitration Association could be used.

In addition, if a contract provides for payment of a royalty, the following special considerations must be weighed:

1. Amount of advance against future royalties.

2. Royalty percentages. For books, carefully check which types of sales permit the publisher to pay a reduced royalty—such as sales by direct mail, sales abroad, sales by coupon advertising, or sales in which a discount greater than 48 to 50 percent is given to the purchaser (usually a jobber who in turn resells to bookstores). Also, royalty percentages often increase with an increased volume of sales.

3. Price on which a royalty is calculated should be the retail price for books, but is usually the wholesale price for manufactured items.

4. Accounting and statements. The artist should have the right to inspect the publisher's or manufacturer's sales records and receive regular reports of sales (at least every six months in the case of manufactured items).

5. Exclusivity. The contract should relate only to the property being sold and not to other properties (such as properties that the artist may create in the future).

6. Subsidiary rights. Secondary uses must be specifically protected (such as the right to make postcards or tee shirts from artwork originally published in a book).

7. Credit line and ownership of copyright.

8. Return of publication rights. If the publisher or manufacturer breaches the contract, or no longer actively sells the work, the usage rights should be returned to the artist.

A thorough introduction to book publishing contracts can be found in *The Writer's Legal Guide* by Tad Crawford, published by Hawthorn/Dutton. For royalty contracts on manufactured items and paper products, refer to *Selling Your Graphic Design and Illustration.*

Copyright

Copyright is the creator's right to control the usage of his or her design or artwork. It is directly related to both pricing and fair trade practices. Since a copyright is a *bundle* of rights, each different usage can be transferred separately and with specific limitations. The greater the copyright usage given to a client, the more the price should be. In terms of trade practices, the copyright law clarifies a number of important protections for the artist.

New copyright law

On January 1, 1978, a new federal copyright law became effective. It reforms the old copyright law in many ways that are favorable to artists, but some pitfalls remain. Application forms, including Form VAa for a work in the visual arts, and a Copyright Information Kit, are available free of charge from the Copyright Office, Library of Congress, Washington, D.C. 20559.

The new law ends the often confusing dual system of state and federal copyright protection by creating a single system of federal protection. An artist has federal copyright as soon as a work is created without putting copyright notice on it or registering it with the Copyright Office. Copyrights created after January 1, 1978, as well as those already existing in work not published or registered, will last for the artist's life plus fifty years, while federal copyrights obtained before 1978 will now run 75 years (but must be renewed on Form RE if renewal would have been necessary under the old law).

Artists' rights

The copyright owner has the exclusive rights to reproduce his or her work, sell his or her work, prepare derivative works (such as a poster copied from a painting), perform his or her work, and display his or her work (except that the owner of a copy of the work can also display it). Anyone who violates these rights is an infringer who can be sued for damages and prevented from continuing the infringement.

There are two limited exceptions concerning the artist's exclusive power to control the uses of work: fair use and compulsory licensing. Fair use permits someone to use a work without permission for a purpose that is basically not going to compete with or injure the market for the work, such as using an illustration in an article about the artist's career. Compulsory licensing permits a noncommercial, educational broadcasting station to use published work without the artist's consent. However, rates for payment have been established by the Copyright Royalty Tribunal in Washington, D.C., and each station is obliged to publish a list of those artists entitled to receive payment. The Guild has urged the repeal of compulsory licensing on the grounds that it deprives the artist of the right to control the use of the work and negotiate a fair price.

Transfer of copyright

Copyright is a *bundle* of rights which can be transferred separately and with specific limitations. All transfers of *exclusive* rights by the creator must be by *written and signed authorization* of the creator or the creator's authorized agent and must specify what rights are being transferred. Only *nonexclusive* rights (which can be transferred to more than one user at the same time) can be transferred verbally. For contributions to collective works (such as magazines, anthologies, encyclopedias, etc.), where there is no signed agreement, the law presumes the transfer of *only* the nonexclusive rights for use in that particular collective work, in any later collective work in the same series (such as a later issue of the same magazine), or in any revision of the collective work. All other rights remain vested in the creator. The new copyright law provides that copyrights are separate from the physical artwork. Selling the physical artwork does not transfer any rights of copyright. Nor does selling a right of reproduction to a client give the client any claim to the physical artwork. The artwork will be temporarily given to the client in order to make reproductions, but the client must take reasonable care of the artwork and return it undamaged to the artist. For a separate fee, of course, the artist could sell the physical artwork to the client or another party who wished to buy it. In any event, when confirming or billing a job, the artist should always state that the physical art is retained by the artist.

Both exclusive transfers of copyrights or parts of copyrights and nonexclusive licenses of copyrights can be terminated by the artist during a five-year period starting thirty-five years after the date of publication or forty years after the date of execution of the transfer, whichever period ends earlier. This right of termination is an important new right which will come into play when transfers or licenses are of exceptionally long duration. It does not apply to works for hire or transfers made by will.

Copyright notice

The artist has copyright as soon as a work is created, but placing copyright notice on the work is important to avoid losing this copyright protection. The copyright notice is Copyright or Copr. or ©, the artist's name or an abbreviation of the name or an alternate designation by which the artist is known, and the year date of first publication. For example, notice could take the form of ©Jane Artist 1981. On useful articles such as jewelry, lamps, or stationery, the year date may be omitted from the notice. The copyright notice can be placed on the back of an artwork or, when it's published, adjacent to the artwork. Other reasonable placements of the copyright notice for published works are specified by the regulations of the Copyright Office. A good practice is to have a rubber stamp made with copyright notice and stamp each work on completion. Pieces in the artist's portfolio should have copyright notice, including published pieces if the artist has retained the copyright.

Also, while the copyright notice at the front of a magazine, anthology, or other collective work will protect the copyright in a contribution from going into the public domain, it is better for the artist to have copyright notice in his or her own name appear with the contribution when published. This makes the artist eligible for a group registration of published contributions and avoids certain risks of infringement.

However, if the artist omits the notice or has it in an incorrect form, the copyright may be protected under the provisions of the new law that save copyrights despite defective notice. In such a case the creator still has five years in which to file for copyright registration while making a reasonable effort to add the copyright notice to all copies that lack it. Only if this is not done does the work then enter the public domain and become freely available to all who wish to copy it. Also, an omission of copyright notice won't affect the validity of protection if the notice is omitted in violation of an agreement that notice accompany the published work.

Registration

All artworks can be registered, published or unpublished. But why pay the $10 fee if an artist already has copyright protection just by creating the work? There are several reasons: (1) registration is necessary to bring a lawsuit; (2) registration is proof that the copyright is valid and the statements in the Certificate of Registration are true; (3) registration is necessary to be eligible for attorney's fees and, special damages (called "statutory damages" and awarded at the court's discretion when actual damages or the infringer's profits would be difficult to prove); and (4) registration can cut off defenses that innocent infringers might otherwise be able to assert.

To cut the cost of registration, the Copyright Office provides that unpublished artworks can be registered in groups. For example, five hundred drawings could be collected in a binder and registered as "Drawings by Jane Artist, Series 1. ' Only one $10 registration fee would have to be paid and the artworks would not have to be registered again when published. A good reason to request copyright notice in the artist's name for contributions to periodicals is that this makes possible an inexpensive group registration of all contributions published in a one-year period with copyright notice in the artist's name. Form GR/CP would be used in addition to form VA for such a registration.

Nor do you have to send original art to the Copyright Office. While the copyrightable content of the artwork must be shown, this can be done with transparencies or photocopies instead of original artwork.

Work-for-hire contracts

The Graphic Artists Guild is emphatically opposed to the use of work-for-hire contracts by art buyers who commission work of freelance artists. When used for such, work-for-hire is an unfair business practice that gives the art buyer benefits and recognition that belong to the creative artist. By signing work-for-hire, an artist becomes a nominal employee for the implicit purpose of circumventing the copyright law and receives no employee benefits such as unemployment, health, medical and dental insurance, sick pay, pension, disability, employee discounts or the like. These contracts devalue the integrity of the artist and his or her work by enabling the buyer to alter the artwork in any way without consulting the artist, and by stripping the artist of any royalties on future use.

The Graphic Artists Guild believes that work-for-hire denies the intent and spirit of the 1978 copyright law, which is called "the creator's law." In all other instances, the law endows the creative artist with all rights to personal stylistic interpretations in tangible visual form. Work-for-hire, meant originally to address a specific need in a specific instance, has become a contradiction to the law and is now used widely for commissioned art works. Work-for-hire denies the artist the opportunity to enter into freely bargained contracts based on a fair value-for-value exchange.

Ownership of original art

Auction prices for artists such as Remington, N.C. Wyeth, and Rockwell, have escalated in recent years by thousands, and in a few cases, tens of thousands of dollars. Well-known illustrators command prices comparable to those paid any other artist selling through galleries. The industry's interest in the ownership question is hardly surprising, and both artist and client should be aware that the sale of the original will normally command compensation *in addition* to the price for reproduction rights. This original art may be exhibited, used as a portfolio piece, given as a gift, or willed as part of an estate. The increasing value of original art provided part of the impetus for the Guild to publish *Protecting Your Heirs and Creative Works,* edited by Tad Crawford. The concern for the protection of original works also stems from recognition among artists that each work reflects something of the personality of its artist and is an essential part of developing and protecting the artist's reputation.

If ownership of the original art is to be transferred, this should be a transaction separate from or in addition to any transfer of reproduction rights. It should, therefore, be explicitly stated if the original art is being sold. Thus, a buyer acquiring "all rights" must still return the original.

However, unlike copyright transfers which must be in writing, transfers of ownership of original art may be by verbal agreement unless state law states otherwise. To avoid any ambiguity based on a verbal agreement, prior course of dealing, or special trade practice; artists will want to make certain that any contracts, invoices, or purchase orders explicitly state that original art belongs to the artist and must be returned undamaged.

Legislation which has passed in New York, California and Oregon (and pending in Massachusetts) provides that, in the sale of reproduction rights, no right to the original is conveyed by the artist unless that is specifically agreed to *in writing.* Such legislation eliminates any misconceptions as to ownership of original art when reproduction rights are sold.

The Guild's goals in reinforcing and extending protections for artists flow from a set of widely accepted principles. As most professionals in the creative community know, the copyright law was designed to protect and encourage creators, and to balance that protection with the needs and perogatives of art buyers.

Free-lance artists' livelihoods depend on their ability to claim "authorship" for the pieces they produce. They build their reputations, and therefore their ability to attract clients, on the basis of past performance. Indeed, artists' careers succeed or fail by their skill and style in translating the ideas and messages society needs to disseminate.

The Copyright Law created, in effect, a bundle of rights inherently vested with the creator, who is defined as the translator of abstract ideas into tangible form. This subdivisible bundle of rights is the basis of all transactions between the creator/seller and the purchaser. That is, the purchaser buys specific rights of usage and/or reproduction as needed, and the unsold rights of usage remain with the creator.

The concept of limited usage for the initial fee is one of basic fairness since no one can be certain what a copyrightable work will ultimately be worth until it has been exploited. Negotiations regarding the price for a commissioned work are normally based on the usage the buyer indicates will be made of the work.

One of government's goals, according to the U.S. constitution, is the protection and and encouragement of creators. The Guild believes that it is in the public interest to see that creators' economic and creative survival is protected to thus ensure the existence of a diverse creative pool and the free flow of ideas and information in the marketplace.

Cancellation fees

When a commissioned job that has been completed is cancelled through *no fault of the artist,* the full fee must be paid. If the artwork is at an unfinished stage at the time of cancellation, the artist may charge a part of the original fee in proportion to the degree of completion. For very preliminary artwork, cancellation fees may be charged at an hourly rate. The buyer usually, but not always, obtains all of the originally agreed upon rights to the use of the work upon payment.

When a buyer rejects commissioned artwork as *not reasonably satisfactory,* the artist must be paid a cancellation fee in compensation for time and effort expended. The fee for completed work is normally at least 66 percent of the original usage fee. If the work is of a complex nature, the cancellation fee should be higher. If only very preliminary work has been done, fees may be charged at an hourly rate. In this situation the buyer foregoes any rights to the use of the artwork. All work and material must be returned to the artist. The buyer also foregoes the use of any concepts provided by the artist and may not commission another artist to complete work on these concepts.

If cancelled preliminary work or completed finishes are later used as finished art, the balance of the original fee must be paid to the artist.

Where royalty arrangements have been entered into, all rights to the artwork, as well as possession of the original art, must revert to the artist upon cancellation. Since payment to the artist was to be based on a percentage of anticipated product sales, rather than a fixed dollar amount, an equitable cancellation fee must be negotiated. Such arrangements often encompass the artist's retention of advances.

In the event of cancellation, all expenses must be reimbursed in full.

Cancellation terms should be stipulated in writing in confirmation forms and purchase orders, or these fees must be negotiated at the time cancellation occurs. Full payment of fees should be made contingent upon receipt of the artwork and not upon publication to cover the possibility of cancellation after acceptance. For a further discussion of Guild policy regarding cancellation fees, refer to page 48.

Expenses

G raphic designers traditionally bill their clients for all the expenses of executing an assignment. Textile designers and illustrators have usually absorbed such expenses as paper, brushes, and paint, because for them the amounts tended to be quite modest. Where, however, the illustrator or textile designer has substantial expenses above the normal expenses (such as extended bookings for a number of models, extensive travel, etc.), clients have begun to accept billings for those items in addition to the fee. As expenses increase in relation to fees, the practice is likely to grow.

Credit lines

A n illustrator usually incorporates his or her signature on an artwork, and that is typically reproduced as part of the piece. For important pieces, especially where a letter of agreement is needed to spell out the terms of usage and payment, artists are making the "credit line" requirement part of the deal.

For some, this may mean a printed credit line; for others merely the reproduction of the signature in the artwork. In some cases, as it has been traditionally with magazines, both credits may be permitted.

This parallels, to a degree, a new development in magazine photography in which a few photographers now require, by contract, that their fees will be doubled if an adjacent credit line is omitted. Their theory is that, given the modest rates for editorial work, the value of the credit line is as important as the basic fee. This activity hardly constitutes a "trade practice," but it may grow in time and could affect designers and illustrators as well.

A copyright notice can be made part of the credit line, simply by adding © before the artist's name, and the year date of publication after the name (©Jane Artist 1981). Such a copyright notice benefits the artist without harming the client.

Reproductions

I t is a courtesy for clients to provide their artists with examples of the finished piece as it was reproduced. This helps build the artist's portfolio and provides the artist with a view of the project in its completed form. Regardless of who owns copyright in the art, the artist's use of his or her own original art in a portfolio is permissible as a fair use (that is, a use that isn't competitive with uses that the copyright owner might make).

Sales tax

T he various states have quite different policies in regard to sales tax. In states that have sales tax, the rate usually ranges from 3 to 8 percent. The tax is levied on the sale or use of physical property in the state. A number of exemptions exist, including special rules for the sale of reproduction rights. The applicable state regulations should be consulted. Many of these laws are unclear as they relate to the graphic communications industry. In any case in which the artist is doubtful whether to collect the tax, it is safest to collect the tax and remit it to the state sales tax bureau. If the artist should collect the tax but doesn't, the artist as well as the client will remain liable for the tax (but, of course, it will be difficult to try and collect the tax from clients on assignments that have been performed in the past). The artist is, in fact, a tax collector for the state.

Liability for portfolios and original art

If an artist's portfolio is lost by an art buyer, the law of "bailments" (the holding of another's property) makes the buyer liable for the reasonable value of that portfolio if the loss arose from the buyer's carelessness. If the portfolio contained original art such as drawings, paintings or original transparencies, the amount in question could be quite substantial. The same potential liability exists with respect to commissioned artwork a client has agreed to return to the artist. A model Holding Form for use by textile designers appears on page 115 and can be modified for use by other disciplines.

There are two ways to minimize these risks. The first is with "valuable papers" insurance. That, however, is not enough. As with any insurance, continued claims will lead to either prohibitive premiums or a complete loss of coverage. Accordingly, buyers also need effective systems for tracking and storing all original art in their offices.

Buyers should make sure that the receipt of every portfolio is recorded and a notation is made of its destination within the organization. If possible, buyers should avoid keeping portfolios overnight and on weekends. All original art should be logged out when it goes to the color separator or printer, and logged in when it returns. Finally, suppliers such as color separators, retouchers and printers should be on notice that they may be held liable for any losses they cause as a result of the damage or disappearance of any original art.

The likelihood of achieving perfection in the handling of original art is remote. That is the reason each buyer must minimize legal risks through the purchase of suitable insurance and, more importantly, the installation of proper record keeping and procedures.

Speculation

The Guild is unalterably opposed to any artist being asked to work on speculation because of the risks to the artist inherent in such requests. Artists who create their own work and then seek to sell it are not in violation of this rule, but art buyers should not ask artists to work on a project unless a fee has been agreed upon. Art contests, except under special circumstances, are also opposed because of their speculative nature. For contest guidelines approved by the Guild, see page 47.

ETHICAL
STANDARDS

Ethical Standards

Introduction

In 1945, a group of artists and art directors in New York City concerned with the growing abuses, misunderstandings and disregard of uniform standards of conduct in their field, met to consider possibilities for improvement. They reached the conclusion that any successful effort must start with widespread backing, and must be a continuing activity. On the group's recommendation, three leading New York art organizations established and financed a committee known as the Joint Ethics Committee.

In 1978 the expanded committee, representing five organizations, revised the code to include the new communications industries. A booklet, *Code of Fair Practice,* was published in response to the many requests for information concerning the operation and scope of the Committee.

One of the paramount reasons for the creation and continued existence of the Guild is its support of ethical standards in all dealings between graphic artists and art buyers. This determination to foster fair business practices can be seen in many facets of the Guild's activities.

The Guild is a sponsor of the Joint Ethics Committee, which mediates or arbitrates disputes between graphic artists and clients in the New York area. It is hoped that the Joint Ethics Committee will become a national organization in the near future. Other sponsoring groups are the Art Directors Club of New York, the American Society of Magazine Photographers, the Society of Illustrators, the American Institute of Graphic Arts and the Society of Photographers and Artists Representatives. The Joint Ethics Committee has formulated its Code of Fair Practice, which the sponsoring groups endorse.

Along with its support of the Joint Ethics Committee, the Guild has its own professional practices and grievance committees which work with members in addressing issues of professional relations between artists and buyers, and assist members in resolving violations of agreements and commonly-accepted trade standards. As with all other Guild programs, these committees draw from members' experiences in the field, track industry standards and publicize any changes in the field that affect contracts and trade practices.

As part of its commitment to make information on standards and practices available throughout the industry, the Guild offers copies of standard forms and contracts to all of its members and, through the *Pricing & Ethical Guidelines,* to anyone in the industry (refer to pages 133-160. These forms and contracts can be used directly or can be amended to meet individual needs.

Personnel

The Joint Ethics Committee is composed of four members with three votes each from the following organizations: Society of Illustrators, Inc., the Art Directors Club, Inc., American Society of Magazine Photographers, Inc., Society of Photographer and Artist Representatives, Inc., the Graphic Artists Guild, Inc. and the American Institute of Graphic Arts appointed by the directing bodies of each organization, but serving jointly in furtherance of the purposes for which the Committee was founded.

Members of the Joint Ethics Committee are selected with great care by their respective organizations. Their selection is based upon their experience in the profession, their proven mature thinking and temperament, and their reputation for impartiality.

Code of fair practice

The Code of Fair Practice, as established by the Joint Ethics Committee, was conceived with the idea of equity for those engaged in the various aspects of creating, selling, buying and using graphic arts.

The Code is reproduced later in this booklet. The Committee zealously upholds the ethical standards set forth in the Code and invites with equal readiness any and all reports of violations.

Action

The Committee meets one or more times a month to read and act upon complaints, requests for guidance, and reports of Code violations. The proceedings and records of the Committee are held in strict confidence. In the interest of the profession typical cases are published periodically without identification of the parties involved.

All communications to the Committee must be made in writing. When a complaint justifies action, a copy of the complainant's letter may be sent, with the complainant's permission, to the alleged offender. In the exchange of correspondence which follows, matters are frequently settled by a mere clarification of the issues, and further action by the Committee becomes unnecessary. In many instances both sides resume friendly and profitable relationships. When, however, a continued exchange of correspondence indicates that a ready adjustment of differences is improbable, the Committee may suggest mediation or offer its facilities for arbitration.

In the case of flagrant violation, the Committee may, at its discretion, cite the alleged offender to the governing bodies of the parent organizations and recommend that they publicize the fact of these citations when (a) the Committee, after a reasonable length of time and adequate notice, receives no response from the alleged offender or (b) when the Committee receives a response which it deems unacceptable.

Mediation

Both parties meet informally under the auspices of a panel of mediators composed of three members of the Committee. If the dispute requires guidance in a field not represented in the Committee's membership, a specially qualified mediator with the required experience may be included. The names of members of the panel are submitted to both parties for their acceptance.

The conduct of a panel of mediators is friendly and informal. The function of the panel members is to guide, not to render any verdict.

The panel's purpose is to direct the discussion along such lines and in such a manner as to bring about a meeting of minds on the questions involved. If mediation fails, or seems unlikely to bring about satisfactory settlement, arbitration may be suggested.

Arbitration

A panel of five arbitrators is appointed. One or more is selected from the Committee, and the remainder are chosen by virtue of their particular experience and understanding of the problems presented by the dispute. Names of the panel members are submitted to both parties for their approval. Both parties involved sign an agreement and take an oath to abide by the decision of the panel. The panel itself is sworn in and the proceedings are held in compliance with the Arbitration Law of the State of New York. After both sides are heard, the panel deliberates in private and renders its decision, opinion, and award. These are duly formulated by the Committee's counsel for service on the parties and, if the losing side should balk, for entry of judgment according to law.

So far, every award has been fully honored. The decisions and opinions of this Committee are rapidly becoming precedent for guidance in similar situations. The Committee's Code has been cited as legal precedent.

Committee scope

The Committee acts upon matters which can be defined by them as involving a violation of the Code or a need for its enforcement.

Upon occasion, the Committee has been asked to aid in settling questions not specifically covered by the Code of Fair Practice. The Committee gladly renders such aid, providing it does not exceed the limitations of its authority.

Committee limitations

The Committee offers no legal advice on contracts, copyrights, bill collecting, or similar matters. But its judgment and decisions as to what is fair and ethical in any given situation, are backed by the support of the entire profession represented by the Committee.

The Committee's influence is derived from widespread moral support. While it has neither judicial nor police powers and cannot punish offenders, nor summon alleged violators to its presence, still, its growing prestige and dignity of operation have made it a highly respected tribunal to which few have failed to respond when invited to settle their differences.

Committee maintenance

The Committee's facilities are not limited to members of its supporting groups. They are available to any individual, business, or professional organization in the field of communications.

The operating expenses of the Committee are defrayed by the sponsoring organizations represented. The time and services of the members are voluntarily contributed without any form of personal gain.

The Joint Ethics Committee Code of Fair Practice for The Graphics Communication Industry

Formulated in 1948 in New York City.

Sponsored by:
Society of Illustrators, Inc.
The Art Directors Club, Inc.
American Society of Magazine
  Photographers, Inc.
Society of Photographers and Artists
  Representatives, Inc.
The Graphic Artists Guild, Inc.
American Institute of Graphic Arts

Relations between Artists and Buyer

ARTICLE 1

Dealings between an artist* or the artist's agent and a client should be conducted only through an authorized buyer.

ARTICLE 2

Orders to an artist or agent should be in writing and should include the specific rights which are being transferred, the price, delivery date, and a summarized description of the work. In the case of publications, the acceptance of a manuscript by the artist constitutes an order.

ARTICLE 3

All changes or additions not due to the fault of the artist or agent should be billed to the purchaser as an additional and separate charge.

ARTICLE 4

There should be no charges to the purchaser, other than those authorized expenses, for revisions or retakes made necessary by errors on the part of the artists or the artist's agent.

ARTICLE 5

Alterations should not be made without consulting the artists. Where alterations or retakes are necessary and time permits and where the artist's usual standard of quality has been maintained, the artist should be given the opportunity of making such changes.

ARTICLE 6

The artist should notify the buyer of an anticipated delay in delivery. Should the artist fail to keep his contract through unreasonable delay in delivery, or nonconformance with agreed specifications, it should be considered a breach of contract by the artist and should release the buyer from responsibility.

ARTICLE 7

Work stopped by a buyer after it has been started should be delivered immediately and billed on the basis of the time and effort expended and expenses incurred.

ARTICLE 8

An artist should not be asked to work on speculation. However, work originating with the artist may be marketed on its merit. Such work remains the property of the artist unless purchased and paid for.

ARTICLE 9

Art contests for commercial purposes are not approved because of their speculative and exploitative character.

ARTICLE 10

There should be no secret rebates, discounts, gifts, or bonuses requested by or given to buyers by the artist or the artist's agent.

ARTICLE 11

Artwork ownership and copyright ownership is initially vested in the hands of the artist.

ARTICLE 12

Original artwork remains the property of the artist unless it is specifically purchased and paid for as distinct from the purchase of any reproduction rights. †

ARTICLE 13

In cases of copyright transfers, only specified rights are transferred in any transaction, all unspecified rights remaining vested in the artist. †

ARTICLE 14

If the purchase price of artwork is based specifically upon limited use and later this material is used more extensively than originally planned, the artist is to receive adequate additional remuneration.

ARTICLE 15

Commissioned artwork is not to be considered as "done for hire" †

ARTICLE 16

If comprehensives, preliminary work, exploratory work, or additional photographs from an assignment are subsequently published as finished art, the price should be increased to the satisfaction of the artist and buyer.

ARTICLE 17

If exploratory work, comprehensives, or photographs are bought from an artist with the intention or possibility that another artist will be assigned to do the finished work, this should be made clear at the time of placing the order.

ARTICLE 18

The publisher of any reproduction of artwork shall publish the artist's copyright notice if the artist so requests and has not executed a written and signed transfer of copyright ownership.**

ARTICLE 19

The right to place the artist's signature upon artwork is subject to agreement between artist and buyer.

ARTICLE 20

There should be no plagiarism of any creative work.

ARTICLE 21

If an artist is specifically requested to produce any artwork during unreasonable working hours, fair additional remuneration should be allowed.

ARTICLE 22

An artist entering into an agreement with an agent or studio for exclusive representation should not accept an order form, nor permit his work to be shown by any other agent or studio. Any agreement which is not intended to be exclusive should set forth in writing the exact restrictions agreed upon between the two parties.

ARTICLE 23

All artwork or photography submitted as samples to a buyer by artist's agents or studio representatives should bear the name of the artist or artists responsible for the creation.

ARTICLE 24

No agent, studio, or production company should continue to show work of an artist as samples after the termination of the association.

ARTICLE 25

After termination of an association between artist and agent, the agent should be entitled to a commission on accounts which the agent has secured, for a period of time not exceeding six months (unless otherwise specified by contract).

ARTICLE 26

Examples of an artist's work furnished to an agent or submitted to a prospective purchaser shall remain the property of the artist, should not be duplicated without the artist's consent, and should be returned to the artist promptly in good condition.

ARTICLE 27

Interpretation of the Code shall be in the hands of the Joint Ethics Committee and is subject to changes and additions at the discretion of the parent organizations through their appointed representatives on the Committee.

*The word artist should be understood to include creative people in the field of visual communications such as graphics, photography, film and television.

†Artwork ownership, copyright ownership, and ownership and rights transfers after January 1, 1978 are to be in compliance with the Federal Copyright Revision Act of 1976.

The Guild's Grievance Committee

The Graphic Artists Guild is committed to raising and maintaining ethical professional standards between graphic artists and art buyers. Most Guild chapters have Grievance Committees to assist local members in resolving violations of agreements and commonly accepted trade standards. These Committees provide Guild members with specific services intended to provide assistance in resolving individual disputes and to prevent the occurrence of grievances in general.

Monitoring industry practices

The Grievance Committee encourages artists and art buyers of all disciplines to communicate instances of unprofessional practices encountered in the field. These reports enable the Committee to monitor business practices within the graphic communications industry. Where such reports are not forwarded, vital information for the industry is missing and such practices are perpetuated.

Report file

The Committee maintains an ongoing record of parties reported for unethical or unfair business practices. This file serves members as a central source for checking whether prospective buyers have violated the Code of Fair Practice. Members who report abuses to the Committee are thus able to forewarn fellow professionals directly and contribute to improving working conditions generally.

"Graphic Artists Beware" column

Buyers reported for flagrant, repeated or unresolved unprofessional practices are selected by the Committee for citation in the "Graphic Artists Beware" column of the Guild's chapter and national newsletters. The intention of citing these companies and individuals is to keep the community of graphic artists aware of these malefactors. At the same time, the Guild puts buyers who use unethical or unprofessional practices on notice that they can no longer exploit artists with impunity.

Committee assistance

The Grievance Committee also provides guidance and assistance to Guild members in their personal efforts to seek resolution of grievances. The Guild is committed to seeing that its members are treated justly and fairly as professionals.

Where a member's grievance is justified, the Committee contacts the member to discuss the case and plan an appropriate strategy for resolution. The Committee directs the member in the use of accepted business and legal procedures. Depending on the unique factors of each case, the Committee's assistance generally involves: (1) guiding the member's personal efforts to resolve the grievance; (2) directing communication with the buyer on the member's behalf; and (3) mediating, if requested by both parties, to achieve a private settlement.

If further action becomes necessary, other relevant alternatives are proposed by the Committee. These may include: (1) arbitration; (2) small claims court; (3) collection methods; (4) lawyer referral; or (5) litigation.

Members who wish to report unprofessional practices should forward them directly to the Grievance Committee at their local Guild Chapter. Members requesting Grievance Committee assistance should also contact their Guild chapter following the procedure on page 173.

The Guild's Professional Practices Committee

The Professional Practices Committee of the Guild seeks to address the issue of professional relations between artists and buyers by fostering an on-going dialogue with all commissioning parties.

The graphic communications industry, much as any other industry, has its instances of misunderstandings and disputes. At times, these are inevitably due to the nature of interaction between people. However, a sizeable degree of contention in artist-buyer relations results from an unawareness or disregard of common standards of professional practices.

It is the Guild's position that such problems can be reduced and that mutually beneficial and productive business practices can be advanced through discussion and negotiation. Both formal and informal communication between the Guild and the industry has existed since the Guild's inception. The Guild has always acknowledged the legitimate concerns of both sides of professional issues. Through the Committee's activities, the Guild seeks to contribute to a broader and fuller understanding and commitment to professional standards of practice.

Media articles

A principal means through which the Committee focuses attention on professional practices is to initiate research into specific issues and produce articles for industry and Guild publications. The selection of topics results from both a monitoring of industry practices and from correspondence received by the Committee.

The Committee intends to expand the publication of its research and writing to reach a wider audience. These publications will take the form of individual articles, a newsletter series (such as the recent seven-part series on dispute-resolution alternatives) and feature columns. Professional associations and trade publishers can contact the Committee at the National Guild office to request articles, reprints, or reference material.

"Graphic Artists Aware" column

The Committee periodically publishes its "Graphic Artists Aware" column as the means of informing the Guild membership of and to acknowledge advancements made in artist-buyer practices.

The column which appears in national and local Guild newsletters, cites individual buyers and companies that have established more equitable terms for art commissions as a matter of policy. Such advances may have resulted through negotiations with the Guild, from communication with the Professional Practices Committee, or have been determined independently.

Inter-industry dialogue

The Committee invites art buyers, their agents and intermediaries, and reps to correspond with them and enter into a dialogue regarding professional practices.

The nature of such discussion should focus on the means for developing professional guidelines policy in the commissioning of artwork (rather than for the purpose of making a determination as to an existing individual misunderstanding or dispute).

PROFESSIONAL
ISSUES

Introduction: Professional Issues

The Graphic Artists Guild is mandated by its constitution to "promote and maintain high professional standards of ethics and practices...to establish, implement and enforce laws, policies, general and specific contracts designed to accomplish these ends."

Monitoring professional practices of graphic artists and their clients or employers has been a Guild activity since its inception and that monitoring has given the Guild a clear set of professional issues. All Guild practices are based on the idea of a value-for-value exchange between artist and client. Like other professionals, graphic artists provide services that clients cannot otherwise obtain. That service (and the special skill necessary to supply it) is the basis on which artists sell their work.

In today's communication industry, graphics presentations are among the most important vehicles that relay messages in our society. In fact, graphic elements are sometimes products as well as messages, as in the case of textile design. A successful illustration can often sell a company's image as well as its products; a successful logo can help with product or company recognition; and packaging can become the key to a product's success or failure on the market. Yet, as with other creative professions, the artist's role in the industry has not always been given the value it deserves. The Guild's goals are to effect a healthy balance between clients' and artists' needs.

Value exchange is denied to an artist who is asked to work on speculation, since the same skills and time are applied to work that is not paid for as for work that is. In other words, artists who could be spending productive, capital-producing periods for assured commissions, are being asked to spend time on projects that can be turned away without payment.

Value is denied when an artist's work is altered, mutilated, damaged or otherwise changed, since an artist's reputation is based on the final commercial use of the work.

Value is denied when an artist, through work for hire or other contract provisions, loses control or further use of his/her creations. The ability to protect the integrity of the artwork and to resell uses is critical to economic survival in the graphics industry.

Creative professionals—actors, musicians, architects, writers, dancers, and graphic artists—occupy a unique place in the society and in the economy. The skills they develop in order to perform their functions are, in some ways, unlike skills other professionals employ. However, like other professionals, artists provide a highly-skilled service, creative input and professional standards and ethics in their roles.

The Guild operates through legislative work, and the development of contract guidelines and ethical standards to insure the highest quality in the industry. It is part of the Guild's goal to encourage both clients and artists to adhere to these standards for the benefit of both parties and the industry.

Legislation

Like most other professional organizations, trade associations and unions, the Graphic Artists Guild monitors and lobbies for laws that affect its members. This activity takes place with member involvement at local, state and federal levels through chapters and the National organization. Since 1976 several legislative issues have been identified by Graphic Artists Guild members: the work-for-hire provision of the federal copyright law, moral rights, fair practices, and the right to make fair market charitable contributions of art under the tax laws.

The Guild has drafted model legislation and lobbied locally and nationally on these issues. Early successes in California, Oregon and New York indicate that Guild concerns are shared widely and its program of legislative goals is sound. In fact, the Guild has worked in tandem with a coalition of creators' organizations that has identified a community of interests encompassing the concerns of artists, photographers and writers. The creators' organization coalition, addressing legislative issues, now numbers

42 organizations with a combined membership of over one hundred thousand creators. Some of these groups have been active locally in lobbying for graphic arts legislation; they all share the Guild's sense of urgency for finding a federal remedy to the work-for-hire problem.

Work for hire

"Work for hire" is a provision of the U.S. copyright law. Under this provision, the employer or other commissioning party is deemed to have created the artwork for the purposes of the copyright law, leaving the artist with no rights whatsoever. And, since the artist is an independent contractor, he/she has no access to traditional employee benefits in this instance.

A work for hire can come into existence in two ways: (1) an employee creating a copyrightable work in the course of employment; or (2) a free-lancer creating a specially ordered or commissioned work in one of several categories verified as a work for hire by a signed contract. Freelance artists will be especially concerned with the following categories that can be covered under work for hire if the artist agrees:

1. A contribution to a collective work, such as a magazine, newspaper, encyclopedia or anthology;

2. A contribution used as part of a motion picture or other audio-visual work;

3. A supplementary work, which includes pictorial illustrations done to supplement a work by another author; and

4. An instructional text.

If no contract is signed stating that a work will be work for hire, it will not be—unless the artist is an employee creating the work in the course of employment. However, even as an employee, an artist may request a written contract which transfers copyright ownership to the artist.

The Graphic Artists Guild opposes the use of work-for-hire contracts and has introduced legislation to close this loophole in the copyright law. This position is supported by the major creators' organizations in the field and is echoed in the Code of Fair Practice, Article 15 (see page 36).

In 1982, California passed legislation on work for hire which states that any artist hired under a work-for-hire contract is eligible for employee benefits for the duration of that contract. This bill was supported by the Graphic Artists Guild and other creators' organizations active in the State. One of the intents of the supporters of this state legislation was to send a strong message to the U.S. Congress to provide a federal remedy for the work-for-hire problem.

Moral rights

The Moral Rights Act's conceptual roots come from the French concept of *Droit Moral:* the intrinsic right of artists to protect the integrity of their creations. California enacted such a law in 1979 for fine arts, and other states (notably Massachusetts) are considering similar proposals. New York State enacted a Moral Rights law in 1983 which protects artists and photographers from unauthorized alterations, defacement and mutilation of their work. It also ensures the creator the right to name credit, and the right to remove the artist's name from a piece that has been altered to its detriment by a client who has bought reproduction rights only.

Most of the cases that brought this problem to the public's attention revolve around the defacement of works of fine art, most notably the dismembering of a hanging sculpture created by Isamu Noguchi for the New York Headquarters of the Bank of Tokyo Trust Company. However, there was a much publicized case in the graphic arts area that involved Antonio Vargas' series, the "Vargas Girls," which ran in *Esquire Magazine.* After the expiration of Vargas' contract with *Esquire,* the magazine continued to run the series under the name, "The Esquire Girls," denying the original creator credit for the work. Vargas brought *Esquire* to court but lost the case. If that case were brought to court in New York State today, he would have a far better chance of winning.

New York law now protects editorial illustrators against reproductions of their work which are badly cropped, used out of the original context to the detriment of the work, recolored or otherwise negatively altered by the client. Since most editorial artists build their reputations through the dissemination of reproductions of their work, they can be severely damaged by unauthorized reproductions.

The right of the artist to protect the integrity of their work is so important and widely recognized that bills have been introduced repeatedly on a federal level to set a national standard in this area. As recognition of our society's interest in protecting our cultural and artistic heritage grows, more local bills will be introduced, which will send a message to Congress of the need for federal action on this issue.

Fair practices

The Fair Practices Act, signed into law in Oregon, 1979; in California, 1982; and in New York, 1983 (pending in Massachusetts); clarifies who owns the original work of art when reproduction rights are sold. The Act provides that an original work of art can become property of a client only if it is sold *in writing*. The passage of this act reinforces one of the premises of the copyright law, which is that works of art have value beyond their reproduction for a specific purpose, and that that value rightly belongs to the artist who creates them. The Fair Practices Act will prevent clients from holding on to originals unless they have written sales agreements with the creator. In Oregon and California, the law provides that if there is any ambiguity as to who owns reproduction rights, the ambiguity shall be resolved in favor of the creator/artist.

For artists whose livelihoods depend on resale of reproduction rights and on sales of original works, this law is critical. It also sets a precedent for clearing up any ambiguity in ownership since a written transfer is now required.

Tax deductions on art

There is a popular misconception that an artist donating his or her art to a charitable organization may deduct the "fair market value" of the work. In fact, the artist may deduct only the cost of producing the work, i.e. the price of the canvas, paint and other materials. If however, the artist sells the original, the buyer may donate the work and deduct the fair market value. As a result, artists have either withheld their valuable originals or sold them to private collectors, limiting public access.

Historically, artists, writers and politicians were able to donate their original art and manuscripts and receive the full market value deduction. In 1969, the situation changed dramatically. Congress sought to prevent politicians from receiving windfalls based on the donations of their papers. Broad legislation was enacted, inhibiting artists and writers as well as politicians. Since 1969, museums, which depend on artists' donations of original art to supplement their

paid acquisitions have documented a sharp drop-off of donations.

Artists and writers have spoken out about this obvious inequity and have received the support of their professional organizations. They have acted in cooperation with museums, universities and libraries whose representatives believe that public access to art is in the public interest.

Speculation: ethical and unethical practices

The Graphic Artists Guild is unalterably opposed to any artist being asked to work "on speculation" because of the inherent risks to the artist in such circumstances. Art buyers should not ask artists to work on a project unless a fee has been agreed upon in advance.

An artist must be equitably compensated at any time he or she is requested to create artwork. Working on speculation places all the risks on the artist without a commitment on the buyer's part.

It is therefore considered an unethical practice, for example, for a buyer to be in the position of deciding only upon completion of the art whether or not to compensate the artist. This situation occurs in agreements where payment becomes dependent on the "buyer's satisfaction" or "on publication."

In royalty arrangements for commissioned art, an advance must be provided. Payment of the advance allows the artist to more timely recoup expenses and to more realistically manage the financial demands of the project.

Similarly, in cancellation of jobs resulting from a buyer's decision, cancellation fees must be paid at all times to compensate the artist for expended professional time, effort and expenses.

Art contests, except under special circumstances, are also opposed because of their speculative nature. For contest guidelines approved by the Guild, see pages 47 to 48.

However, when the artist creates artwork on his or her own initative and then seeks to sell it to a buyer for speculative marketing, it is considered ethical speculation and not in violation of this rule.

Where an artist in this type of situation, for example, has entered a royalty arrangement in a book contract, both artist and publisher are taking a mutual risk in their investment. The compensation to both parties is "speculative"—that is, the compensation to both being dependent on the market response to their product.

Contests and competitions

Illustrators and designers share the enticement of the competition in common with other creative professionals—musicians, ballerinas, painters and sculptors.

Each year in the United States several hundred unethical art contests are held in the field of illustration alone. There are, however, almost a dozen art competitions recognized and respected by professional artists.

Art contests, in contrast with art competitions, are usually the creation of organizations or clients who wish to see a vast array of artistic solutions to a specific problem—at low or no cost. As you may see clearly in the Code of Fair Practice (refer to page 38), the Guild opposes such contests because of their speculative and exploitative nature.

In 1980, a New York group called Designers Saturday (DS) approached the Guild seeking a solution to their dilemma: designers they had hired in the past to create graphics for their annual showroom tour had not, they felt, met the challenge of creating an exciting, inspired design.

Taking the concept of audition used by other creative professionals, the Guild suggested the creation of an ethical contest as a vehicle for encouraging healthy competition *and* increased publicity for Designer's Saturday. The cornerstone of the initial call for entry would be an "audition" of portfolios.

Designer's Saturday selected a jury that included three highly revered professionals, Massimo Vignelli, Arthur Drexler and Helmut Krone. They then gathered 45 designers' names from various design organizations. The designers were made aware of the rules of the audition and the rewards of selection. At the audition, three finalists were chosen from the portfolios submitted. Each finalist was allowed one interview with DS to be briefed on the needs of the project and to discuss the problems involved (see page 160), which specified a fee for the submission of a comprehensive design.

After the entries were assessed, it was clear that the process was a success. The winner, Gilbert Lesser, designed a long, shiny box from which a sponge rubber arm chair popped out when opened.

The jury, DS, and ultimately the consumer were all pleased, amused and impressed. Gilbert Lesser was paid an additional fee to complete production on his winning entry, and all other terms of the contract were fulfilled.

This success sparked the Guild's interest in pursuing a more thorough study of the need for and interest in art contests and competitions held within the United States.

At this writing, an NEA grant study has been in progress for over a year. The study will result in specific guidelines for contest and competition holders and entrants. In the case of art contests, several models will be developed based on the audition concept. Below is a step-by-step outline of the components of the Designer's Saturday Contest, which will be used as the model for professional design contests open or limited call for entries:

1. The call for entries should request existing printed pieces to be submitted and indicate these pieces will not be returned. It should also clearly define the contest and prizes, including the form of letter of agreement to be used.

2. The review of the samples should reduce the number of artists to those whose work is appropriate for a portfolio review.

3. The portfolio review, depending on the number of portfolios and geographic areas involved, may be held several different ways: (1) the submission of slides; (2) the submission of a portfolio (if feasible); (3) in-person interviews (if only a small number of artists are involved). If slides or a portfolio are submitted, the sponsor should sign and return to the artist a holding form in which the sponsor agrees to take reasonable care of the material in its possession. Ideally, the sponsor should provide insurance for such materials. If insurance is provided by the sponsor, the holding form should advise the artist of this.

4. The appropriate jury will be designated by the sponsors with one member of the jury designated as the "art buyer."

5. The number of artists selected after portfolio review and asked to submit sketches or comprehensives should be small and depend on the nature of the prize. If the prize is money, all the artists asked to submit sketches or comprehensives should receive some portion of the prize. If the prize is an award, all these artists should receive awards. In this way the speculative nature of the contest is avoided.

6. Letters of agreement should be

issued to each artist asked to work on the project. The Guild's contracts or equivalents should be used. This must include terms covering ownership of art, the nature of the credit line, copyright ownership, and the price to be paid to the artist. It should also define the job clearly.

7. Commencement of the project will begin once the artists have received their letters of agreement. The process for approving sketches and the requirements for the complexity and tightness of the comprehensives shall be agreed to by the artist and sponsor prior to the commencement of work. If the prize is an award, all expenses should be reimbursed and the letter of agreement should so provide.

8. When viewing the comprehensive the jury or the art buyer should review the final submissions and select the winner. The winner shall, depending on the object of the contest, go to camera-ready art and on to a printed piece, if it is appropriate.

.9. The prize or award should be significantly greater for the winner who has completed the project than for the other finalists who have done less work.

The problem of art competitions is quite different from that of art contests. There are several reputable, established annual competitions that the Guild is using as a reference for standard guidelines. Two organizations, the Society of Illustrators and the American Institute of Graphic Arts (AIGA), who are also sponsors of regular competitions have already shown significant support for this project. The study will result in clear procedures that already exist in some of the larger annual competitions, but which have never been standardized.

As with Designer's Saturday, the Guild continues to offer a service to contest and competition holders that includes a review of guidelines, recommendations for changes, and when the standard has been met

Cancellation fees

The Graphic Artists Guild strongly supports the *Code of Fair Practice* article that condemns the practice of commissioning artists to work on speculation. All assignments should provide for a fee, even in the event of cancellation. The written agreement between artist and buyer should contain a "cancellation provision" based on the following guiding principles:

Cancellation fees The client agrees to pay the artist a cancellation fee if the assignment is cancelled.

1. If cancellation occurs after the completion of finishes and is due to any reason other than the finishes not being reasonably satisfactory, the cancellation fee shall be 100% of the original usage fee. (If the cancellation is due to finishes not being reasonably satisfactory, the fee shall be no less than 66% of the original usage fee.)

2. If cancellation occurs prior to the completion of finishes, the cancellation fee shall be no less than 50% of the original usage fee if cancelled for reasons other than the work not being reasonably satisfactory. (The cancellation fee shall be no less than 33% if cancelled work is not reasonably satisfactory.)

3. If cancellation occurs during or after the completion of preliminary work, the client shall pay the artist a cancellation fee based on the artist's hourly rate.

4. All necessary and related expenses shall be paid in full.

5. In the event of cancellation, the client obtains all of the originally agreed-upon rights to the use of the artwork (except royalty arrangements) if the work was cancelled for reasons other than the work not being reasonably satisfactory. (Where work is cancelled for not being reasonably satisfactory, the artist shall retain ownership of all artwork, concepts, and rights of copyright.)

6. If cancelled preliminary or incomplete work is later used as finished art, the client will pay the unpaid balance of the original usage fee.

7. Both artist and client agree to submit any dispute regarding cancellation fees to the Joint Ethics Committee or other forum for binding arbitration.

The cancellation fees shown in these guidelines are commonly accepted. These fees are flexible. If preliminary work is unusually complex or the assignment was required to be done on a very short deadline, the artist could reasonably expect higher cancellation fees.

The Guild monitors abuses that take place with regard to cancellation fees. Even if contracts are verbal (or written but lack a cancellation provision), clients and artists should follow the accepted trade practices reflected in the Guild's cancellation guidelines. Any failure to follow these standards should be reported immediately to the Grievance Committee of the local Guild chapter.

PRICES
AND TRADE CUSTOMS

General Illustration

Ggeneral illustrators are graphic artists who create visuals for print media in many different styles and many different markets. Most illustrators are freelance artists as opposed to salaried artists. They maintain their own studios, frequently in their homes. While advertising artists often have representatives to promote their work with advertising agencies, editorial illustrators most often represent themselves.

The illustrator uses a variety of techniques such as air brush, pastel, pen and ink, water color, mixed media and computer-generated work. Live models, clip files of reference material and books are among the many resources needed in planning and completing illustration. It is important for an illustrator to have some knowledge of the various printing and separation methods in order to maintain the quality of the final printed piece.

Illustrators work almost exclusively with art directors, editors, designers and other graphics professionals, either through their representatives or directly. Most illustration is sold on the basis of usage and reproduction rights. That is, the price quoted on a project is based on the standard factors of deadline, overhead, complexity of style, *intended usage* and *intended market.* The original artwork, unless sold separately, is the property of the illustrator.

Usage rights sold are generally based on the client's needs. Other non-competitive uses for an artwork may be sold as long as they do not compromise the commissioning client's market. In any event, it is recommended that the client only buy rights particular to his/her project, leaving the illustrator to sell other rights the client chooses not to buy.

It is imperative that, in judging the context of the Guild's pricing survey, the chapters preceding and following the Prices be studied thoroughly.

Where this symbol ★ appears:
Suggested prices from data in 1980 and 1983 national surveys do not reflect fluctuating regional inflationary and cost-of-living increases. It is recommended that consideration be given to this fact when estimating prices.

Advertising illustration

Aan *advertising illustrator* is a graphic artist who works with the art director, account executive, copywriter, and/or creative group head of an agency to illustrate products or services for specific advertising needs. The agency often asks the illustrator to work in a specific style represented in his or her portfolio. The illustrator often follows a sketch supplied by the agency and approved by the client. The terms and fee for the art are often negotiated by the illustrator or the artist's representative with the agency's art buyer.

The premium prices for illustration are paid in the advertising field where the highest degree of professionalism and performance is expected from the artist working within unusually strict time demands. Changes and last minute alterations are not uncommon. The illustrator may need to create work that will please several people of varying opinions since many advertisements are created by committee. Prices are negotiated strictly on a *use* basis with extra dividends for complexity of style, tighter deadlines, residual rights sold, and "buy-outs."

The three categories of magazines used in the tables are discussed in the Editorial Illustration section. Examples of each can also be found in that section.

All prices for illustration in the *Guidelines* are based on a nationwide survey which was then reviewed by a group of experts through the Graphic Artists Guild. The prices represent average fees for work done by most professional illustrators. These figures are meant as a point of reference only and do not necessarily reflect such important factors as deadlines, job complexity, research, reputation and experience of a particular artist, technique or unique quality of expression, and extraordinary or extensive use of the finished illustration.

The prices here represent *only the specific use for which the illustration is intended* and do not necessarily reflect any of the above considerations. The buyer and seller are free to negotiate, taking into account all the factors involved. By their nature, however, advertisements are conceived of with multiple appearances in mind. Therefore, it's understood that the specific use may refer to unlimited use in a specific area, within a specified time period. This must be made clear before the project starts and the price is agreed upon.

The following standard trade practices should be adhered to:

1. It is of the utmost importance that the intended use of the art be made clear in a purchase order, contract or letter of agreement stating the price and terms of sale.

2. Normally, the artist sells only first reproduction rights unless otherwise stated.

3. If a piece of art is to be used for other than its original purpose, price should be negotiated as soon as possible. It is quite conceivable that the secondary use may be of *greater* value than the primary use so there is no formula for reuse fees.

4. An illustrator should negotiate reuse arrangements with the original commissioning party with speed, efficiency, and all due respect to the client's position.

5. Return of original artwork to the artist should be automatic unless otherwise negotiated.

6. The use of art always influences the price. If the advertising is to be featured over an extensive area or is a buyout, fees should be significantly higher than when it is used locally or within a selected area.

7. Fees for work required in a very short period of time should be higher than the figures listed here. Regular overtime figures may be used as a rule of thumb.

8. A rejection fee is negotiable but should always be paid. The rejection fee for finished work should be upwards of 50 percent of the full price depending on reasons for rejection and complexity of the job. When the job is rejected at the sketch stage, a fee of one-third of the original price is customary. This fee may be less for quick, rough sketches and more for highly rendered, time-consuming work.

9. A cancellation fee should be agreed upon if a job is cancelled through no fault of the artist. Depending upon the stage at which the job is terminated, the fee paid should cover all work done.

10. Any form of speculative work is absolutely rejected not only by the Graphic Artists Guild but by every other national professional organization.

11. The Graphic Artists Guild is unalterably opposed to the use of work-for-hire contracts.

12. Unusual props, costumes, models' fees, travel costs, production expenses, consultation time, etc. should be billed separately to the client. These fees should be agreed upon and set down in the original written agreement or as an amendment of the agreement.

13. In judging the context of the Guild's pricing survey, it is imperative that Part One of the *Guidelines* and the Code of Fair Practice be studied thoroughly.

Comparative fees for comprehensive illustration

Magazine advertising	Black and White	Full Color
Major national account Full page	$250	$375
Spread	400	500
Smaller regional account Full page	200	250
Spread	250	300

Television storyboards (per frame)

	Black and White	Full Color
National account, 3¾" × 2¾" (Miniboards)	30-40	35-50
Local account, 3¾" × 2¾" (Miniboards)	20-25	25-35
National account, 5" × 5"-5" × 7"	40-50	45-55
Local account, 5" × 5"-5" × 7"	30-40	45-55
National account, 8" × 10"	65-75	100-120
Local account, 8" × 10"	50-65	75-90

Comparative fees for point-of-purchase illustration (counter card, display, in-store promotion)

	Black and White*	Color
Complex	$2000	$2500
Simple	1200	1500

*Add 25 percent for each color overlay.

Comparative fees for packaging illustration*

Major company with national distribution	Black and White†	Color
Complex	$2500 + *	$4000 +
Simple	1800	2500

Smaller company with regional distribution		
Complex	2000 +	2500 +
Simple	1200	2000

*In this category, the size of the print order is the best method of determining the fee. Illustrations for packages produced for test marketing only should be priced accordingly; 100 percent payment should be specified for the eventuality of full production.

†Add 25 percent for each color overlay.

Comparative fees for major city transit-car card illustration

	Black and White	Color
Major corporation	$2000	$3000
Smaller corporation	1500	2000

Comparative fees for 24-sheet outdoor billboard advertising illustration

National campaign in major cities	$4500 +
Regional campaign in large cities	3000 +
Local campaign in one small city	1200

Comparative fees for film and audiovisual illustration

Television commercial

Styling of a 30- or 60-second animated spot including backgrounds and key illustrations, depending on complexity of illustrations and number of key illustrations required	$3500–12,000

Animatics

Depending on amount of illustrations and required use (animatics usually have a limited use)	$2000–4500

Audiovisual presentation*

Per color slide	$150
Per black-and-white slide	100

*Typical audiovisual presentations are meant to be quick and effective. The illustrations commissioned for this category are generally quite simple in style. More complexity would of course demand a higher fee.

Comparative fees for collateral advertising illustration

Major national account (Fortune 500)	Full Color
Cover and interior (4 pages)	$5000-8000
Cover only	4500-5000
Interior page	1500-2000
Interior page (multiple illustrations)	1750-2000
Spot	300-750

Smaller companies and regional divisions	Black and White	Full Color
Cover and interior	$1500-2000	$2000-3000
Cover only	1200-1500	2000
Interior (multiple illustrations on page)	1500-2000	2000-2500
Interior page	1200	1500
Spot/interior	500-750	600-800

Comparative fees for theater poster illustration ☆

	Major Production	Small Production
Broadway	$3500	$2000
Off-Broadway and regional theater	2500	1000

Comparative fees for consumer newspaper advertising illustration

National account	Black and White Only
Full page	$3000
Spread	3750
Half page	1750
Smaller than half page	1250
Column and lineage	500-750

Local account	
Full page	—
Half page	700-800

Trade publications (business to business) (nat. circ. 50,000)	Black and White	Full Color
Full page	1250	1750
Spread	1500	2000
Half page	1100	1500
Smaller than half page	500	1000

Comparative fees for motion picture poster illustration☆

Extra large-budget	$12,000–25,000 +
Major production	5000 – 7000
Small-budget film with independent financing	1500 – 4000

*The following factors should be taken into consideration for pricing. Many independently produced films have major studio distribution. Some small-budget films with independent distribution become quite successful. A royalty agreement with an advance payment may be appropriate in these cases. Sketch fees and nonreproduction fees should be decided upon before commencing work; many posters never go to finish or are never used.

Comparative fees for advertising illustration; based on one year campaign

National consumer magazine	Black and White	Full Color
Full page	$3000	$4500
Spread	4000	5000
Half page	2000	2500
Spot	1000	1250
Local newspaper magazine supplements		
Full page	1750	2500
Spread	2225	3250
Half page	1100	1500
Spot	800	1000

Comps, animatics, and TV storyboard illustration

Artists who specialize in audiovisual work mainly service the advertising industry and are usually called upon to produce very high caliber professional work within extremely tight deadlines. Although some tend to specialize, nearly all of these artists are engaged in three main areas of audiovisual graphics: comprehensives, or "comps" as they are generally called; animatics; and TV storyboards.

Comps are visual renderings of proposed advertisements and folders including headlines, body text, and a "visual," which is the sketch of the illustration or photo to be used in the finished piece. An *animatic* is a limited, animated film using camera movements, a select number of drawings, and a sound track, and is usually produced for the purpose of testing a proposed "spot" or TV commercial. The demand for animatics is currently on the rise due to the increased desirability of test marketing for advertisers. A *TV storyboard* is a visual presentation of a proposed commercial using a limited number of frames and usually drawn on a telepad.

Fees in this field depend on job complexity, including factors such as the degree of finish required, the number of subjects in a given frame, the type of background required, and so on.

Rush work is billable at a minimum of 25 percent more than the regular fee. Day rates are not encouraged and flat fees should be carefully priced on a per-frame basis which considers all of the factors involved.

All the prices for illustration in the *Guidelines* are based on a nationwide survey which was then reviewed by a group of experts through the Graphic Artists Guild. The prices represent average fees for work done by most professional illustrators. These figures are meant as a point of reference only and do not necessarily reflect such important factors as job complexity, research, reputation and experience of a particular artist, technique or unique quality of expression, and extraordinary or extensive use of the finished illustration.

The prices here represent *only the specific use for which the illustration is intended* and do not necessarily reflect any of the above considerations. The buyer and seller are free to negotiate, taking into account all the factors involved. By their nature, however, advertisements are conceived of with multiple appearances in mind. Therefore, it's understood that the specific use may refer to unlimited use in a specific area, within a specified time period. This must be made clear before the project starts and the price is agreed upon.

The following standard trade practices should be adhered to:

1. It is of the utmost importance that the intended use of the art be made clear in a purchase order, contract or letter of agreement stating the price and terms of sale.

2. Normally, an artist sells only first reproduction rights unless otherwise stated.

3. If a piece of art is to be used for other than its original purpose, price should be negotiated as soon as possible. It is quite conceivable that the secondary use may be of *greater* value than the primary use so there is no formula for reuse fees.

4. An illustrator should negotiate reuse arrangements with the original commissioning party with speed, efficiency, and all due respect to the client's position.

5. Return of original artwork to the artist should be automatic and timely unless otherwise negotiated.

6. The use of art always influences the price. If the illustration is to be featured over an extensive area or is a buyout, fees should be significantly higher than when it is used locally or within a selected area.

7. Fees for work required in a very short period of time should be higher than the figures listed here. Regular overtime figures may be used as a rule of thumb.

8. A rejection fee is negotiable but should always be paid. The rejection fee for finished work should be upwards of 50 percent of the full price depending on reasons for rejection and complexity of the job. When the job is rejected at the sketch stage, a fee of one-third of the original price is customary. This fee may be less for quick, rough sketches and more for highly rendered, time-consuming work.

9. A cancellation fee should be agreed upon if a job is cancelled through no fault of the artist. Depending upon the stage at which the job is terminated, the fee paid should cover all work done.

10. Any form of speculative work is absolutely rejected not only by the Graphic Artists Guild but by every other national professional organization.

11. The Graphic Artists Guild is unalterably opposed to the use of work-for-hire contracts.

12. Unusual props, costumes, models' fees, travel costs, production expenses, consultation time, etc. should be billed separately to the client. These fees should be agreed upon and set down in the original written agreement or as an amendment of the agreement.

13. In judging the context of the Guild's pricing survey, it is imperative that Part One of the *Guidelines* and the Code of Fair Practice be studied thoroughly.

Comparative fees for audiovisual graphics and illustration☆

Comprehensives in black & white	Major National Account	Regional Account, Limited Market
Single page	$175	$125
Double-page spread	350	250
Comprehensives in color		
Single page	350	200–250
Double-page spread	450–600	350–450
Television storyboards for animatics		
Per frame	125	175-200
Flat fee (30 seconds, 12 frames)	1750	2500
TV Storyboards (per frame)		
Miniboards*	20–25	10–15
Telepad†	35–50	20–25
4 × 5 inches	60–70	35–45
5 × 7 inches	65–75	40–55
8 × 10 inches	100	70–80

*Miniboards are less than 2¾ × 3¾ inches.

†Telepads are 2¾ × 3¾ inches.

Institutional and corporate illustration

An *institutional* or *corporate illustrator* is a graphic artist who works with a graphic designer or art director to create illustrations for use in annual reports, in-house magazines or newspapers, and similar material. Often the illustrator is given responsibility for conceiving the concept and determining the style of the illustration. In annual reports particularly, illustration becomes a showcase in which the client enhances the institution's or corporation's image.

All the prices for illustration in the *Guidelines* are based on a nationwide survey which was then reviewed by a group of experts through the Graphic Artists Guild. The prices represent average fees for work done by most professional illustrators. These figures are meant as a point of reference only and do not necessarily reflect such important factors as job complexity, research, deadline, reputation and experience of a particular artist, technique or unique quality of expression, and extraordinary or extensive use of the finished illustration.

The prices here represent *only the specific use for which the illustration is intended* and do not necessarily reflect any of the above considerations. The buyer and seller are free to negotiate, taking into account all the factors involved. By their nature, however, advertisements are conceived of with multiple appearances in mind. Therefore, it's understood that the specific use may refer to unlimited use in a specific area, within a specified time period. This must be made clear before the project starts and the price is agreed upon.

The following standard trade practices should be adhered to:

1. It is of the utmost importance that the intended use of the art be made clear in a purchase order, contract or letter of agreement stating the price and terms of sale.

2. Normally, an artist sells only first reproduction rights unless otherwise stated.

3. If a piece of art is to be used for other than its original purpose, price should be negotiated as soon as possible. It is quite conceivable that the secondary use may be of *greater* value than the primary use so there is no formula for reuse fees.

4. An illustrator should negotiate reuse

arrangements with the original commissioning party with speed, efficiency, and all due respect to the client's position.

5. Return of original artwork to the artist should be automatic and timely unless otherwise negotiated.

6. The use of art always influences the price. If the illustration is to be featured over an extensive area or is a buyout, fees should be significantly higher than when it is used locally or within a selected area.

7. Fees for work required in a very short period of time should be higher than the figures listed here. Regular overtime figures may be used as a rule of thumb.

8. A rejection fee is negotiable but should always be paid. The rejection fee for finished work should be upwards of 50 percent of the full price depending on reasons for rejection and complexity of the job. When the job is rejected at the sketch stage, a fee of one-third of the original price is customary. This fee may be less for quick, rough sketches and more for highly rendered, time-consuming work.

9. A cancellation fee should be agreed upon if a job is cancelled through no fault of the artist. Depending upon the stage at which the job is terminated, the fee paid should cover all work done.

10. Any form of speculative work is absolutely rejected not only by the Graphic Artists Guild but by every other national professional organization.

11. The Graphic Artists Guild is unalterably opposed to the use of work-for-hire contracts.

12. Unusual props, costumes, models' fees, travel costs, production expenses, consultation time, etc. should be billed separately to the client. These fees should be agreed upon and set down in the original written agreement or as an amendment of the agreement.

13. In judging the context of the Guild's pricing survey, it is imperative that Part One of the *Guidelines* and the Code of Fair Practice be studied thoroughly.

Company magazines and in-house organs

In recent times, with the growth of national corporations and conglomerates (corporations with diverse holdings), we are seeing the emergence on a much larger scale of the company magazine. Often the audience is comparatively small but the budgets are much larger than those of many consumer magazines. The company magazine does not depend on circulation and advertising-page revenues for income but rather works with a budget directly funded by the parent corporation.

Nonprofit or *not-for-profit corporations* are groups and associations that incorporate for purposes other than private profit. These corporations raise their operating funds from membership dues, grants, and contributions. The Ford Foundation, Common Cause, religious organizations, labor unions, and the Graphic Artists Guild are examples of nonprofit organizations.

Fortune double-500 companies are 1000 of the largest corporations in the world ranked by net worth in an annual survey by *Fortune* magazine. They generally have more than 100 employees, though they are ranked by net worth rather than the number of employees.

Annual reports

An *annual report* is the yearly fiscal report of a major company. It usually reflects the image of the company which its board of directors and officers wish to present to the stockholders and the financial community.

In this field, illustrators are often called upon to do thoughtful, provocative, and interesting illustrations to offset the dry written and financial material that is being presented. Annual reports turn out to be highly effective vehicles of the company's self-promotion.

Fees are relative to the size of the corporation and the nature of the annual report. Modestly produced reports in two colors generally do not have the budgets that more lavish annual reports have printed in four colors on expensive stock. Fees are usually negotiated on a one-time use basis only.

Corporate calenders

Prices for illustration for company calendars can vary greatly. Usually, the fee is dependent on the size of the company and the complexity of the subject.

Comparative fees for company magazines and in-house organs☆

Fortune double-500 company	Black and White*	Color
Cover	$2000	$2500
Spread	1700	2200
Full page	1200	1500
Half page	600	1000
Quarter page	400	500
Spot	250	300

Small corporation

	Black and White*	Color
Cover	1200	1500
Spread	1000	1500
Full page	750	1000
Half page	450	600
Quarter page	300	350
Spot	175	200

Nonprofit corporation

	Black and White*	Color
Cover	750	1000
Spread	600	750
Full page	450	600
Half page	300	400
Quarter page	175	250
Spot	100	150

*Add 25 percent for each color overlay.

Comparative fees for annual report illustrations☆

Fortune double-500 company	Black and White	Color
Cover	$ —	$4000
Full page	1700	2500
Half page	1000	1500
Quarter page (approximate)	600	850

Smaller companies, including nonprofit

	Black and White	Color
Cover	—	2800
Full page	800	1200
Half page	500	750
Quarter page (approximate)	350	500

*Add 25 percent for each color overlay.

Comparative fees for twelve illustrations for company calendars☆

	Black and White	Color
Fortune double-500 company	$ —	$12,000 – 15,000
Small company	6000	9000

Book jacket illustration

Book jacket illustration and design is the second most important ingredient in the promotion and sale of a book, superceded only by the fame and success of the author.

The publishing business has undergone a period of tremendous growth and change in the last decade and many of the large publishing houses have been acquired by conglomerates. Still, the publishing business is flourishing, and prices for book jacket and paperback cover illustration have risen accordingly.

It is a complex area of illustration for pricing, so strict attention should be paid to all the factors involved. For example, paperback covers generally pay better than hardcovers simply because the paperback market is much larger. Also many book jacket illustrators act as both designer and illustrator and so their method of doing business is structured somewhat differently (book jacket designer/illustrators should refer to the Book Jacket Design section for further information).

It is important to note that illustrators who specialize in the book jacket field tend to receive lower fees than illustrators who do only several covers a year. Illustrators known for their painterly, highly realistic, or dramatic styles may command much higher fees than those whose style is more graphic and design oriented. Although this practice is prevalent in the entire illustration field, it is particularly evident in publishing.

Major paperback houses sometimes put illustrators under contract to do a specified minimum number of covers per year at per-cover fees from $1500 to $3500 and more plus expenses. In such cases, contract terms must be clearly understood or checked by an attorney. Such contracts may prohibit the illustrator from working for other publishers.

Paperback publishers often give very specific instructions on every assignment including the art director's rough notes from a cover conference. If the illustrator is required to read a lengthy manuscript in search of illustrative material and then produce sketches subject to approval by editors and an art director, the estimated time should be taken into account when negotiating the fee.

Other factors requiring additional fees are as follows: (1) The publisher may change approach and direction after sketches are completed, and require new sketches: (2) Art is used in promotional material above and beyond what is the common trade practice (when art is used separately from the cover it is considered advertising): (3) An extremely tight color comprehensive is specified (for sales meetings and catalogs). All of these contingencies ought to be understood and negotiated by buyer and seller before the assignment is confirmed.

All the prices for illustration in the *Guidelines* are based on a nationwide survey which was then reviewed by a group of experts through the Graphic Artists Guild. The prices represent average fees for work done by most professional illustrators. These figures are meant as a point of reference only and do not necessarily reflect such important factors as job complexity, research, reputation and experience of a particular artist, technique or unique quality of expression, and extraordinary or extensive use of the finished illustration.

The prices here represent *only the specific use for which the illustration is intended* and do not necessarily reflect any of the above considerations. The buyer and seller are free to negotiate, taking into acount all the factors involved. By their nature, however, advertisements are conceived of with multiple appearances in mind. Therefore, it's understood that the specific use may refer to unlimited use in a specific area, within a specified time period. This must be made clear before the project starts and the price is agreed upon.

The following standard trade practices should be adhered to:

1. It is of the utmost importance that the intended use of the art be made clear in a purchase order, contract or letter of agreement stating the price and terms of sale.

2. Normally, an artist sells only first reproduction rights unless otherwise stated.

3. If a piece of art is to be used for other than its original purpose, price should be negotiated as soon as possible. It is quite conceivable that the secondary use may be of *greater* value than the primary use so there is no formula for reuse fees.

4. An illustrator should negotiate reuse arrangements with the original commissioning party with speed, efficiency, and all due respect to the client's position.

5. Return of original artwork to the artist should be automatic and timely unless otherwise negotiated.

6. The use of art always influences the price. If the illustration is to be featured over an extensive area or is a buyout, fees should be significantly higher than when it is used locally or within a selected area.

7. Fees for work required in a very short period of time should be higher than the figures listed here. Regular overtime figures may be used as a rule of thumb.

8. A rejection fee is negotiable but should always be paid. The rejection fee for finished work should be upwards of 50 percent of the full price depending on reasons for rejection and complexity of the job. When the job is rejected at the sketch stage, a fee of one-third of the original price is customary. This fee may be less for quick, rough sketches and more for highly rendered, time-consuming work.

9. A cancellation fee should be agreed upon if a job is cancelled through no fault of the artist. Depending upon the stage at which the job is terminated, the fee paid should cover all work done.

10. Any form of speculative work is absolutely rejected not only by the Graphic Artists Guild but by every other national professional organization.

11. The Graphic Artists Guild is unalterably opposed to the use of work-for-hire contracts.

12. Unusual props, costumes, models' fees, travel costs, production expenses, consultation time, etc. should be billed separately to the client. These fees should be agreed upon and set down in the original written agreement or as an amendment of the agreement.

13. In judging the context of the Guild's pricing survey, it is imperative that Part One of the *Guidelines* and the Code of Fair Practice be studied thoroughly.

Mass market and trade

Mass market books are mysteries, spy stories, gothics, fantasy and science fiction, historical and modern romance novels that appeal to a wide audience. Trade books are books of poetry, serious fiction, biography, how-to books, and more scholarly works that appeal to a special audience.

Mass market books obviously pay higher fees because of the larger print runs and profitability; leading mass market books command the premium prices.

Size of the print order should always be taken into account.

A hardcover assignment might also include paperback rights, for which a minimum of 50 percent of the original fee should be charged. A considerably larger paperback reprinting should amount to 100 percent of the original fee and possibly more.

Domestic book club rights are usually included in the original hardcover fee. Foreign reprints and foreign book club rights usually pay 25 to 50 percent of the original fee.

All other residual rights, especially movie and television rights, should be negotiated separately.

Comparative fees for book cover illustrations☆

	Wrap-around Cover	Front Cover Only
Trade paperback, major publisher with major distribution	1600	1200
Trade paperback, small publisher with independent distribution	1000	850
Mass market paperback, major publisher with major distribution	3000	2500–2700
Mass market paperback, small publisher with independent distribution	1500	1000
	Black and White *	Color
Paperback text, major publisher with major distribution	600	850
Paperback text, small publisher with independent distribution	400	600

*Add 25 percent for each color overlay.

Comparative fees for book jacket illustrations☆

	Wrap-around Cover	Front Cover Only
Hardcover, mass market, major publisher with major distribution	$3000	$2500
Hardcover, regular trade, major publisher with major distribution	1700	1200
Hardcover, small publisher with independent distribution	650–1000	500–800
Hardcover, trade, young adult, major publisher with major distribution	1200	1000

	Black and White*	Color
Hardcover text, major publisher with major distribution	$650	$1000
Hardcover text, small publisher with independent distribution	450	700

*Add 25 percent for each color overlay.

Book illustration

A *book illustrator* is a graphic artist who works with an editor, art director, or book designer to create illustrations for a trade or text title. Book illustration varies from simple, instructional line drawings for textbooks to full-color spread illustrations for picture books. The book and its related elements is considered a package. The importance of illustration to the package may be minor or major depending on the needs of the book as determined by the publisher. Book illustrators are sometimes authors and/or designers as well. Occasionally, they create the entire package.

In cases where a publisher has a larger budget for a book and the visuals are of major importance, endpapers, die cuts, pop-ups, and other elements may be considered possible.

The artist has long been recognized as an important ingredient to the editorial value of a book as well as a promotional force in its sale. This extensive field of illustration offers myriad assignments to artists; however, artists' relations with publishers have often suffered from tradition-bound restrictions. The size of the print order, use of art in promotional material, and reprint and reuse of artwork are all legitimate points for price negotiations. Other factors affecting fees in this complex area include:

1. When inside illustrations require extensive research, props, renderings, or model fees, additional payment should be made. The price range is often dictated by the type of book and the importance of the author.

2. The size of the contemplated print order and the artist's reputation and record of commercial success should be taken into consideration when determining the fee.

3. When asked to do color separations (or overlays), the artist should be paid *as much as or more than* the price of full-color illustrations; in effect, the artist is doing the engraver's work, thus reducing engraving costs. Unless otherwise negotiated, original art should be returned to the illustrator, who normally sells only first reproduction rights.

4. When art is reused, an additional fee must be negotiated. It is customary for illustrators to receive one-half of the original price for the reuse of their art. If the art is to be widely used in promotional material, then this factor should be taken into account *when negotiating the original fee.*

5. Long, time-consuming projects (books with many illustrations) require payment to the illustrator as work progresses. For example, one-third the total fee should be paid upon approval of sketches, one-third upon delivery of finished art, and the remainder within thirty days of delivery of finished art.

All of the prices for illustration in the *Guidelines* are based on a nationwide survey which was then reviewed by a group of experts through the Graphic Artists Guild. The prices represent average fees for work done by most professional illustrators. These figures are meant as a point of reference only and do not necessarily reflect such important factors as job complexity, reputation and experience of a particular artist, technique or unique quality of expression, and extraordinary or extensive use of the finished illustration.

The prices here represent *only the specific use for which the illustration is intended* and do not necessarily reflect any of the above considerations. The buyer and seller are free to negotiate, taking into account all the factors involved. By their nature, however, advertisements are conceived of with multiple appearances in mind. Therefore, it's understood that the specific use may refer to unlimited use in a specific area, within a specified time period. This must be made clear before the project starts and the price is agreed upon.

The following standard trade practices should be adhered to:

1. It is of the utmost importance that the intended use of the art be made clear in a purchase order, contract or letter of agreement stating the price and terms of sale.

2. An illustrator should negotiate reuse arrangements with the original commissioning party with speed, efficiency, and all due respect to the client's position.

3. Fees for work required in a very short period of time should be higher than the figures listed here. Regular overtime figures may be used as a rule of thumb.

4. A rejection fee is negotiable but should always be paid. The rejection fee for finished work should be upwards of 50 percent of the full price depending on reasons for rejection and complexity of the job. When the job is rejected at the sketch stage, a fee of one-third of the original price is customary. This fee may be less for quick, rough sketches and more for highly rendered, time-consuming work.

5. A cancellation fee should be agreed upon if a job is cancelled through no fault of the artist. Depending upon the stage at which the job is terminated, the fee paid should cover all work done.

6. Any form of speculative work is absolutely rejected not only by the Graphic Artists Guild but by every other national professional organization.

7. The Graphic Artists Guild is unalterably opposed to the use of work-for-hire contracts.

8. In judging the context of the Guild's pricing survey, it is imperative that Part One of the *Guidelines* and the Code of Fair Practice studied thoroughly.

Children's picture books

An advance against royalties is usually paid; one-half is paid on signing the contract and one-half on delivery of artwork. The royalty and amount of the advance against the royalty are determined by the illustrator and publisher based on the illustrator's reputation, experience, and desirability of talent rather than number of pages to be illustrated or whether the color is to be preseparated or done in full color.

The publisher usually suggests color limitations and size, but the illustrator often has a say on how the books will be produced. When doing color separations on books with a fourth color, that color should be negotiated as additional work since most preseparated books are two or three colors.

Advance against royalties are negotiable, and it is not advisable to accept the first offer from the publisher. Obviously, it is to the illustrator's advantage to obtain as large an advance as possible, since a considerable time period can pass before royalties are actually paid, and a publisher usually will be more committed to the sale of a book when a higher advance has been paid. An advance against royalties should always be paid, otherwise the work is considered speculative in nature.

The jacket art is usually wraparound, and is considered part of the total negotiated price for the book.

The following prices indicate the range of advances against royalties prevailing in the marketplace.

Publishers usually pay less to one person who writes and illustrates a book (author/illustrator) than they pay in total to an author and an illustrator working on a book together. This is not very logical and sometimes works to the *advantage* of the publisher, but it is currently a trade practice which the Guild opposes.

Paperback editions should be negotiated separately. Usually, illustrators are not offered any additional advance when their books are reprinted in paperback, and the royalty is less than the hardback edition. However, an advance for paperback rights *is a negotiable item and should be negotiated at the time of the original contract.*

The contract for a picture book can be a complicated legal agreement. It is advised that the illustrator seek professional advice before signing. The Guild strongly recommends that an attorney look over the contract if the illustrator is unfamiliar with or is uncertain about what is being signed. Remember, a contract is a *negotiated* agreement between the illustrator and the publisher and is legally binding.

Young adult picture books

Usually, no advances or royalties are paid in this category. All books are done for a straight fee. A typical book includes a full-color wraparound jacket and from 8 to 14 black-and-white interior illustrations of various sizes.

Juvenile workbooks

Most workbooks are given out through brokers or agents who generally work directly with the publisher at pricing out each book. Brokers and agents specializing in this field represent many illustrators who work in varied styles. Workbooks usually are priced out per page, per half page, or per spot; although fees are quite low, an entire workbook can add up to a considerable amount of work. Artists who are able to turn out this kind of artwork at a fast rate (obviously, one must work in a simple style) may find this type of assignment quite lucrative and feel secure in knowing that months of work lie ahead. Often, a single book needing a considerable amount of illustration is divided up among several illustrators in order to meet its publishing date.

Budgets for workbooks vary considerably depending on the size of the publisher, locality, publication schedules and experience of the artist.

Fees for young adult hardcover books ☆

Full-color book jacket

Front only	$600
Wraparound	1000

Interior illustrations in black-and-white*

Spread	600
Full page	350†
Half page or smaller	200†

*Add 25 percent for each color overlay.
†Fee depends on complexity.

Comparative fees for interior illustrations for trade paperback and adult paperback ☆

Major publisher with major distribution	Black and White
Spread	$500
Full page	300
Half page	200
Quarter page	150
Spot	100

Small publisher with independent distribution	
Spread	350
Full page	200
Half page	150
Quarter page	100
Spot	75

Comparative fees for interior illustrations for college and young adult textbooks ☆

Major publisher with major distribution and large print runs	Black and White*	Color
Spread	$600	$750
Full page	500	600
Half page	350	400
Quarter page	250	300
Spot	150	200

Major publisher with major distribution	Black and White*	Color
Spread	450	600
Full page	350	450
Half page	250	300
Quarter page	175	200
Spot	125	150

Small publisher with independent distribution	Black and White*	Color
Spread	350	450
Full page	250	350
Half page	150	250
Quarter page	100	175
Spot	75	100

*Add 25 percent for each color overlay.

Royalty for paperback rights

Author/illustrator: 8 percent
Author and illustrator separately: 4 percent

Comparative fees for interior illustrations for trade and adult hardcover books ☆

Major publisher with major distribution and large print runs	Black and White*	Color
Spread	$1000	$1500
Full page	750	850
Half page	400	500
Quarter page	300	400
Spot	200	250

Major publisher with major distribution	Black and White*	Color
Spread	500	750
Full page	350	450
Half page	250	350
Quarter page	200	250
Spot	125	150

Small publisher with independent distribution	Black and White*	Color
Spread	350	450
Full page	250	300
Half page	175	200
Quarter page	125	150
Spot	75	100

*Add 25 percent for each color overlay.

Advances against royalties for children's picture books*☆

	Text and Illustrations	Illustrations Only
First book (previously unpublished)	$3000–3500	$2000–2500
Previously published	4000–4500†	2500–3000‡

*Standard royalty arrangements are 10 percent up to 15,000 copies and 12½ percent thereafter for an author/illustrator; 5 percent up to 15,000 copies and 6¼ percent thereafter for the author and illustrator separately.

†Can go as high as $6000 to 8000 for an illustrator with a notable reputation or a very complex style.

‡Can go as high as $8000 to 10,000 for an author/illustrator with a notable reputation or a very complex style.

Comparative fees for juvenile workbooks☆

Major publisher	Spirit Duplicating Master*	Color
Full page	$ —	$ 300+
Half page	—	250
Quarter page	—	150
Spot	25	40
Small publisher		
Full page	—	250
Half page	—	185
Quarter page	—	100
Spot	15	25

*Black and white line.

Editorial illustration

An *editorial illustrator* is a graphic artist who works with the editor and art director of consumer and trade magazines and newspapers to illustrate specific stories, covers, columns, or other editorial material. The editor, art director, and illustrator discuss the use, slant, and intended impact of the piece or pieces of art before sketches are prepared by the illustrator. Often the illustrator prepares several sketches to explore a range of approaches to the problem. Editorial art is often commissioned under tight deadlines, especially in news publications.

Fees for editorial illustration have traditionally been lower than fees in the advertising field. This is generally true for all the creative services in the editorial area, including fees and salaries paid to writers, photographers, and editors. Fees for illustration in this field particularly have changed very little in the last ten to twenty years despite inflation and ever-rising production costs such as the cost of paper, printing and binding, and mailing. Fees currently paid by many national magazines are substantially lower than their fees for the same work twenty years ago. Newspapers, however, have always paid on the low end of the scale despite the coming of age of four-color supplements, weekend magazines, and special sections.

On the positive side, the editorial area always has provided a showcase for illustrators just coming into the field and an opportunity for more experienced illustrators to try new techniques and styles. In a sense, it has been a trade-off, albeit an inequitable one.

All prices for illustration in the *Guidelines* are based on a nationwide survey which was then reviewed by a group of experts through the Graphic Artists Guild. The prices represent average fees for work done by most professional illustrators. These figures are meant as a point of reference only and do not necessarily reflect such important factors as job complexity, research, reputation and experience of a particular artist, technique or unique quality of expression, and extraordinary or extensive use of the finished illustration.

The prices here represent *only the specific use for which the illustration is intended* and do not necessarily reflect any of the above considerations. The buyer and seller are free to negotiate, taking into account all the factors involved. By their nature, however, advertisements are conceived of with multiple appearances in mind. Therefore, it's understood that the specific use may refer to unlimited use in a specific area, within a specified time period. This must be made clear before the project starts and the price is agreed upon.

The following standard trade practices should be adhered to:

1. It is of the utmost importance that the intended use of the art be made clear in a purchase order, contract or letter of agreement stating the price and terms of sale.

2. Normally, an artist sells only first reproduction rights unless otherwise stated.

3. If a piece of art is to be used for other than its original purpose, price should be negotiated as soon as possible. It is quite conceivable that the secondary use may be of *greater* value than the primary use so there is no formula for reuse fees.

4. An illustrator should negotiate reuse arrangements with the original commissioning party with speed, efficiency, and all due respect to the client's position.

5. Return of original artwork to the artist should be automatic unless otherwise negotiated.

6. The use of the art always influences the price. If the illustration is to be featured over an extensive area or is a buyout, fees should be significantly higher than when it is used locally or within a selected area.

7. Fees for work required in a very short period of time should be higher than the figures listed here. Regular overtime figures may be used as a rule of thumb.

8. A rejection fee is negotiable but should always be paid. The rejection fee for finished work should be upwards of 50 percent of the full price depending on reasons for rejection and complexity of the job. When the job is rejected at the sketch stage, a fee of one-third of the original price is customary. This fee may be less for quick, rough sketches and more for highly rendered, time-consuming work.

9. A cancellation fee should be agreed upon if a job is cancelled through no fault of the artist. Depending upon the stage at which the job is terminated, the fee paid should cover all work done.

10 Any form of speculative work is absolutely rejected not only by the Graphic Artists Guild but by every other national professional organization.

11. The Graphic Artists Guild is unalterably opposed to the use of work-for-hire contracts.

12. Unusual props, costumes, models' fees, travel costs, production expenses, consultation time, etc. should be billed separately to the client. These fees should be agreed upon and set down in the original written agreement or as an amendment of the agreement.

13. In judging the context of the Guild's pricing survey, it is imperative that Part One of the *Guidelines* and the Code of Fair Practice be studied thoroughly.

Magazines

Three categories of magazines are presented below: (1) national, (2) regional and mass trade, and (3) specific trade and limited audience. Obviously, magazines don't always fall completely into one of the three categories. *Time* and *Reader's Digest* are undoubtedly national magazines. *Forbes* is a national magazine, yet it falls into the regional and mass trade category because of its rather specialized audience and lower circulation. *New York* magazine is a regional magazine. Most women's service magazines are mass trade, although *Family Circle* would be considered a national magazine because of its high circulation. *Psychology Today* would fall somewhere in between the regional and mass trade and specific trade and limited audience categories. A magazine like *Popular Mechanics,* however, would more clearly fall into the specific trade and limited audience category. In all cases, discretion must be used. Figures on circulation and readership are available from the advertising and subscription departments of most magazines.

Spot illustrations are usually considered to be one column in width and quite simple. Although quarter-page illustrations are not spots, low budget magazines often make no distinction between the two.

Newspapers

Newspaper illustrations are usually paid according to published size, which is measured in agates and column width. For example, a medium-sized illustration is approximately 65 agates.

Newspapers like the *New York Times*

and *Washington Post* are considered national publications (for the purpose of pricing) because they are very large circulation daily papers and are national in scope. A great share of their readership is outside the city where they are published, and these newspapers also publish foreign editions. Medium circulation newspapers generally are regional in nature, sell outside the city where they are published, most often carry national news, and publish four-color supplements and weekend magazines. Local newspapers, naturally, have the lowest circulation. However, even in this category the size of readership varies widely and must always be taken into account when determining price.

It is worth mentioning again that this is one of the lowest-paying fields of illustration and has its value mostly as a trade-off for the excellent exposure that large daily newspapers provide the beginning talent. Still, the Guild maintains that these prevailing prices are unfair, and that they take advantage of inexperienced and emerging talent.

Comparative fees for consumer magazine illustration

Circulation under 100,000	Black and White	Full Color
Cover	—	$1300
Spread	1100	1400
Full page	450	500
Half page (or smaller)	300	350
Spot	125	250

Circulation 100,000-250,000		
Cover	1200	1300
Spread	—	1500
Full page	600	1200
Half page (or smaller)	325	450
Spot	180	225

Circulation 251,000-999,000		
Cover	—	1400
Spread	900	1700
Full page	750	1300
Half page (or smaller)	375	500
Spot	200	240

Circulation 1,000,000 +		
Cover	—	2500-3500+
Spread	1300	2750
Full page	1000	2000
Half page (or smaller)	300	725
Spot	200	400

Comparative fees for trade magazines

Circulation under 100,000	Black and White	Full Color
Cover	$500-750	$750-1000
Spread	—	675-1000
Full page	450	600
Half page (or smaller)	230	350
Spot	125	180

Circulation 100,000-350,000		
Cover	—	1000-1250
Spread	—	600-1000
Full page	—	450-600
Half page (or smaller)	350	450-500
Spot	125-150	150-175

Comparative fees for newspaper illustrations ☆

National and major circulation newspapers	Front Page and Covers	Large Size	Medium Size	Spots
Arts and leisure	$450	$350	$250	$100
Book review	500	350	250	125
Business and finance	350	300	200	125
Home	450	300	250	250
Living	500	350	250	150
Op-ed	—	350	250	150
Special city	400	300	200	150
Travel	350	300	200	150
Week in review	450	350	250	150
Sunday magazine and special supplements, color	1200	800	500	300
Sunday magazine and special supplements, black and white	—	600	400	175
Regional and medium circulation newspapers				
Sunday magazine and special supplements, color	750	450	350	175
Sunday magazine and special supplements, black and white	600	350	250	150
Special sections	350	300	200	100
Local and small circulation newspapers				
Sunday magazines, color	500	300	250	125
Sunday magazines, black and white	350	250	200	100
Special sections	250	200	150	60–75

*Add 25 percent for each color overlay.

Fashion illustration

A *fashion illustrator* is a graphic artist who illustrates clothed figures and accessories within a certain style or "look" which they create for a store, agency, or manufacturer. Occasionally, fashion illustrators work in the editorial area for fashion magazines or newspapers.

Sometimes, the fashion illustrator is required to draw a clothed figure with only the garment at hand (i.e., the illustrator must invent the model, pose, and background).

Factors affecting pricing include model fees, props, photography, research, and special materials.

The market for clothing and accessory illustration has become smaller in recent years. This decline has been offset in part by growth in the beauty and cosmetic area, which includes product and package illustration.

Most clothing illustration is paid on a per-figure basis, with an additional charge for backgrounds. *Model fees are always a billable expense.* Most accessory illustration is paid on a per-item basis. When more than one item is shown, additional items can be charged at a lower unit price. With the exception of specialized work, accessory illustration rates are generally 50 to 75 percent of per-figure prices.

The price ranges reflect rates for women's, men's, and children's illustration. Prior price differentials (higher for men, lower for children) have become gradually blurred. The ranges do not reflect complexity of style and fees for the new, highly rendered and photographic style of fashion illustration, which commands a 50 percent premium over the high end of the range in all categories. The particular illustrator's experience and desirablility is, of course, always an important factor in determining the specific fee. All the prices for illustration in the *Guidelines* are based on a nationwide survey which was then reviewed by a group of experts through the Graphic Artists Guild. The prices represent average fees for work done by most professional illustrators. These figures are meant as a point of reference only and do not necessarily reflect such important factors as job, complexity, reputation and experience of a particular artist, technique or unique quality of expression, and extraordinary or extensive use of the finished illustration.

The prices here represent *only the specific use for which the illustration is intended* and do not necessarily reflect any of the above considerations. The buyer and seller are free to negotiate, taking into account all the factors involved. By their nature, however, advertisements are conceived of with multiple appearances in mind. Therefore, it's understood that the specific use may refer to unlimited use in a specific area, within a specified time period. This must be made clear before the project starts and the price is agreed upon.

The following standard trade practices should be adhered to:

1. It is of the utmost importance that the intended use of the art be made clear in a purchase order, contract or letter of agreement stating the price and terms of sale.

2. Normally, an artist sells only first reproduction rights unless otherwise stated.

3. If a piece of art is to be used for other than its original purpose, price should be negotiated as soon as possible. It is quite conceivable that the secondary use may be of *greater* value than the primary use so there is no formula for reuse fees.

4. An illustrator should negotiate reuse arrangements with the original commissioning party with speed, efficiency, and all due respect to the client's position.

5. Return of original artwork to the artist should be automatic unless otherwise negotiated.

6. The use of the art always influences the price. If the illustration is to be featured over an extensive area or is a buyout, fees should be significantly higher than when it is used locally or within a selected area.

7. Fees for work required in a very short period of time should be higher than the figures listed here. Regular overtime figures may be used as a rule of thumb.

8. A rejection fee is negotiable but should always be paid. The rejection fee for finished work should be upwards of 50 percent of the full price depending on reasons for rejection and complexity of the job. When the job is rejected at the sketch stage, a fee of one-third of the original price is customary. This fee may be less for quick, rough sketches and more for highly rendered, time-consuming work.

9. A cancellation fee should be agreed

upon if a job is cancelled through no fault of the artist. Depending upon the stage at which the job is terminated, the fee paid should cover all work done.

10 Any form of speculative work is absolutely rejected not only by the Graphic Artists Guild but by every other national professional organization.

11. The Graphic Artists Guild is unalterably opposed to the use of work-for-hire contracts.

12. Unusual props, costumes, models' fees, travel costs, production expenses, consultation time, etc. should be billed separately to the client. These fees should be agreed upon and set down in the original written agreement or as an amendment of the agreement.

13. In judging the context of the Guild's pricing survey, it is imperative that Part One of the *Guidelines* and the Code of Ethics be studied thoroughly.

Comparative fees for fashion illustration☆

Newspapers	Black and White	Color
Major department store, small ad	$125—200	$ —
Major department store, full page	300—500	—
Large specialty shop/small ad	150—250	—
Small specialty shop/small ad	125—200	—
Mat service, any size	75—100	—
Major advertising agency	200—400	—
Small advertising agency	125—200	—
Trade-manufacturer	100—175	—

Magazines	Black and White	Color
National, one-third page	350—500	—
National, full page	500—800	600—1000
Local, one-third page	100—175	—
Local, full page	150—225	175—250
Trade-manufacturer	100—175	175—400

Other	Black and White	Color
Mailers and brochures, trade or consumer	$100—150	$ 200—300
Store catalog	150—200	200—275
Patterns	100—135	140—250

Note: Prices are based on one figure. Accessories are usually 50 to 75 percent of the per-figure price, depending on complexity of the accessories .

Technical illustration

A technical illustrator is a graphic art
ist who creates highly accurate renderings of machinery, charts, instru-
ments, scientific subjects (such as biological
studies, geological formations, and chemical
reactions), space technology, cartography
(maps), or virtually any subject that requires
precision of interpretation in illustration.
The technical illustrator often works directly
with a scientist or technician to achieve the
most explicit and accurate visualization of
the subject.

Technical illustration is used in all areas
of graphics communication in this age of
high technology. Some of the areas most
commonly requiring this specialized art are:
annual reports, special interest magazines,
and industrial publications.

The technical illustrator is often trained
in airbrush techniques, mechanical drafting,
and mathematics and can interpret diagrams
and blueprints.

The factors affecting pricing of technical illustration include: (1) research and consultation time, (2) travel, (3) reference
materials, (4) complexity of project. All
prices for illustration in the *Guidelines* are
based on a nationwide survey which was
then reviewed by a group of experts through
the Graphic Artists Guild. The prices represent average fees for work done by most
professional illustrators. These figures are
meant as a point of reference only and do
not necessarily reflect such important factors as job complexity, research, reputation
and experience of a particular artist, technique or unique quality of expression, and
extraordinary or extensive use of the finished illustration.

The prices here represent *only the specific use for which the illustration is intended*
and do not necessarily reflect any of the considerations above. The buyer and seller are
free to negotiate price, taking into account
all the factors involved.

The following standard trade practices
should be adhered to:

1. It is of the utmost importance that
the intended use of the art should be clearly
outlined in written form before work is
started. This is essential to avoid future confusion and misunderstanding on the part of
both the buyer and the artist.

2. A purchase order or contract is
recommended at the beginning of each and
every project.

3. If a piece of art is to be used for other
than its original purpose, price should be
negotiated as soon as possible.

4. Normally, an artist sells only first
reproduction rights unless otherwise
stipulated.

5. Return of original artwork to the artist should be automatic unless otherwise
negotiated.

6. The use of the art always influences
the price. If the editorial use is to be
featured over an extensive area or is buyout, it should pay significantly more than
when it is used locally or within a selected
area.

7. Work required in a very short period
of time should pay more than the figures lis'
ed here. Regular overtime figures may be
used as a rule of thumb.

8. A rejection fee is negotiable but
should always be paid. The rejection fee for
finished work should be close to the full
price depending on reasons for cancellation
and complexity of job. When the job is cancelled at the sketch stage, a fee of one-third
of the original price is customary. This fee
may be less for quick, rough sketches and
more for highly rendered, time-consuming
work.

9. Because the individual artist is not
like a capitalized corporate entity, payment
for work should be made within thirty days.

10. Any form of speculative work is absolutely rejected not only by the Graphic
Artists Guild but by every other professional
group in this field.

11. The Graphic Artists Guild is unalterably opposed to the use of work-for-hire
or done-for-hire contracts.

12. Unusual props, costumes, models'
fees, travel costs, production expenses, etc.,
should be billed separately to the client.

In judging the context of the Guild's
pricing survey, it is imperative that Part One
of the *Guidelines* and the Code of Ethics be
thoroughly studied.

Comparative fees for technical advertising illustration ☆

National magazine	Black and White	Color
Spread	$3500	$5000
Full page	2500	3700
Half page	1800	2500
Quarter page	1200	1500
Spot	750	1000

Regional and mass trade magazine

	Black and White	Color
Spread	2200	3500
Full page	1700	2500
Half page	1200	1700
Quarter page	750	1200
Spot	500	800

Specific trade and limited audience magazine

	Black and White	Color
Spread	1500	2000
Full page	1200	1700
Half page	1000	1500
Quarter page	750	1000
Spot	350	600

National newspaper advertising campaign †

	Black and White	Color
Spread	3000	—
Full page	2500	—
Half page	1500	—
Two column (quarter page)	1000	—

Newspaper supplement	Black and White	Color
Spread	$ —	$3500
Full page	—	3000
Half page	—	2000
Two column (quarter page)	—	750

*Add 25 percent for each color overlay.
†No specific prices are available for small town local newspapers. A broad range of fees are negotiable depending on budgets and the artist's reputation.

Comparative fees for technical editorial illustration ☆

In-house publication	Black and White	Color
Cover	$ —	$1000–1500
Spread	1250	1500–1800
Full page	1000	1250

Magazines

	Black and White	Color
Spread	1500–1800	2500–3000
Full page	1000	1500

Books

	Black and White	Color
Full page, complex	750	1200
Full page, simple	400	500

Consultation fees ☆

Per hour $75—125   Per diem   250—400

Novelty and miscellaneous products illustration

The greeting card and the paper novelty fields generally are currently experiencing a great business boom with unprecedented sales, new greeting card companies, and fresh card lines entering the market constantly. Success and failure in this business is based entirely upon the whim of the public and so lends itself perfectly to a royalty arrangement. Royalty agreements for calendars and posters are handled in the same manner as royalty agreements in the book field (see Book Illustration section for further information).

All the prices for illustration in the *Guidelines* are based on a nationwide survey which was then reviewed by a group of experts through the Graphic Artists Guild. The prices represent average fees for work done by most professional illustrators. These figures are meant as a point of reference only and do not necessarily reflect such important factors as job complexity, reputation and experience of a particular artist, technique or unique quality of expression and extraordinary or extensive use of the finished illustration.

The prices here represent *only the specific use for which the illustration is intended* and do not necessarily reflect any of the above considerations. The buyer and seller are free to negotiate, taking into account all the factors involved. By their nature, however, advertisements are conceived of with multiple appearances in mind. Therefore, it's understood that the specific use may refer to unlimited use in a specific area, within a specified time period. This must be made clear before the project starts and the price is agreed upon.

The following standard trade practices should be adhered to:

1. It is of the utmost importance that the intended use of the art be made clear in a purchase order, contract or letter of agreement stating the price and terms of sale.

2. Normally, an artist sells only first reproduction rights unless otherwise stated.

3. If a piece of art is to be used for other than its original purpose, price should be negotiated as soon as possible. It is quite conceivable that the secondary use may be of *greater* value than the primary use, so there is no formula for reuse fees.

4. An illustrator should negotiate reuse arrangements with the original commissioning party with speed, efficiency, and all due respect to the client's position.

5. Return of original artwork to the artist should be automatic and timely unless otherwise negotiated.

6. The use of the art always influences the price. If the illustration is to be featured over an extensive area or is a buyout, fees should be significantly higher than when it is used locally or within a selected area.

7. Fees for work required in a very short period of time should be higher than the figures listed here. Regular overtime figures may be used as a rule of thumb.

8. A rejection fee is negotiable but should always be paid. The rejection fee for finished work should be upwards of 50 percent of the full price, depending on reasons for rejection and complexity of the job. When the job is rejected at the sketch stage, a fee of one-third of the original price is customary. This fee may be less for quick, rough sketches and more for highly rendered, time-consuming work.

9. A cancellation fee should be agreed upon if a job is cancelled through no fault of the artist. Depending upon the stage at which the job is terminated, the fee paid should cover all work done.

10 Any form of speculative work is absolutely rejected not only by the Graphic Artists Guild but by every other national professional organization.

11. The Graphic Artists Guild is unalterably opposed to the use of work-for-hire contracts.

12. Unusual props, costumes, models' fees, travel costs, production expenses, consultation time, etc. should be billed separately to the client. These fees should be agreed upon and set down in the original written agreement or as an amendment of the agreement.

13. In judging the context of the Guild's pricing survey, it is imperative that Part One of the *Guidelines* and the Code of Ethics be studied thoroughly.

The fees listed in this section represent nonreturnable advances figured on a projection of the first year's royalties. The average royalty is 5 percent of the retail price, and this increases to 7.5 percent after a certain number of items are sold. This number depends upon the particular item and its market costs. It is advisable to seek the advice of an attorney before signing a royalty agreement, which is a binding contract.

Novelty merchandising

Art for T-shirts, towels, mugs, tote bags, and other such items should be sold under a royalty-type agreement called *licensing.* Spin-offs from nationally known and highly developed characters like *Peanuts* and B. Kliban's Cats are sold in this manner. Royalties for licensing rights vary from 2 to 10 percent according to the fame of a particular character, art, or artist and type and price of retail product. It is recommended that in this field of novelty merchandising a large royalty percentage is generally more desireable than a smaller royalty percentage with a larger advance. It is advised that an attorney always be retained to negotiate a licensing contract. (See the discussion of royalty in the Book Illustration category for more information.)

Limited edition prints

Art for limited edition prints may be created by the artist independently or under a contract with a gallery or publisher. Payment is either on a commission or royalty basis, and an advance is usually included. Both the advance and the ultimate payment to the artist will vary depending on the size of the print run, the number of colors printed, the selling price, and other factors. A typical arrangement for a limited edition of prints is for an advance against 50 to 67 percent of gross sales revenues (i.e., the gallery's commission is 33 to 50 percent).

For an unlimited, mass market print, the royalty with the publisher would be from 2 to 10 percent of net sales revenues. Net sales revenues here means the total income to the buyer minus all costs incurred by the buyer. Such buyer costs include production, marketing, and distribution expenses.

If the publisher or gallery is responsible for all production costs (i.e., platemaking, etching, proofing, paper, ink) including advertising and promotion, the artist will receive less than if the artist pays these costs. Under such an agreement, the artist is entitled to a limited number of "artist's proofs" to use in any way the artist may wish. A typical edition will range from 100 to 250 prints, and each print is usually numbered and signed by the artist. An attorney should always be consulted before entering into any contract or agreement.

In all cases, marketing can make or break the venture. Market research should be done prior to making a binding agreement or making significant outlays of money or investment of time in creating the art. Keep in mind also that the market for limited edition prints is regulated by law in a number of states, including New York, California, and Illinois. Extensive disclosures or disclaimers may have to accompany limited edition prints sold in these states.

Comparative fees for greeting cards and novelty products * ☆

	Black and White	Color
Greeting cards	$350†	$500–700
Calendars for sale (approx. 12 illus.)	3500	5000
Posters for sale (litho or silkscreen, three to five colors)	—	2000

Fees listed are nonreturnable advances against royalties.   †Add $50 for each color overlay.

Record album illustration

The demand for engaging, forceful, and highly creative record album packaging has attracted the best of today's talented editorial and advertising illustrators, who have in turn created a new art form. Many record album covers have become collector's items. Several books have been published recently on record album cover art, and an ongoing market has developed for collecting the originals.

Commissions for record album illustration can sometimes be extremely lucrative. Fees tend to vary widely, however, depending on recording artists, particular label and recording company, and the desirability and fame of the illustrator.

When the record producer needs to rely on the talents of a particularly well-known illustrator, a much higher fee is paid than normally. For complex record packages, fees have gone higher than $10,000. This kind of assignment, however, requires many meetings, sketches, and changes.

Most recording companies produce under different labels depending on the recording artist and type of music.

The minor labels of major recording companies are usually reserved for less commercially saleable records and reissues of previous recordings. There is no discernable difference between fees paid by West Coast companies (Capital, Warner Bros.) as opposed to East Coast companies (Columbia, Motown, Atlantic). In all cases, only record company publication rights are transferred, and the original art is returned. Sometimes, tie-in poster rights are included.

All the prices for illustration in the Guidelines are based on a nationwide survey which was then reviewed by a group of experts through the Graphic Artists Guild. The prices represent average fees for work done by most professional illustrators. These figures are meant as a point of reference only and do not necessarily reflect such important factors as job complexity, reputation and experience of a particular artist, technique or unique quality of expression, and extraordinary or extensive use of the finished illustration.

The following standard trade practices should be adhered to:

1. It is of the utmost importance that the intended use of the art should be clearly outlined in written form before work is started. This is essential to avoid future confusion and misunderstanding on the part of both the buyer and the artist.

2. A purchase order or contract is recommended at the beginning of each and every project.

3. If a piece of art is to be used for other than its original purpose, price should be negotiated as soon as possible.

4. Normally, an artist sells only first reproduction rights unless otherwise stipulated.

5. Return of original artwork to the artist should be automatic unless otherwise negotiated.

6. A rejection fee is negotiable but should always be paid. The fee for finished work should be upwards of 50 percent of the full price depending on reasons for cancellation and complexity of job. When the job is cancelled at the sketch stage, a fee of one-third of the original price is customary. This fee may be less for quick, rough sketches and more for highly rendered, time-consuming work.

7. Because the individual artist is not like a capitalized corporate entity, payment for work should be made within thirty days.

8. Any form of speculative work is absolutely rejected not only by the Graphic Artists Guild but by every other professional group in this field.

9. The Graphic Artists Guild is unalterably opposed to the use of work-for-hire or done-for-hire contracts.

10. *Unusual* props, costumes, models' fees, travel costs, production expenses, etc., should be billed separately to the client.

11. In judging the context of the Guild's pricing survey, it is imperative that Part One of the *Guidelines* and the Code of Ethics be thoroughly studied.

Comparative fees for record album cover illustrations☆

	Popular and Rock	Classical and Jazz
Major recording company	$2500–4000	$1500–2500
Small recording company and or minor label	–	1200–1800

Medical illustration

A medical illustrator is a highly specialized graphic artist who has usually studied anatomy, pathology, and physiology at the postgraduate level in order to create accurate, realistic, and imaginative medical illustrations of anatomical subjects. Microanatomy and surgical procedures are also areas covered by medical illustrators. The medical illustrator has a full library of medical journals and books which must be constantly maintained. Free-lance medical illustrators generally work in their studios from reference, although students and staff illustrators often draw from life in the operating room. Most medical illustrators work closely with physicians, especially when creating editorial artwork for textbooks. Advertising agencies often hire medical experts to review the preliminary sketches and finished art created by the medical illustrator. Accurate and literate interpretation are the key words in medical illustration. For advertising purposes, medical illustration often requires more imaginative, fresh approaches with emphasis on impact rather than on information.

Factors affecting pricing include: research, complexity of the project, expenses such as models or reference.

Comparative fees for medical illustrations for publication☆

Medical journals, controlled circulation publications, medical texts	Black and White	Color
Cover	$ —	$600–800
Full page, line	500–750	—
Full page, tone	600–850	800–1000
Quarter page, line	100–175	—
Quarter page, tone	150–275	200–300

Large circulation magazines directed to general readership	Black and White	Color
Cover	—	1000–2500
Full page	—	600–1000
Half page	—	400–600
Quarter page	150–275	200–350

Advertising	Black and White	Color
Spread	$ —	$1750–2000
Full page	—	1500–1750
Half page	100–500	500–1000
Spot detail	75–150	100–250

Comparative fees for other medical illustration☆

Television	
Background painting	$600–1500
Cell overlays	50–75

Medicolegal	
Graphics for courtroom, black and white	200–500
Testifying as expert witness, per hour	75–100 Plus expenses

Consulting	
Per hour	75–125

ANIMATION
PRICES
AND TRADE CUSTOMS

Animation

Animators are graphic artists whose skills entail creating the illusion of movement. Knowledge of movement and technical film details are essential for the animator. In the process of animation, the animator begins with a layout, which gives the "path" for movement. Following the model sheets of characters, which are based on the designer's concepts and are usually supplied by an agency, the animator creates specific movement based on the written directions and camera instructions. These directions and instructions, along with any dialogue, music, or sound effects, are broken down frame by frame for 35-mm film. Often, the animator will physically stage the action.

Generally, animators work for a studio but there are those in the Animators Union who free-lance. There are nonunion animators, but union membership is required in order to work in unionized studios.

Animation has a range of uses such as television commercials, medical and educational films, television specials, titles, feature films, special effects, and the familiar Saturday morning cartoons. There are also independent animated films which are an entirely different art form with a broad spectrum of styles. Usually these are shown in film festivals or competitions that serve as showcases for the artist's work.

A factor affecting pricing is whether one is a free-lance or on staff. If the animator is free-lancing, pricing is also affected by what category the animation falls under (e.g., the intricacy of the movement, how much movement there is, and how intricate the drawings must be). This is decided upon before work is begun.

There is a category in the union titled *graphic film artist* which involves knowledge of cameras and film. An image is taken and a computerized camera figures the movement of that image for the desired effects. The most common examples of this are the television station and network logos broadcast with movement and "glowing halo" effects.

Animation is a highly specialized field, but advancement is possible according to one's skills. There are animators who also work in other areas; some are illustrators, designers for film, and cartoonists. It does not follow that cartoonists or illustrators have the skill or patience to be animators. Most are satisfied with seeing their drawings animated by someone else's hand. Occasionally, artists who supply a design may want to try animating it.

In showing work, portfolios of storyboards, backgrounds, model sheets, and similar items are useful to animators who have expertise and seek work in these areas. The animator's samples, however, are usually condensed onto a film reel or a video cassette in order to show the true nature of one's ability in animating movement.

Most animation in this country is done with drawings that are then inked and painted onto cels. Other techniques of commercial value are cut-outs, which are moved under the cameras; flat, hinged puppets, which are also moved under the camera; kinesthesis or filmographs, which require figuring camera moves to extend movement in a single piece of artwork such as a photograph; pixilation, or trick photography, in which objects are manipulated and appear to be speeding through the frame; computer animation, which can be hard edged, geometric, abstract, or figurative; and three-dimensional animation, which has clay figures or puppets or any other three-dimensional object used to narrate a story; and highly realistic miniatures used in special effects.

Pay scales of temporary animation workers*

Classification	Weekly	Hourly
Director	$1,260.00	$ 36.00
Story, story sketch	905.63	25.88
Layout	905.63	25.88
Animator †	945.63	27.00
Assistant animator	590.63	16.88
Inbetweeners	511.88	14.63
Production coordinator	650.48	18.59
Preplanner/checker (animation)	590.63	16.88
Junior checker (ink and paint)	464.63	13.28
Inkers	464.63	13.28
Painters	448.88	12.82
Background	776.48	22.19
Graphic film artist I	708.75	20.25
Graphic film artist II	647.33	18.50

Animator

Limited footage, 14 ft @ $10.50	—	147.00
Light footage, 7 ft @ $26.25	—	183.75
Medium footage, 5 ft @ $42.00	—	210.00
Heavy footage, 4 ft @ $57.75	—	231.00

Assistant animator	Per Diem	Weekly
Light footage, 7 ft @ $15.75	—	$110.25
Medium footage, 5 ft @ $25.20	—	126.00
Heavy footage, 4 ft @ $34.65	—	138.60
Light footage 7 ft @ $19.69	—	137.83
Medium footage 5 ft @ $31.50	—	157.50
Heavy footage 4 ft @ $43.31	—	173.24

*Temporary work scale is at time-and-one-half of regular salary. See salaried Staff section for staff salaries. All animation figures were supplied by the Animators Union and represent the union pay scale.

CARTOONING
PRICES
AND TRADE CUSTOMS

Cartooning

Magazines

Magazine cartoons are created by free-lance cartoonists who almost always conceive the idea (although gag writers are used at times), draw it, and then offer it for sale to magazines. Generally, cartoonists market their work in order of rate paid, with higher-paying publications given first look.

Cartoonists bring a unique blend of writing and drawing skills to bear on every cartoon they create. They know how to stage a cartoon as graphic theater with setting, characters, and sitution instantly communicated. A successful cartoon says it faster than a paragraph of descriptive words, with more impact, and most importantly, it makes you laugh.

The magazine cartoon is probably the most popular of the graphic arts. Media surveys invariably place cartoons among readers' first preferences. Because of their mass accessibility and their relative simplicity in conception and style, cartoons appear deceptively simple to create. On the contrary, cartooning is a highly demanding specialization with a long "apprentice" period required to reach the point where all the various elements involved can be brought together consistently and sharply. In fact, free-lance cartooning taken in all its forms, is still a rather small field of highly skilled artists. Besides magazine cartoons, free-lance cartooning includes work in syndicated comic strips and panels; advertising; humorous illustration for text, trade and children's books; television; public relations; and sales promotion.

Syndication

Many free-lance cartoonists develop comic strips or panels for distribution to newspapers by national and international syndicates. Since the number of newspapers using syndicated material and the space alloted to it are limited, the field is highly competitive. Very few strips or panels are introduced in any given year and then often only when an existing feature is dropped. It is therefore very tempting for the cartoonist whose strip or panel is accepted by a syndicate to sign the first contract offered.

Because a syndicated cartoonists' earnings are based on the number of newspapers carrying his or her strip or panel and the circulation level of the papers, the assumption is that syndicates use fairly standard contracts and that it's in the artist's self-interest to make as few waves as possible.

Syndicate contracts are complicated and vary considerably among the major firms in the field. As in all other business relationships, it is expected that each party to the contract will seek to attain the most favorable terms through negotiation. Cartoonists owe it to themselves and their creations to prepare as well as they can for this process.

An important educational aid available to anyone interested in syndication is the Cartoonists Guild's "Syndicate Survival Kit." A detailed analysis of six major syndicate contracts with commentary by the Guild; the kit also outlines how artists can get maximum protection in such contracts. The cost is $6.00, payable by check to the *Graphic Artists Guild*.

Should a cartoonist be offered a contract by a syndicate, it is also essential to get the best legal representation possible. A lawyer with expertise in cartooning, visual arts, copyright, and/or literary property contracts is recommended. Experience proves that there is no substitute for knowledgeable counsel in contract negotiations.

Editorial cartooning

Editorial cartoonists are usually salaried staff artists on individual daily newspapers. Salaries range greatly with the circulation and status of the paper and the reputation and experience of the cartoonist. In some cases, however (i.e.: Herblock, Mauldin, Oliphant, Auth), the work of editorial cartoonists is syndicated nationally, although they continue to remain on staff with their base papers. Usually their papers require that they do two locally oriented cartoons per week and the syndicates want at least three cartoons a week relating to national issues. As with comic strip or panel artists, the earnings that editorial cartoonists net from syndication depend on their contract and, based on that, the number and size of the newspapers using their work regularly. (See Syndication above).

Sometimes free-lance cartoonists sell their work to major daily newspaper op-ed pages or to weeklies. Rates differ a good deal, but are generally established based on column width of the work used and whether the drawing is an original or reprint. Or, rates may be open to negotiation. In either case, it's best to check with individual papers regarding their interest in free-lance contributions before sending work for consideration.

Books

In addition to collections of the published work of one or more cartoonists, there has been a recent trend toward publishing original cartoon works. Book contracts vary as much as syndication contracts, so it is a good idea to consult a qualified literary agent or lawyer. In fact, book publishers prefer to negotiate terms with a knowledgeable author's representative. Cartoonists should insist on an advance on royalties at contract signing. For a first-time cartoonist-author, the advance usually ranges from a minimum $3000 up to $10,000.

Licensing and merchandising

Another burgeoning aspect of cartooning is licensing and merchandising. When cartoon characters, such as Snoopy, Kliban's Cats, or Superman are licensed for a range of products from toys and apparel to designer sheets and stationery the creator stands to earn considerable additional income *if* he or she retains all or a significant percentage of the subsidiary rights in the property.

It is generally assumed that only nationally known syndicate characters are sought by licensing agents or manufacturers. With the fast growth in this area, however, there are now possibilities for cartoonists to develop characters specifically for product use. Cartoonists interested in pursuing this potentially lucrative application of their work should seek counsel with an attorney specializing in this field so that adequate copyright protection is achieved *before* presenting work to licensers or manufacturers. In May 1980 the first trade show in the character licensing and merchandising field was held in New York City. This show brought together creators, licensers, syndicates, and manufacturers and provided a place to explore business opportunities. Similar shows are already scheduled in the future on the east and west coasts and could become an important meeting ground for cartoonists seeking to expand in this field.

Pricing of magazine cartoons

The pricing of free-standing magazine cartoons is different from that of other forms of illustration because they are purchased as complete editorial elements—similar to free-lance feature articles—at fixed rates. Generally, all black-and-white or color cartoons published at a particular unit size are paid for at the same rate. The exception is a handful of magazines (e.g., *The New Yorker*) that additionally compensate those cartoonist-contributors closely identified with their magazine. In these instances, an annual signature fee may be paid for first look at cartoons produced for magazines, as well as bonuses and, in a few cases, fringe benefits.

A number of factors affect prices for magazine cartoons. Among them are: finished art in black and white or color; unit size cartoon is published; national vs. regional distribution; circulation, impact, and influence of the magazine; importance of cartoons as a regular editorial element; the extent of rights being purchased; and the national reputation of the cartoonist. Since the list is composed of objective and subjective factors and the mix in each case is different, rates vary considerably among magazines. Consequently, this presentation is limited to a pricing range on captioned or uncaptioned magazine-type cartoons, not humorous illustrations, comic strips, or the other cartoon forms mentioned elsewhere in this section. Requests for additional information on cartooning may be addressed to the Cartoonists *Graphic Artists Guild* 30 East 20th Street New York, New York 10003, (212) 777-7353

Basic terms of sale

1. Payment should always be made on acceptance of the work, not on publication.

2. First reproduction rights only should be sold, unless otherwise negotiated.

3. Under the new copyright law cartoonists retain copyright ownership of all work they create. Copyright can only be transferred in writing.

4. Cartoonists should never send the same original drawing to more than one U.S. publisher at a time. Multiple photocopy submissions are acceptable to many European and other overseas publishers.

5. Purchasers should make selection(s) promptly—within two to four weeks at the most—and return the unpurchased cartoons immediately to avoid tying them up.

6. All original art should be returned to the artist immediately after reproduction, regardless of rights purchased.

7. No work-for-hire provisions should be included in purchase agreements covering free-lance cartoons.

8. Terms of sale should be specified in a contract or on the bill. For example, if work is to be reprinted in a textbook, the following should be included:

"For one-time, non-exclusive, English language, North American print rights only, in one hardcover edition, to be published by_____, entitled "_____." All additional request for usage by your organization or any other publication, except as specified above, are to be referred to _(name of artist)_ to determine the appropriate reprint fee."

Refer to model illustration contract.

Comparative fees for cartoon reprints

Consumer magazines

National, one column	$200 and up
National, two or more columns	250 and up
Other	100 and up

Trade magazines

Major	200 and up
Other	100 and up

Textbooks

North American one-time rights, English language	150 and up
World one-time rights, English language	200 and up
Foreign language rights	50 additional
All future editions or revisions	200 and up (in addition to fees for other rights)

Other trade hardcover and paperback books

One-time rights	100 and up

Cartoon anthologies

Advance on royalties

Comparative fees for cartoons for national magazines*

Single panel	Black and White	Color
Quarter page or less	$150–350	$300–500
Full page	350–600	500–1200

Multipanel	Single-panel rate plus an additional rate per panel.

*These figures reflect the different rates now being paid for the purchase of first North American serial rights only by various general or special-interest magazines regularly using cartoons. For the reasons stated in the text of this section, listing average figures in each category would be unrealistic and misleading.

This section of the Guidelines is dedicated to the memory of Jan Giolito. Jan's commitment to the members of the Guild and her contributions to the Textile Design Discipline have enriched our profession.

TEXTILE
PRICES
AND TRADE CUSTOMS

Textile Design

A textile designer is a graphic artist who creates illustrations, designs, or patterns to be used on surfaces, usually in repeat. Textile designers work in many areas including apparel, decorative, and home furnishings. Knowledge of the reproduction or printing methods, markets and trends is essential to textile designers.

Most free-lance textile designers create individual designs which they sell to manufacturers, often stipulating a specific use or combination of uses. Designers are often commissioned to create a line of textile designs.

Factors for determining an appropriate price for a textile design include: (1) rights transferred; (2) credit on the selvage of the printed piece; (3) complexity of the design; (4) research; and (5) return of the original to the artist. In addition to the comparative fees and trade practices listed below, textile designers should be aware of the following conditions:

Quantity orders The Guild discourages reduced fees for large orders. Each textile design is individual in nature, and industry fee scales are already low.

Royalties The usual advance against royalties is often close to the fees listed in the table. Working without an advance against royalties is strongly discouraged by the Guild. There is no guarantee of income with such an arrangement, and it therefore amounts to speculation.

Commission The standard commission for an agent or representative who sells a textile designer's work is between 33⅓ and 40 percent.

Trade practices

The free-lancer's perspective The following trade practices are relevant to the free-lance textile designer (see the textile design business and legal forms on page 149).

Work orders All work ordered by a customer should be recorded in writing in a work order form provided by the Guild or by a studio.

Holding work Individual judgement is necessary in this area. Previous work experience with a client who wishes to hold work helps establish reliability. The Guild discourages consenting to an extended holding time; shorter holding times help protect against damage, loss, or unauthorized reproduction of work. A maximum of five days is preferred by most artists; some limit holding to one day. As always, a written holding form should be used.

Billing for a sale An invoice form is written at the time of sale. Payment to a textile designer should be prompt and negotiated at the time of sale. Because the major portion of the work represents labor, all invoices are payable in fifteen days (although thirty days is standard industry practice).

Appropriate speculation The creation of work initiated by a textile designer for presentation and sale is standard practice in the industry. However, it is also standard practice to obtain a written guarantee of payment for creating *any* new work specifically requested by clients. The Guild opposes creating new work without such a guarantee accompanying the request.

Kill fees When artwork commissioned by a client is not purchased, the artist should charge a cancellation fee which is based on the amount of labor invested in the work. Ownership of all copyright and artwork is retained by the artist. If a job is cancelled and is based on work belonging to a client (such as a repeat or coloring), a labor fee will be charged and the work will be destroyed.

Client responsibilities: Include additional payment to the artist when: (1) artwork changes are requested by the client, but were not part of the original agreement; (2) extra expenses arise from the assignment including, but not limited to, photostats, mailings, shipping charges, and shipping insurance; (3) ordered corners are not developed into purchased sketches; a cancellation fee will be charged and ownership of all copyright and artwork is retained by the designer; and (4) sales taxes must be included on all artwork except when original work is returned to the designer or a resale certificate, signed by an officer of the company, is provided to the designer.

Royalties Payments based on a percentage of the income earned by a design are becoming more common between clients and textile designers, but must be negotiated to include advance payment at the time of sale. Percentage rates range from 2 to 10 percent and depend largely on wholesale costs, sales volume of fabric house, and how much involvement the textile designer has in the project.

Limitations The Guild strongly recommends limiting, in writing, the rights being sold to the client's specific needs; the textile designer retains all other rights. For example, if the design is sold for sheets and pillowcases only, those words are written out on the order form and the textile designer can sell the same design in other markets (e.g., for bath items, toweling, etc.).

Be sure to read any agreement carefully and try to restrict selling rights to specific markets. This can be done by crossing out inappropriate sections (see page 26.) A word of caution, be sure to check any agreement for the words "work for hire," under this contract, you may be signing away "authorship" and all rights forever. See page 45 for more information on "Work for hire."

Artist/agent contracts The Guild has developed a standard form for textile designer/agent contracts (pages 154-158). An agreement, even verbal, is legally binding, but it is an advantage to both parties to have the agreement in writing. Textile designers should have receipts for all work left with an agent.

Return of artwork The Guild encourages textile designers to request the return of artwork. Textile designers are making these requests to obtain additional exposure (such as by display of designs as artwork).

Credit to artist This is another practice that is becoming more prevalent in the industry. In particular, some designers receive credit on the selvage after they are known in the marketplace by designing a line or collection.

Artist/agent responsibilities In the textile design industry, the cost of shipping is usually billed to the client. In cases where the client is not billed, the agent pays—not the designer.

The Guild strongly recommends that a designer work for an agent strictly on a commission basis agreed upon by both parties in writing.

Knock-offs A textile designer cannot ethically copy or "knock-off" a design by another artist. Although it is common practice, artists should be aware that it is illegal to infringe on anyone else's designs, and that infringement can lead to legal liability. It is unlikely that a client who commissioned the work would support a freelance artist in a court of law.

(Refer to page 125 for information on staff artists)

Comparative fees for textile design

Prices shown are low/average/high

	Corner ☆
Apparel	
Men, Women, Children	
Specialty-Apparel	
Men's ties, * *Markers, Engineered designs*	
Scarves	175-350-600
Hand-painted	175-350-600
Lingerie (per garment)	200-300
TV Costume (per garment)	1000 or commission
Home Decorative	
Wallpaper, Drapery, Upholstery, Bedspreads	50-125-300
Domestics * *	
Sheets	50-100-200
Pillow case	45-80-150
Hand towel	
Bath towel	
Bath sheet	
Face cloth	
Specialty/domestics	
Tablecloth	
Tea towel	
Place mat	
Shower curtain	
Rug design (¼ of rug)	

Design or Sketch (croque)	Repeat	Design in Repeat	Coloring
250-300-450	225-275-500	250-400-600	45-60-125
200-400	225-275-500	275-475	
250-350-600	200-250-375	300-375-600	35-65-150
175-400		250-450-750	
450-525-800	225-350-850	675-850-1200	80-100-175
300-550-850	250-635-1000	500-800-1200	60-100-200
300-500-600	300-450-650	450-650-900	75-100-150
200-425-600	200-400-600	450-610-900	50-75-125
300-500-650	350-600-800	500-675-900	50-75-125
300-500-800	350-750-1200	550-850-1000	50-100-125
200-400-800	225-425-700	300-400-650	50-75-125
375-650	350-650	500-750	50-75-125
350-750	275-600	350-600-800	50-75-125
150-400	125-300	400-800	30-50-75
450-600-800	250-500-750	675-750-1200	75-150
300-600-900		375-600-900	75-125

Comparative fees for textile design (continued)

Specialty— Home decorative	Design or Sketch	Repeat	Design in Repeat	Coloring
Kitchen accesories	125-350	225-600	375-550-600	50-75-100
China/giftware/ barware	200-300-700	175-450	325-550-800	65-75-125
Desk accessories Giftwrap/greeting cards	250-750-800	250-500	225-400-600	75-150

Woven design***

Sample weaving	$35-60 per piece 20-35 per hour
Analyses (pick-out)	30-45 per hour
Jacquard sketch	$250-600
Coloring / One color	$45-55 per piece
Several colors for one design	$750-1500
Prints developed for Jacquard	$500-750 per design
Developing a 'colorline' for solids	$1,000
Developing a group of wovens 'styling a line'	$2,000-10,000 per season
Contract	$25 per hour—$140 per diem
Consultation fee	$20-35 per hour

Special

Commissioned work and special orders	$20-30 per hour
Rug design consultation fee	$20-30 per hour
Consultation fees (plus expenses)	$35-50 per hour
Royalty arrangements	1½-2-5 percent of net sales per yard

Styling	*per diem*	*per week*
Apparel	$80-100 (8 hours)	$350-450 (35 hour week)
Home decorative	80-150 (7 hours)	350-625 (35 hour week)
Mill work *Excluding expenses*		
Apparel	125-175 (12 hours)	750-1050 (60 hours)
Home decorative	125-200 (12 hours)	750-1200 (60 hours)
	150-250 (16 hours)	1500-1600 (80 hours)

Overhead
(design related expenses) $4200 an average per year

These are average ranges. The higher fee can go much higher depending on the complexity of design and reputation of the designer.

☆As to tracing layouts and corners, there are labor charges only. All artwork remains property of designer and no reproduction rights are transferred.

*The above prices are based on items being part of a total domestic package. If they are sold individually, prices must be increased accordingly.

***Home furnishings work here will be slightly higher due to size and complexity of work.

NEEDLEART
PRICES
AND TRADE CUSTOMS

Needleart design

A *needleart designer* is a graphic artist who creates designs and/or objects in a wide range of needleart media such as knitting, crochet, needlepoint, embroidery, lace, sewing, patchwork, applique, quilting, soft sculpture, macrame, weaving, basketry, braiding, latch hook, and punch needle. The needleart designer works in many commercial markets, including publishing, advertising, apparel, decorative and home furnishings, toys, and novelties.

Most needleart designers are commissioned to create one-of-a-kind items for editorial, educational, promotional, or advertising use or as prototypes for multiple reproduction. Designers also work as industry consultants to develop and/or expand new or existing educational programs, product lines, needleart techniques and skills. Needleart designers also create items individually or in multiples for resale in stores and/or galleries.

Rights sold

The terms of sale for a design vary with the needs of the client and designer. They can range from a one-time use to a buyout of all reproduction rights. Fees for reproduction rights do not include purchase of the original artwork *unless specified in writing*. This manner of selling rights applies whether the original design is reproduced photographically, as in editorial; or reproduced by a manufacturer, as in product design.

For editorial purposes, one-time use generally refers to first North American reproduction rights. Additional rights to be sold may refer to publication in other geographic areas, markets, and mediums; reuse rights, or the right for use for promotional purposes. If rights for publishing are not used within one year of delivery, they revert back to the artist. And, any rights not specified in a written contract remain the property of the artist. In the case of prototypes for manufacturing, rights should be enumerated and a royalty agreement should be negotiated at the beginning of the project. This applies to books, kits, leaflets, toys and home furnishings.

Many factors are used in determining an appropriate price for the sale of a needleart design or concept. They include: (1) complexity of design or concept ; (2) complexity and/or multiplicity of techniques used; (3) uniqueness of design or concept and/or technique(s) used; (4) research and development time; (5) designer reputation, range, skill, and ability; (6) rights transferred; and (7) return of original art to designer.

In addition, the fee should reflect reimbursement for out of pocket expenses including materials and supplies, messengers, toll telephone calls, transportation and travel, shipping and insurance. It is customary to increase the fee for rush delivery deadlines. The designer should be compensated for sketches and swatches done to the specifications of a client that do not result in a commission, and designs rejected by a client remain the property of the designer. Changes requested by a client once a project has been undertaken should be compensated for at the designer's hourly rate. Complexity of instructions (e.g. grading of patterns, conversions to knitting machies, etc.) will also affect pricing. If the designer is called in for consultations on a project beyond the initial project conference, a fee for consultation should be charged (please refer to pricing chart for fees).

Contracts

Since the transfer of rights is based on contractual agreement, it is imperative that the terms be clear to both client and designer. The written contract may be a document. in either case, the written document is legally binding. It is recommended designer to decide which form is most appropriate for the situation. It is recommended that designers do not begin a project before a contract or letter of agreement has been negotiated and signed.

Any contract should specify the conditions of sale in addition to enumerating rights that are transferred upon receipt of full payment. When a design is sold for publication, the contract should include the form of credit to be given. Name credit on, the page where the design appears is expected. For limited reproduction rights, credit is in the form of a copyright notice in the designer's name and should appear adjacent to the work.

Specifications regarding the return of the original artwork are included when reproduction rights are being sold. Artwork should be returned in an undamaged condition within an agreed upon period from the date of delivery or the date of publication. The client should be billed for full market value if the work is lost, damaged or not returned.

The delivery date of any assignment is predicated on the receipt of all materials to be supplied by the client, by the agreed upon date.

Payment and delivery schedules are included in the contractual agreement. *Payment in full within thirty days of delivery* is standard, not upon publication (which may be delayed). If the major portion of the project represents labor and payment is preferred within fifteen days, it should be negotiated at the beginning of the assignment and included in the contract. A percentage increase (1½ to 2 percent) on the fee for payment received after thirty days can be put in the contract and specified on the invoice at the time of delivery.

Other conditions that may be included in the contract are: conditional clauses to account for non-publication of the project and changes requested after delivery, etc.

Comparative fees

The comparative fees in the accompanying tables are arranged according to the category of the purchaser. *Consumer products/magazine editorial* refers to work that will be photographed and reproduced in conjunction with specific editorial content of a magazinel. *Advertising art* refers to any agency producing commercial advertising for printed publications, television media, etc. The fees listed are for work specifically commissioned for an advertising program. The designer may offer existing work to an agency for a rental fee of 10 to 15 percent of the market value of that work. The client is responsible for returning the work in its original condition. If damaged or lost, the client is liable for the full market value of the artwork. *Prototypes for manufacturers* refers to any market entity that produces any product entity in multiples (e.g., kits, books, leaflets, toys, novelties, clothing, home furnishings) or work related to packaged consumer goods.

As used in the tables, *average* refers to a design of normal intricacy in any one of the needleart media. *Complex* refers to a design of greater intricacy or scale. Extremely simple designs requiring less than average development and execution and extremely complex designs should be priced accordingly.

The Needleart Designer's Confirmation form appears on page 140.

Comparative fees for needleart design creating a textile structure or completely covering a textile surface

Garments	Consumer Products/ Magazine Editorial	Advertising Art	Prototype for Manufacturer
Half-body, average	$300-600	$600-1200	$400-600
Half-body, complex	600-1250	1200-3000	500-1000
Whole-body, average	600-800	1000-1500	500-800
Whole-body, complex	800-1500	1500-3000	800-1000
Accessories, average	150-350	400-600	350-500
Accessories, complex	350-1000	600-1000	500-1000
Soft sculpture			
Three dimensional	300-800	500-2000	
Props	300-800	500-2000	
Puppets	300-1000	500-2000	

Comparative fees for needleart design creating a textile structure or completely covering a textile surface (continued)

Environmental furnishing	Consumer Products/ Magazine Editorial	Advertising Art	Prototype for Manufacturer
Accessories, average	150-250	300-500	
Accessories, complex	300-400	500-1000	
Tableware, average	200-800	500-1000	
Tableware, complex	800-2000	1000-2500	
Window/wall treatment, average	200-800	500-1000	
Window/wall treatment, complex	800-2000	1000-2500	
Blankets or afghans, average	450-650	800-1500	
Blankets or afghans, complex	650-1500	1500-3000	
Quilts, average	500-1000	1000-3500	
Quilts, complex	1000-3500	1200-2500	
Bedspreads, average	300-500	600-1000	
Bedspreads, complex	500-2000	1000-3000	
Banners, average	300-500	500-1000	
Banners, complex	500-2000	1000-3000	
Floor coverings, average	400-800	500-1000	
Floor coverings, complex	800-2500	1000-3000	

Logos and insignias

	Consumer Products/ Magazine Editorial	Advertising Art	Prototype for Manufacturer
Literal translation	300-500	1000-2000	
Creative interpretation	500-1000	1500-3000	

Comparative miscellaneous needleart fees

Consulting			$25-50
Instruction writing			20-35
Technical drawing			15-35
Pattern drafting			25-35

Toys and novelties

	Consumer Products/ Magazine Editorial	Advertising Art	Prototype for Manufacturer
Average	300-500	500-800	
Complex	500-1500	800-2000	

DESIGN
PRICES
AND TRADE CUSTOMS

General graphic design

A *graphic designer* is a graphic artist who creates communication tools incorporating the spectrum of graphic elements such as typography, illustration, photography, production and printing, to achieve the appropriate impact and message.

Unlike free-lance illustrators, graphic designers generally work within a studio that they may own, and through which they may employ other graphic designers, illustrators, mechanical artists or photographers on a salaried or free-lance basis. In that respect, graphic designers are actually studio owners and it would be misleading to consider them free-lancers. Almost all such graphic designers buy *and* sell art.

Many graphic designers handle a range of projects and refer to themselves as general graphic designers. The specialized areas of design are described on the following pages. Trade customs and practices that are part of a specialized design area have been noted. Otherwise, the standards used by general graphic designers apply.

Graphic designers generally estimate the cost of each anticipated expense before starting work on a major project. The client is then presented with a proposal that reflects many of the following factors: (1) printing requirements (supervision, handling of printing); (2) research; (3) complexity of style required by the project; (4) art and/or copy that must be developed by the designer; (5) typography, production, retouching that must be commissioned by the designer; (6) intended use of the printed piece.

Often a client may choose to select a graphic designer with whom a long-term relationship may be established. This arrangement is appropriate when there is a string of projects which need a continuity of design. Another advantage for the client who develops a working relationship with a designer is that during the early stages of a project the designer may be consulted for help in planning the visual thrust and the time and cost schedules.

As a professional consultant, the graphic designer can determine the feasibility of a project by incorporating his or her knowledge of the technical resources available. Often clients choose to develop projects and *then* bring in the designer. This can be an inefficient use of the designer's capabilities since many decisions may already have been made that the designer should have been consulted on. The result can be unnecessary delays, additional costs, and inadequate design solutions. The sooner the designer is called in to consult on a project, the easier it is for the designer to help steer the project to the best graphic solution.

It is customary for the project description and cost proposal to be submitted to the client free of charge; however, any fees and expenses incurred on the client's behalf and with the client's consent are billable.

After the proposal is accepted by the client, the project is discussed at length and a direction is decided upon by the designer and the client. The designer then proceeds to develop the direction and make decisions as to size, length, color, visuals (e.g., illustration or photography), paper, printing methods, and the specific "look" of the piece or package. A presentation of a tight or loose comprehensive(s) is then shown to the client; the comprehensive indicates what can be expected of the finished piece. Alterations or additions are made at this point. It is only after the approval of the comprehensives that the designer proceeds to incur major expenses. It is important to note that changes that come after this stage can be expensive to the client and make the completion of the project difficult. It is relatively easy and inexpensive to change a comprehensive.

In many situations, graphic designers are entitled to credit and copyright, depending on the contractual arrangement. When other creative professionals are involved in a project through the designer, they may also be deserving of the same acknowledgment and rights on the piece or package of pieces.

When a graphic designer handles the printing of a job, it is a widely practiced custom for all subsequent printings and changes to be made through the designer as well. This allows the designer to control the quality of the piece.

Since the graphic designer works with so vast an array of graphic resources, it is imperative that all conditions and expectations be spelled out before the work commences. Note the following points:

Payment In larger projects the standard system of payment is one-third upon commencement of work, one-third upon approval of design comprehensives, and one-third within thirty days of delivery of mechanicals or printed pieces.

Markups The graphic designer's standard markup to cover handling of billable expenses is from 15 to 25 percent of each expense.

Consultation fees When a graphic designer is called in by a client to give advice on a project or design decision, a consultation fee is charged according to the designer's hourly rate. Such a fee is usually from $40 to 100 per hour.

The Graphic Designer's Estimate Confirmation/Invoice Form appears on pages 104–105.

It is imperative that, in judging the context of the Guild's pricing survey, the chapters preceeding and following the Prices be studied thoroughly.

Corporate graphic design

A graphic designer specializing in corporate design is involved in the design of annual reports, corporate communications and identity programs, signage, newsletters and annual reports.

The corporate designer generally works on a staff with a studio that includes a team comprised of a principal of the studio, a production manager, a copywriter, and possibly an account executive. Most graphic design studios are owned by graphic designers. The nature of the projects that corporate design studios are commissioned to handle often involves much more long term research and development than other areas of graphic design (see page 19). Many corporate design studios work on a retainer basis acting as design consultants in peripheral areas besides their main projects. Consequently, corporate designers often are brought in at the early stages of a project and may be integrally involved in directing the project through fruition.

Of particular concern to corporate design studios is the somewhat complicated issue of copyright. In some instances, individual artists own copyright on the work they create, not the client. Quite often, the studio contracts with free-lance illustrators, designers and photographers on a limited use basis for specific projects. It is not uncommon, therefore, for copyrights to be held by different individuals within a project. The studio negotiates with the client on behalf of the talent within the scope of the art budget the client has agreed to. Studios occasionally allow free-lance artists to deal with the client directly on terms and fees. However, the project cost can get out of hand if too much freedom is allowed, unless that direct client contact expedites matters.

Since many clients commissioning corporate design groups don't buy art on a regular basis, it is often the responsibility of the studio to educate the client on the intent, content and ethics of the copyright law. The studio frequently prepares a document explaining sub-contractor relationships, billing procedures and contract terms.

In addition to copyright concerns, the studio's terms and conditions are clearly outlined in writing and generally are reviewed prior to the first commission. These standard customs are contained in the contract, letter of agreement or confirmation of engagement form (see page 133 for standard contracts).

Most corporate design studios work in "phases."

Phase 1, programming: consists of all necessary research to determine a time schedule and clearly-defined program. A great deal of time is spent in this phase with the client defining the needs and problems that are to be solved. A rough budget is often prepared, showing a range of fess plus flexible expenses. A portion (normally 1/3) of the total budget is paid before the project begins.

Phase 2, schematic design: after a meeting of minds between design and client in phase 1, visual solutions are pursued that solve stated problems. Much of phase 2 is idea development (see page 19), which results in a presentation showing *only* those ideas that the design team feels are viable, appropriate and meet the prescribed criteria.

Phase 3, design development: at this stage, the design team refines the accepted design. A final presentation is then offered explaining the applications, tighter budget and time schedules. This phase is optional if the conditions are agreed upon prior to Phase 3.

Phase 4, design production: at this point, decisions are final. Illustrations, photography, typography, copy and mechanicals are finalized and all other pre-print production elements are locked into place. Any client changes after this point become billable as "client alterations."

Phase 5, product production: depending on the end product(s) the studio has been commissioned to produce, this phase may be a matter of going on press and/or supervising the manufacturing of products. Supervision is the key to this phase since all depends on the precision and quality achieved in this final phase. After the end product is approved, the project is considered billable.

A separate issue is ownership of preprint production materials such as type, film, and mechanicals. The studio normally retains control of design alterations, corrections and printing.

Billing

Billing expenses and fees may be handled in a number of ways. The studio arranges to bill on an hourly or project basis during the first phase. Expenses are always billed with handling charges or markups included. Sales tax and freight are never included in estimates and are normally billed at the end of the project along with client alterations, which are billed at a predetermined studio or principal's hourly rate.

The printing or manufacturing part of the project may be billed by the studio or directly to the client. This depends on the practice of the studio principals.

Regardless of who the invoice is sent to, the printer and all other professionals working with the design studio regard themselves as employed by the studio and are ethically bound to the studio's direction while working on the project. This, of course, becomes a matter of practicality since the designer is orchestrating many elements and must control them all to insure consistency.

It is imperative that, in judging the context of the Guild's pricing survey, the chapters preceeding and following the Prices be studied thoroughly.

Comparative fees for letterhead design*

	One or Two Colors
Corporate extensive use	$1500-2000
Corporate limited use	1000-1250
Nonprofit organization	1000-1250
Institution	1000-1500
Personal	750-1000

*Based on presentation of three versions of letterhead, card and envelope using an existing logo or simple typography; production charges are *not* included.

Comparative page rates for corporate annual reports*

	Text		Financial	
Corporate extensive use	*Two Color*	*Full Color*	*Two Color*	*Full Color*
Simple design	$250-500	$350-750	$200-400	$300-500
Complex design	300-750	400-850	300-600	350-750
Corporate limited use				
Simple design	$200-400	250-650	150-350	250-450
Complex design	250-500	300-750	250-500	300-650
Nonprofit organization				
Simple design	$150-350	200-500	150-300	200-350
Complex design	200-400	250-600	200-400	250-500
Institution				
Simple design	$150-350	200-500	150-300	200-350
Complex design	200-400	250-600	200-400	250-500

*Based on a 24 page annual report, broken down to 4 pages of financial and 20 pages of text; including client consultation, concept and design, research and presentation, rough tissue layouts and finished comprehensive dummy; production charges are *not* included.

Comparative fees for logo design*

	Research and Presentation	Development of Logo: Stationary Application	Development of Corporate Identity†
Corporate extensive use	$2500-7500	$1500-3500	$3500-10,000
Corporate limited use	1500-5000	1000-3000	1500-5000
Nonprofit organization	750-2500	750-1750	1000-3000
Institution	750-2500	750-1750	1000-3000

*Based on the presentation of three comprehensive layouts, rough tissue layouts, research, concept and design plus client consultation throughout the project; production charges are *not* included.

†Corporate identity includes standardization of identity and manual.

Comparative fees for newsletter design*

	Simple		Complex	
	4 pages	*12 pages*	*4 pages*	*12 pages*
Corporate, extensive use	$1250-2500	$1500-3000	$1500-3000	$2000-3500
Corporate, limited use	1000-2000	1250-2500	1250-2500	1500-3000
Consumer, extensive use	1250-2500	1500-3000	1500-3000	2000-3500
Consumer, limited use	1000-2000	1250-2500	1250-2500	1500-3000
Nonprofit organization	750-1500	1000-2000	1000-1750	1250-2500
Institution	750-1500	1000-2000	1000-1750	1250-2500

*Based on original concept and design including rough tissue layouts, three comprehensive layouts indicating masthead page, single page and spread format, and client consultation; production charges are *not* included.

Production charges*

Principal's hourly rate	$50-100
Studio staff hourly rate	25-50

Overtime rate is twice the above.

*Based on an hourly fee billable for unanticipated client consultations; selection, handling and super vision

Collateral advertising design

A graphic designer who specializes in collateral material is one who handles the design of catalogs, packaging, brochures, press kits and direct mail packages.

Advertising agencies generally handle the main campaign for products and/or services of a client. But often the client will commission or retain a design studio to handle its collateral material. Studio designers understand the print capabilities better because they specialize in that area. In general, they also are required work on tighter deadlines with less design latitude and with more controls than other design areas.

From a practical standpoint, collateral advertising is targeted to elicit a specific response. The graphic designer must therefore have a more sophisticated awareness of advertising, marketing, and sales than other designers.

Since the client or advertising agency is apt to supply the designer with existing art or photography, it is important to know the rights that the artist transferred. If additional rights must be purchased, this should be negotiated *before* the design or production stage. It is normal for an agency to purchase rights for many uses of art or photography to avoid the necessity of renegotiating each use.

It is also standard for the designer to sell uses to the client, for first time print runs or extended uses if that is appropriate.

Comparative fees for brochure and self mailer brochure design*

	Simple		Complex	
Major company	Two Color	Full Color	Two Color	Full Color
One fold	$450-900	$650-1000	$600-1200	$750-1500
Four folds	500-1000	750-1500	750-1500	1500-3000
Smaller company				
One fold	$300-750	$400-850	$350-1000	$500-1200
Four folds	500-1000	750-1500	750-1500	1000-2000
Nonprofit Organization				
One fold	$250-500	$350-750	$300-750	$450-1000
Four folds	400-750	500-1000	500-1000	750-1500
Institution				
One fold	$250-500	$350-750	$300-750	$450-1000
Four folds	400-750	500-1000	500-1000	750-1500

*Based on concept and design, rough tissue layouts, shooting format and final comprehensive layout; production charges *not* included.

Comparative fees for direct mail package design*

	Simple		Complex	
	Two Color	*Full Color*	*Two Color*	*Full Color*
Major company	$1500-3000	$2500-4000	$2000-4000	$3000-5000
Smaller company	1250-2500	1750-3000	1500-3000	2000-3500
Nonprofit organization	750-1750	1000-2000	1000-2000	1250-2500
Institution	1000-2000	1250-2500	1250-2500	1500-3000

*Based on design of a basic package including envelope, letter and brochure, reply card and return envelope; client consultation; rough tissue layouts showing format; comprehensive layout; production charges *not* included.

Production charges*

Principal's hourly rate	$50-100
Studio staff hourly rate	25-50

Overtime rate is twice the above.

*Based on an hourly fee billable for unanticipated client consultations; selection, handling and supervision of photography, illustration or printing; corrections.

Comparative fees for press kit design*

	Simple		Complex	
	Two Color	*Full Color*	*Two Color*	*Full Color*
Major company	$2000-3000	$3000-4000	$2500-4000	$3500-5000
Smaller company	1500-2500	2000-3500	2000-3500	2500-4000
Nonprofit organization	1000-2000	1500-2500	1500-2500	2000-3500
Institution	1000-2000	1500-2500	1500-2500	2000-3500

*Based on design of a basic kit including press kit cover or folder, insert sheets showing, for example, advertising ideas, promotional and display material and additional data; client consultation plus concept and design, rough tissue layouts and a comprehensive layout; production charges *not* included.

Comparative page rates for product and service catalog design*

Major company	8-16 Page Rate	24 Page Rate	48 Page Rate	Over 48 Page Rate
Color	$200-300	$150-275	$150-250	$150-250
Black and white	150-250	150-225	150-200	150-200
Smaller company				
Color	150-250	125-250	125-200	125-200
Black and white	150-200	125-200	100-175	100-175
Nonprofit organization				
Color	125-200	125-200	125-175	125-175
Black and white	100-175	100-175	100-150	100-150
Institution				
Color	125-200	125-200	125-175	125-175
Black and white	100-175	100-175	100-150	100-150

*Based on concept and design, rough tissue layouts showing format of spread, single page and cover design and final comprehensive layout. Price should be adjusted depending on the number of products required to be shown; production charges *not* included.

Advertising and promotion design

A graphic designer who specializes in advertising and promotion design is one who handles the design and placement of magazine and newspaper advertising, poster, billboards, press kits, letterhead, and promotion campaigns. In many areas studios must have agency status in order to place ads with magazines and newspapers.

More and more studios are taking on advertising particularly for clients who don't make advertising their main thrust for generating sales. Advertising designers must have a sophisticated knowledge of marketing, sales and, obviously, advertising print production.

Advertising designers hire other graphic artists on a free-lance basis, and purchase art and photography on behalf of their clients. They must have a good working knowledge of advertising illustration and photography, including trade customs that govern both. In terms of expense, these two areas are at the top of the list. In the case of illustration this is partially due to the demands that are required of the illustrator in an advertising project. For photography, there is an additional factor of overhead costs: studio time, equipment and staff.

The investment a client makes in advertising is often sizeable. Because of the value of advertising relative to the sales it produces, the risks must be calculated. This puts limits on the creative input that the designer might have, sometimes to the *detriment* of the client. The designer's role is to work as part of a team comprised of a copywriter, possibly an account executive and/or client representative such as a public relations person. The proposal given to the client should present a strategy as well as a design solution.

It is imperative that, in judging the context of the Guild's pricing survey, the chapters preceeding and following the Prices be thoroughly studied.

Comparative fees for consumer product package design*

	Simple		Complex	
New product line	*Two Color*	*Full Color*	*Two Color*	*Full Color*
Consumer, extensive use	$1500-2000	$2000-3000	$2000-3500	$2500-5000
Consumer, limited use	1250-1750	1500-2000	1750-2500	2000-3500
Corporate, extensive use	1500-3000	2000-4000	2000-4000	2500-6000
Corporate, limited use	1250-2000	1500-3000	1750-3000	2000-4000
Existing product line				
Consumer, extensive use	$1250-1750	$1500-2000	$1500-2500	$2000-4000
Consumer, limited use	1000-1500	1250-1750	1250-2250	1750-3000
Corporate, extensive use	1250-2000	1500-3000	1500-3000	2000-5000
Corporate, limited use	1000-1750	1250-2500	1250-2500	1750-3500

*Based on development of one logo in application to three products; mock-ups; production charges *not* included.

Comparative fees for magazine advertising design*

	Full	Half	Less than Half Page	Spread	Cover
National consumer	$2000-5000	$1500-3000	$1000-1500	$3500-6000	$2500-5500
Regional consumer	1500-2500	1000-1750	750-1250	2500-3500	2000-3000
Trade publication	1000-2000	750-1500	600-1000	1500-3000	1750-2500
Specialized audience	750-1750	600-1250	500-750	1500-2500	1750-2000
In-house magazine	650-1250	500-1000	400-700	1250-2000	1000-1750

*Based on concept and design of a maximum of three rough tissue layouts plus final comprehensive layout using the elements of photography or illustration, headline, subhead, body copy and company logo or sign off; production and art charges *not* included.

Comparative fees for newspaper advertising design*

	Full Page	Half Page	Less Than Half Page
National advertising campaign	$1500-3000	$1000-2000	$750-1500
Regional advertising campaign	1000-2500	750-1750	500-1250
Weekly newspaper	500-1250	350-1000	250-750

*Based on concept and design of a maximum of three rough tissue layouts; one final comprehensive layout using the elements of photography or illustration, headline, subhead, body copy and company logo or sign off; production and art charges *not* included.

Comparative fees for advertising and promotional campaign design*

	Simple	Complex
Corporate, extensive use	$1750-3500	$2500-4500
Corporate, limited use	1250-2500	2000-3000

*Based on concept and design including rough tissue layouts, comprehensive layout through to finished presentation; production charges *not* included.

Comparative fees for television advertising design*

National advertising campaign	$5000-10,000
Regional advertising campaign	3000-7500
Local area advertising campaign	2000-5000

*Based on client consultation; concept and design including storyboards.

Comparative fees for billboard design*

Major company	$1000-2500
Smaller company	750-1750
Nonprofit organization	500-1250
Institution	500-1250

*Based on concept and design including rough tissue layouts and comprehensive layouts; client consultation; production charges are *not* included.

Comparative fees for public transportation advertising design*

Major company	$750-1500
Smaller company	500-1250
Nonprofit organization	500-1000
Institution	500-1000

*Based on concept and design including rough tissue layouts and comprehensive layouts; client consultation; production charges are *not* included.

Comparative fees for record album design*

	Front Only	Front and Back
Major label	$2500-3500	$3000-5000
Other	1500-2500	2000-3000

*Based on concept and design including rough tissue layouts, one finished comprehensive layout, supervision of photography or illustration; production charges *not* included.

Production, consultation, and supervision charges*

Principal's hourly rate	$50-100
Studio staff hourly rate †	25-50

*Based on an hourly fee billable for unanticipated client consultations; selection, handling and supervision of photography, illustration or printing; corrections.

†Overtime rate is twice the above.

Display and novelty design

Geneneral graphic designers, needle-artists, and illustrators often handle display and novelty design, although there are some artists who specialize in this field. Display and novelty design includes such items as posters, greeting cards, gift or boutique-type items, holiday decorations, eyeglass covers and the like.

Since manufacturing materials, resources and requirements for production of these items often limit the type of display and design, research into those factors can be an important part of an assignment of this type. The resourcesfulness of the designer in combining these limits with creative design is often the key to a successfully marketed display or novelty item.

It is imperative that, in judging the context of the Guild's pricing survey the chapters preceeding and following the Prices be studied thoroughly.

Comparative fees for point-of-purchase display material design*

	Simple		Complex	
	Two Color	*Full Color*	*Two Color*	*Full Color*
Counter cards				
Consumer, extensive use	$500-1750	$750-2000	$750-2000	$1000-2500
Consumer, limited use	400-1250	500-1500	500-1500	750-2000
Posters				
Consumer, extensive use	750-1500	1000-2000	1000-2500	1500-3000
Consumer, limited use	600-1250	750-1500	850-1750	1250-2000
Banners				
Consumer, extensive use	650-1250	750-1500	750-1500	1000-1800
Consumer, limited use	500-1000	650-1250	500-1200	750-1500
Motion picture, extensive use	500-1250	750-1500	750-1500	1000-1800
Motion picture, limited use	450-1000	600-1250	600-1250	750-1500
Shopping bags				
Consumer, extensive use	500-1250	750-1500	750-1350	1000-2500
Consumer, limited use	400-1000	500-1250	600-1200	750-1500

*Based on design and concept including rough tissue layouts and a final comprehensive layout; production and art charges *not* included.

Comparative fees for design of exhibit display material*

	Simple		Complex	
Posters	Two Color	Full Color	Two Color	Full Color
Corporate, extensive use	$1250-2000	$1500-2500	$1250-2500	$1500-3000
Corporate, limited use	750-1500	1000-2000	1000-2000	1250-2500
Motion picture, extensive use	1250-2500	1500-3000	1250-3000	1500-3500
Motion picture, limited use	1250-2000	1500-2500	1000-2500	1500-3000
Theater	750-1500	1000-2000	1000-2000	1500-2500
Nonprofit organization	500-1000	750-1000	750-1500	1000-2000
Institution	750-1000	1000-1500	1200-2000	1500-2500
Banners				
Corporate, extensive use	500-1250	750-1500	750-1500	1000-1800
Corporate, limited use	450-750	500-750	500-850	750-1000
Theater	450-1000	600-1250	750-1250	1000-1500
Nonprofit organization	450-1000	600-1250	850-1500	1000-2000
Institution	450-1000	600-1250	850-1500	1000-2000
Billboards				
Corporate, extensive use	750-2000	1000-2500	1000-2500	1500-3000
Corporate, limited use	500-1300	750-1500	750-1500	1000-1800
Motion picture, extensive use	750-2000	1000-2500	1000-2500	1500-3000
Motion picture, limited use	500-1500	750-2000	750-2000	1000-2500
Theater	500-1500	750-2000	750-2000	1000-2500
Nonprofit organization	500-1250	1000-1500	750-1500	1000-2000
Institution	500-1250	1000-1500	750-1500	1000-2000

*Based on design and concept including rough
tissue layouts and a final comprehensive layout.

Publication design

Publication designers create the formats and "look" of magazines or tabloids. These publications have an editorial point of view and often contain advertising.

While most publication design is done on staff within a parent company, there are free-lance publication designers. For staff design information, please refer to page 125.

A publication designer may, on a free-lance basis, design the format for a magazine or tabloid, and be retained as a consultant for periodic oversight of the publication. In this case; the role filled by the publications designer is called art director.

Working with the art director may be one or more associate art directors, assistant art directors, and/or designers and mechanical artists.

At the planning stages for each issue of the publication, the key editorial staff (most often the editor-in-chief, section editors and key writers for the issue) meet with the art director and appropriate staff to hold a story and cover conference. In this session, the strategy for several issues is mapped out, with the major focus on the current issue. A direction is established and concepts may be determined at this time. From this point on, the art director commissions art for the issues within the yearly budget constraints. However, the editor of the publication has approval over dummies and storyboards, since he/she is accepted as the authority for the publication. In all instances the publisher has final approval over the package.

Free-lance artists who are commissioned to work on publications are often expected to sell on an all rights or work-for-hire basis, which limits the pool of talent available to publications, and thus the visual content of the piece.

There are independent studios that produce magazines and/or tabloids on a periodic basis, but they are not the norm in the field.

Frequently, free-lance or independent designers are commissioned to redesign an existing magazine and continue on as consultants, either on retainer or fee based on an estimated number of hours per issue.

It is imperative that, in judging the context of the Guild's pricing survey, chapters preceeding and following the Prices be studied thoroughly.

Comparative fees for editorial magazine design*

Existing format	Masthead and Cover	Spread	Single Page
Extensive circulation, black and white	$750-1500	$350-500	$250-400
Extensive circulation, color	1500-2000	650-850	350-500
Limited circulation, black and white	600-1200	300-450	200-350
Limited circulation, color	1200-1500	500-750	300-450
Trade publication, black and white	600-1200	300-450	200-350
Trade publication, color	1200-1500	500-750	300-450
Special interest, black and white	500-1000	250-400	200-350
Special interest, color	750-1500	400-550	250-400
Corporate in-house, black and white	500-1000	250-400	200-350
Corporate in-house, color	750-1250	400-550	250-400
Institution, black and white	500-1000	250-400	200-350
Institution, color	750-1500	400-550	250-400
Nonprofit organization, black and white	500-1000	250-400	200-350
Nonprofit organization, color	750-1500	400-550	250-400

Comparative fees for editorial magazine design (continued)*

New format	Masthead and Cover	Spread	Single Page
Extensive circulation, black and white	$1000-2000	$500-750	$350-500
Extensive circulation, color	1800-2500	750-1000	500-750
Limited circulation, black and white	750-1500	400-650	300-450
Limited circulation, color	1400-2000	600-850	400-650
Trade publication, black and white	750-1500	400-650	300-450
Trade publication, color	1400-2000	600-850	400-650
Special interest, black and white	600-1200	350-600	250-400
Special interest, color	1000-1750	500-750	350-600
Corporate in-house, black and white	600-1200	350-600	250-400
Corporate in-house, color	1000-1500	500-750	350-600
Institution, black and white	600-1200	350-600	250-400
Institution, color	1000-1750	500-750	350-600
Nonprofit organization, black and white	600-1200	350-600	250-400
Nonprofit organization, color	1000-1750	500-750	350-600

*Based on concept and design including rough tissue layouts and comprehensive layouts; client consultation; production charges are *not* included.

Production, consultation, and supervision charges*

Principal's hourly rate $50-100

Studio staff hourly rate   25-50

Overtime rate is twice the above.

*Based on an hourly fee billable for unanticipated client consultations; selection, handling and supervision of photography, illustration or printing; corrections.

Miscellaneous design

The entertainment industry has innumerable types of packages such as video cassettes and record album covers, that require design. Because of the newness of some of these mediums, there is not enough information available to publish statistically relevant pricing data.

Record albums, as you can see from the accompanying table, represents a standard design area. A peculiarity exists here, however, that should be noted. Unlike most packaging, album covers are not normally seen as advertising by the record industry. Its unclear if there is a standard category that they can be slotted into.

Presentations are included here as well since they are another non-specific area. The value, design attitude and production problems of presentations are virtually impossible to elaborate on since they are unique to the project.

It is imperative that, in judging the context of the Guild's pricing survey, chapters preceding and following the prices be studied thoroughly.

Comparative fees for record album design ☆

	Front Only	Front and Back
Major label	$2500-3500	$3000-5000
Other	1500-2500	2000-3000

*Based on concept and design including rough tissue layouts, one finished comprehensive layout, supervision of photography or illustration; production charges *not* included.

Production, consultation, and supervision charges*

Principal's hourly rate	$50-100
Studio staff hourly rate †	25-50

*Based on an hourly fee billable for unanticipated client consultations; selection, handling and supervision of photography, illustration or printing; corrections.

†Overtime rate is twice the above.

Comparative fees for shopping bag designs*

	Simple		Complex	
	Two Color	Full Color	Two Color	Full Color
Corporate, extensive use	$650-1300	$750-1800	$850-1500	$1000-2000
Corporate, limited use	500-750	650-1000	750-1250	850-1500
Motion picture, extensive use	650-1500	750-2000	1250-1750	1500-2500
Motion picture, limited use	500-1000	650-1750	1000-1500	1200-2000
Theater	650-850	750-1000	1000-1500	1250-2000
Nonprofit organization	400-750	500-850	750-1100	850-1250
Institution	400-750	500-850	750-1100	850-1250

*Based on concept and design including rough tissue layouts and comprehensive layouts; production charges *not* included.

Book jacket design

A *book jacket designer* is a graphic artist who creates the look of the jacket or cover of a book or series of books using the graphic elements of typography, illustration, photography, and/or designed letterforms.

The book jacket designer works in a way similar to the graphic designer, usually taking the project through to camera-ready mechanicals. Generally, printing of the jacket or cover is handled by the publisher.

After terms and fees are agreed upon by the publishing house's art director and the designer, one comprehensive is prepared for presentation. If additional comprehensives are required, it is customary for an additional fee to be paid. Once the comprehensive is approved, the designer proceeds to execute or commission illlustration, lettering, or other graphic elements used in the finished art.

Generally, the comprehensive is as close as possible in appearance to the finished piece. Such a tight comprehensive often entails expenses for typesetting, photostats, or color keys to achieve a finished look. All out-of-pocket expenses are billable to the client in the sketch and finish stages. Because of the nature of publishing, there is a high rate of rejection. This is accepted as a risk by the designer and publisher. It should be noted however, that the rejection fee is always considered separate from the expenses; the rejection fee reflects the amount of work completed at the time of termination of the project and the expenses are additional.

In cases where the designer's influence is apparent in the jacket or cover, the copyright of the design should appear in the designer's name. Copyright and credit for the designer should be agreed upon before work is commenced. If other creative elements (e.g., illustration or lettering) appear on the cover, they must be recognized as well. If the publisher is preparing the flaps of the jacket or the back cover where the copyright will appear, it is imperative that all credit be noted on the mechanical but outside of the reproduction area. When the rest of the jacket or cover is set in type, the credit will naturally be added. Otherwise, it is easily overlooked. In any event, when confirming a job and on the invoice, it is essential that a book jacket designer specify that artwork is prepared only for the named edition and title. Designers usually sell one-time reproduction rights. The designer should receive additional payment for use of art by other domestic or foreign publishers and book clubs, or by film, television, or other sources of communication.

Production costs such as (but not necessarily limited to) photographic processing, type, mechanically reproduced lettering, and photostats should be billed by the designer over and above the design fee, or such costs shall be directly assumed by the client.

It is suggested that a 15 to 25 percent handling fee be applied to expenses incurred (type, photostats, etc.) by the designer for a jacket design, if the publisher does not pick up these costs directly.

Additional rights for use of finished art by the original client are usually limited to use in advertising and promoting sale of the original book in the edition initially contemplated. If any other rights are conveyed, it is imperative that the designer state on his or her bill specifically what those rights are and for what editions. It should also state specifically that all other rights are reserved to the designer and that original art should be returned to the designer.

Comparative fees for book jacket design concepts ☆

	Hardcover and Trade Paperback	Mass Market Bestseller
One concept for front jacket or cover with supplied mechanical for front and spine	$400–650	$500–1000
Additional concepts (per sketch)	150–250	150–350
One concept followed by voluntary termination	50% of original fee (minimum)	50% of original fee (minimum)

*Some distinction should be made as to the difference of fees of 2-color and 3-color graphic designs, full-color spot design, and full-color bleed art. For juvenile book jackets, see Juvenile Book section.

Book design

A *book designer* is a graphic artist who develops the style and visual flow of a book by using the graphic elements of typography, illustration, and photography and applies these elements through production techniques. The functions of the book designer range from the highly creative to the purely mechanical. Before dealing with the creative aspects of a job, it is necessary to analyze the project in order to prepare a design brief that includes the information outlined below. The design brief may be prepared either by the publisher or by the free-lance book designer. The prices in the book design categories are based on preparation of the design brief by the publisher. When the designer's assignment includes this responsibility, it should be reflected by an increase in design fee.

The design brief

The *design brief* includes: (1) a copy of the manuscript, with a selection of representative copy for sample pages and a summary of all typographic problems, copy areas, code marks, etc.; (2) an outline of the publisher's manufacturing program for the book: the compositor's name and method of composition, the printer's name and method of binding; and (3) a description of the proposed physical characteristics of the book (e.g., trim size, page length, number of columns, number of colors if more than one) and the projected list price and quantity of the first printing. The publisher should also indicate whether any particular visual style is expected.

The following prices are based on preparation of as many layouts as the designer feels are necessary to show major design elements. When the client wishes to see highly detailed layouts showing elements which could just as easily be communicated to the compositor by typemarking of the sample manuscript pages, an increase of the fee is in order. Any additional considerations (such as a book in two or more colors) should also be reflectd in an increase in the fee.

After the fee is agreed upon by the publisher and the book designer, sketches are prepared. The book designer may prepare pencil tissues of chapter openings, title page, double-page spread of the text, and pages incorporating illustrations, photographs, or tables. These typical examples of pages clearly show the design to the publisher and are used as a guide in production.

Most publishers use in-house or the compositor's production facilities to take the book from sketches to page makeup. With complicated layouts, the publisher may request that the book designer dummy the book. *Dummying* is actually taking copies of galleys and placing them in position on dummy sheets. The dummy may then be used by the production staff or designer to prepare mechanicals for the printer.

Occasionally, a writer and book designer may team up to create a package for a publisher. Such a package includes camera-ready mechanicals or pasteups, and the publisher is thereby relieved of these production responsibilities. This way of working is generally used when the idea of the book originated with the writer or designer. It may also be used when the publisher requires a unique design that must be completed by the designer chosen to work on the project.

Book design categories

The table below provides typical fees for simple, average, and complex book design format categories. The categories are defined as follows:

Simple A straightforward book such as a novel or short book of poetry. Design includes a layout showing a title page, a chapter opening, and a double spread of text.

Average Basic textbooks, nonfiction trade books, or simple books that require an especially stylish or deluxe presentation (e.g., art books, books of photographs, or picture books). Design includes frontmatter (half-title, ad card, title, copyright, dedication, acknowledgments, preface, contents, list of illustrations, introduction), part opening, chapter opening, text comprising from three to six levels of heads, tabular matter, extracts, footnotes, and simple backmatter such as a bibliography. The design, exclusive of the frontmatter, is usually set into sample pages.

Complex These are books such as workbooks, catalogs, and elaborate art or picture books, instruction manuals, foreign langue texts, two-color basic texts, cookbooks, poetry or drama anthologies, or other books of greater complexity than in the previous category.

The book designer should be aware that the following items are not included in the basic design fee and should be billed at the designer's hourly rate: manuscript analysis for design brief, checking of proof, alterations, and sizing of illustrations (usually billed on a per-unit basis). Page dummies are billed at $4-8 per page (the low figure is for a single color book, the higher for 4-color books). Illustration sizing is generally billed at $4 per illustration, which includes mounting. Any additional labeling or redrawing of illustrations should be billed accordingly.

It is imperative that, in judging the context of the Guild's pricing survey, chapters preceeding and following the Prices be studied thoroughly.

Comparative fees for book design*

	Simple Format		Average Format		Complex Format	
	Low Usage	High Usage	Low Usage	High Usage	Low Usage	High Usage
Textbook						
Usual fee	$475	$500	$650	$800	$750	$1000
Highly stylized	520	600	720	900	1000	1200
Unique design	600	700	750	1000	1100	1500
Each additional book in series	25%	25%	33%	33%	50%	50%
Trade book						
Usual fee	500	550	650	700	750	850
Highly stylized	550	650	700	800	1000	1400
Unique design	650	750	750	1000	1500	1750
Each additional book in series	25%	25%	33%	33%	50%	50%

*See the text above for elaboration on the meaning of the range of formats.

Comparative fees for design of cover and interior text of juvenile books

	Type Layout after Illustrated Dummy	Format and Type Design	Format and Type Design Plus Art Illustration Direction
Trade Book	$700	$900	$1500*
Textbook	600	800	1100*

*Alternatively, a flat fee may be charged for the format and type design and then the art direction of illustration is billed at the rate of $25-35 per hour.

Computer-generated art

Due to the relatively un-
chartered area of business
practices for computer technology, pricing for computer-assisted art
must start with the final applications for the
work: that is, whether the art will be used
as an illustration, text design, in broadcast,
etc. The applications covered here are
primarily for work done on a personal computer or for videotex broadcasting. Work
created on larger and more powerful paint
and animation systems are best priced by
referring to the other pricing sections of
this book that apply to the final product.

Because of the overlap between conventional technology and the new areas of
digital format, any pricing structures are
preliminary. However, any work generated
on computer for conventional print or
media should be billed at current rates *plus
consideration of the unique value of the computer.*

One more point, a computer is not a
"self-functioning" tool. Like pencils, air-
brushes and other graphics tools, com-
puters do not generate work of and by
themselves. *Any computer-generated art is
the result of the artist's talent, skill, experience
and knowledge of software.*

The work done on personal computer
and videotex is in digital format, i.e. it remains in the form produced by the computer. Whereas other uses of computer-
generated works require conversion into
more commonly-known applications such
as 35 mm film, slides and videotape, etc.

Broadcasting is an area where computer-generated work has been most commonly used. Computer technology is used
to create and augment titles and commercials through both illustration and animation. However, even though the original
work is created on computer, the final product is displayed on 35mm film or videotape. The technology to produce computer-
generated art directly on hardcopy is not of
high enough print quality for standard
printing techniques at this time. Similarly,
business graphics and presentations are
created on computer and then photographed onto film. Therefore, any use of
computer-generated art for print illustration
must employ the "raster lines" of the
monitor as part of the aesthetic of the style
and requires conversion of the computer
image into some form of "hardcopy" that is
photographable.

Applications

Hardcopy includes all applications for
standard print illustration. Follow illustration pricing sections for any work that will
be used in conventional print or media applications.

Broadcast and audio-visual refers to
presentation and business graphics such as
charts and graphs, broadcast graphics and
commercials. Refer to pricing sections for
broadcast and audio-visual art.

Software and electronic publishing includes title page illustration, interior illustration, structured or formated pages, game title pages and interior screens.

Artists working in this area will be
creating illustrations or designs on specific
operating systems (i.e. Apple, Atari, IBM).
The most realistic way to work with these
systems is to use a system that includes an
electronic digital drawing board, rather
than trying to write complex and time con-
suming programs. Art created for software
will follow very standard print models: title
and chapter screens for games and programs, illustrations, and formated pages
(pages laid out for text with borders, win-
dows, etc.).

In all probability, publishing will use
electronic downloading digital information
via telephone services before 1985. Because
of this, artists should establish royalty payment structures for art used in software
and electronic downloaded publishing.

Videotex is a broadcast industry that
uses vertical band intervals to transmit
digital information. Services in this area include advertising, public bulleting boards,
games and information services. Videotex
should also require royalty arrangements
since it is billed by per-frame use. Even
though Videotex has not become the giant
in the industry that it was projected to be, it
will be a job source for artists in the next
decade. Whatever its final form, the concept is one of interactive digital-based information and entertainment services through
which artists will illustrate game screens,
title screens and advertisement screens.

Consideration should be given to the
potential use of the work when pricing.
Royalties should be established for the
work if it is to be used for continued resale.

Copyright. Work for use in digital format—software, electronic publishing, and videotex—is copyrightable. In fact, it can be copyrighted as text (printed source code), as graphic art (hardcopy printout, photo, etc) and as an audio visual work. In most instances, registering a work as an audio-visual is the choice of the artist.

The contract for computer-generated art appearing in this book is applicable to software, electronic publishing and videotex. Because of the newness of the field, the contract is a starting point, which can be amended as the technology and industry practices change.

Software Illustration
Screen Design
Software Animation

Type of screen	Educational		Entertainment		Business	
	Large Company	Small Company	Large Company	Small Company	Large Company	Small Company
Title screen	$700	$350	$800	$200	$800	$200
Secondary title screen	600	300	700	150	700	150
Illustration screen	350	250	400	250	400	200
Formatted screen	200	150	300	250	350	250

Hourly rate $60.

Letterforms

A *hand letterer* is a graphic artist who uses the characters of the alphabet and numbers to create graphic forms or original alphabets. Hand lettering includes calligraphy, built-up letterforms, designed letterforms, and alphabets.

The hand letterer works in a way similar to the illustrator. Upon agreement of the terms and fee for the project, the letterer prepares sketches of possible solutions to a specific problem. Upon acceptance of the comprehensive or sketches, finished art is prepared for reproduction.

Hand lettering is used in all areas of the communications industry: advertising, corporate identity and promotion, publishing, and institutional.

Many hand letterers are also graphic designers or illustrators. In fact, it is rare to find a graphic artist who does hand lettering only except in the area of calligraphy.

The dramatic development of photo and film lettering in recent years has, of course, made it necessary to restructure the pricing concepts for the creative professional letterers and alphabet designers. Among the many factors affecting the prices of lettering are the following: (1) the amount of design work involved; (2) the size of the original art; (3) medium to be used (pen, brush, ink paint); (4) styled lettering (typeface modification); (5) surface upon which it is to be executed (paper, color print, box, bottle, can); (6) distortions (perspective, condensing); and (7) number of comprehensives required.

The prices below reflect the average hand letterer's fee. All expenses are additional. The prices to a client may be higher if the lettering is being commissioned through a designer or art director because the end price must accommodate their additional participation.

It is imperative that, in judging the context of the Guild's pricing survey, the chapters preceeding and following the Prices be studied thoroughly.

Alphabet design

Alphabet design is a rather complex situation to make a determination about price arrangements. Most corporations have contracts that take complete possession of the design and continue to pay royalties for the sale to other corporations for extensive uses. It is up to the designer to communicate with the alphabet buyer (corporation) to negotiate changes in the contract. An advance against royalties of at least $500 is usually paid by the corporations for accepted alphabet designs.

Comparative fees for alphabet design* ☆

	Low	*Medium*	*High*
Corporate	$3000	$4500–5000	$6000–7500 +
Type house†	—	—	—
Magazine or publication	2000	4000	5000

*Includes upper- and lowercase and numerals in one weight (approximately seventy characters); unlimited rights, but not for resale.

†$100 advance is paid on delivery and a royalty arrangement is negotiated based on unit sales. The advance should be negotiated based on the number of characters, the weights, slants, small capitals, numerals, and upper and lowercases required. No outright sales is suggested for a purchase price less than $5000.

*A survey was conducted in 1983 which resulted in insufficient statistically-relevant pricing data to warrant changes in this pricing section. The prices reflected here are the results of the survey conducted in 1980.

Comparative fees for letterforms ☆

	Low	Medium	High
Publication titling *(one comprehensive, one finish)*			
Major magazine	$350	$500	$800
Specific audience or minor publication	350	450	550
Publication masthead design logotype *(three comprehensives, one finish; unlimited rights)*			
Major magazine	2000	2500	5000
Specific audience	350	500	750
Small publication (newsletter, in-house organ)	300	400	600
Hardcover book jacket lettering *(one comprehensive, one finish; one-time rights limited to specific editions involved)*			
Mass market	300	450–650	700–900
Specific market	300	400	600
Paperback cover lettering *(one comprehensive, one finish; one-time rights limited to the specific edition involved)*			
Mass market	350–400	500–650	800–1000
Specific market	300	450	700
Logotypes *(three comprehensives, one finish; unlimited rights)*			
Corporate	1500	—	—
Individual	500	750	1000

Rough lettering: $3 to 4 per word

Rough lettering on acetate: $4 to 10 per word

Comprehensive lettering: $6 to 12 per word

Calligraphy on certificates or envelopes: $2 per word or line, depending on the height and weight of the words and the quality required

Reworking or altering letterforms *(in house):* $30 to 45 per hour

Advertising *(including packaging, television and film):* See advertising illustration section for comparable prices for any built up, designed or calligraphic letterforms

Retouching

A *retoucher* is a graphic artist who alters, enhances, or adds to a photograph by using bleaches, dyes, brush, or airbrush techniques. The resulting photograph usually appears to have never been touched. This "invisible art" requires a highly skilled hand and eye in order to be successful. Therefore, the retoucher most often specializes in one area of retouching and concentrates on the techniques, skills, and technical knowledge of that area.

When pricing a retouching project, many factors come into play:

Surface Most color work of high quality is done on transparencies, or chromes, or dye transfers because of the subtleties that can be achieved on these surfaces. A retoucher uses dyes and bleaches when working on a chrome. C prints are often used for presentation purposes but when extreme detail is required, often lack the dependability of chromes and dye transfers for the printer to use as reproduction art. Brush, pencil, dyes, bleaching, etching, and airbrush techniques are used in retouching on all surfaces. In black-and-white retouching, photographic prints of high quality are most commonly used as a surface to be retouched.

Complexity Retouching can run the gamut of change in the photo: from simply adding a few highlights to actually creating photorealistic, hand-wrought backgrounds, shapes, or figures, or stripping two or more photos together to create a montage.

Expenses Typography, photography, props, and other out-of-pocket expenses are considered to be additional, billable expenses.

Overtime Retouching, by its nature, should not be a last-minute project. It's important, therefore, to know how the retoucher charges for extraordinary time requirements. Normal timing for any average-size project is three days. Overtime rates for less than three days turnover are figured at: two days—50 percent more; one day—100 percent more (rush job status). If the job requires evening, weekend, or holiday time, there is often a 100 percent overtime charge.

Rights Unlike the other graphic artists, retouchers always work on an existing piece of art and are usually not entitled to copyright or reuse fees. The fee that they charge initially represents the total income from that project, unlike artists who are working on the basis of selling future rights.

Studio A retouching studio has full equipment and staff to provide multiple talents, flexibility in handling larger projects, and accessibility. Studio rates are higher than free-lance rates.

Free-lance Free-lance retouchers handle each project themselves and generally work out of their own studios. They rarely work on the client's premises. Since free-lancers often have less overhead, rates may reflect it.

Hourly rates for retouching*☆

	Studio	Free-lance
Color, chromes or dye transfers	$50–80	$30–50
Color, C prints	50–80	30–60
Black and white, prints	40–60	20–40

*The above prices are based on average job, working conditions, talent, and client as the guide. Deviations from average may reflect in higher or lower prices and/or rates.

Comparative fees for retouching* ☆

	Corporate and Advertising		Editorial	
Automotive	*Spot*	*Large*	*Spot*	*Large*
National, color	$800	$2000	$500	$1000
National, black and white	350	800	250	500
Regional, color	600	1500	350	700
Regional, black and white	250	500	150	350
Beverage				
National, color	700	1500	400	900
National, black and white	450	700	250	450
Regional, color	550	1000	300	600
Regional, black and white	250	400	150	300
Tobacco				
National, color	800	1700	500	1000
National, black and white	350	600	250	550
Regional, color	600	1200	350	800
Regional, black and white	250	500	150	350
Cosmetics				
National, color	700	1200	400	800
National, black and white	300	500	250	450
Regional, color	500	900	300	650
Regional, black and white	200	400	125	325
Fashion				
National, color	800	1600	450	950
National, black and white	250	500	200	350
Regional, color	600	1000	350	750
Regional, black and white	175	350	150	300
Industrial, pharmaceutical, and general markets				
National, color	500	1000	300	600
National, black and white	250	500	175	350
Regional, color	350	700	250	500
Regional, black and white	175	350	125	275

Production

A *production artist* is a graphic artist who executes the finished mechanical or pasteup for a graphic designer or art director to his or her layout specifications. The production artist, in short, makes the project camera ready for the printer. The subtle decisions and interpretations that a production artist must make on the board determine the final product. The details are critical.

Advanced production artists are adept at keyline ruling, overlays, and all other complicated production techniques.

Some of the considerations a production artist uses in determining the cost of producing a mechanical or pasteup are: (1) condition of the job and tightness of the layout; (2) extent of responsibility in gathering materials for the job; (3) location of job (on site or in own studio); (4) complexity of style; and (5) deadline (amount of overtime involved).

Most production artists base their prices on their hourly rates. Occasionally, prices are worked out on a per-page rate.

Hourly rates for preparing camera-ready art ☆

Pasteups

Corporate	$16–18
Publishing	10–16
Advertising	20–25

Mechanicals

Corporate	18–22
Publishing	12–18
Advertising	23–28

SALARIED
PRICES
AND TRADE CUSTOMS

Salaried Artists

For more detailed descriptions of positions mentioned in the pricing section of this chapter, please refer to the appropriate free-lance sections, which describe the role of each discipline. The positions included here are those that do not appear in those free-lance sections.

The main difference between salaried graphic artists and those who are exclusively free-lance is the scope of the commitment. Many free-lance graphic artists have the same clients for many years, and such graphic artists thereby develop a strong sense of commitment to the people and companies for whom they work. The salaried graphic artist is usually employed solely by one company. Unless contractual arrangements are made to the contrary, all art created on company time is considered work for hire. In the more creative jobs, often it is considered unethical to moonlight for a competitor. Generally, the scope of employment limits the income for the salaried graphic artist to that artist's employing company.

Many of the disciplines listed below are not exclusive of each other. For instance, an art director may also produce illustrations, designs, or letterforms. In fact, very few salaried graphic artists specialize so rigidly as to only have talents in one given area. The needs of the position must, therefore, dictate the talents required. Using the primary role to be filled, the salaries outlined below should give an idea of the ranges that can be expected by the professional artist being interviewed for a staff position.

These salaries are based on a standard 35-hour week with a benefits package including health insurance, vacation pay, holiday and sick pay. Bonuses, stock options, and retirement plans are negotiable. The jobs described are creative positions and do not include purely executive or supervisory functions.

Generally, larger companies hire full-time art staff (i.e., companies that produce a significant amount of graphic art in-house such as catalogs, textile designs, advertising, packaging, or corporate graphics). Free-lance talent is often used to supplement an art staff. At times, independent agencies or studios are on retainer when there is no art staff or the company chooses to subcontract large areas of concern (e.g., advertising, corporate identity programs, or annual and quarterly reports).

Employment conditions

When applying for a full-time salaried position, artists should consider conditions of employment along with salary and type of work. Among the conditions generally accepted as standard for full-time workers are:

Staff policy: Many employers have written staff policies that outline the way in which a company relates to its employees. In fact, New York State companies are required by law to notify employees "in writing or by publicly posting" policy on sick leave, vacation, personal leave, holidays and hours. Other items that may be included in staff policies are: maternity/paternity leave, employee grievance procedures, criteria for salary increases and promotions, cause for firing, etc. A staff policy can often give a potential employee an impression of an employer's attitude towards his/her staff, so it is useful to know before deciding to accept a job.

Job benefits: Most companies offer some benefits packages to their employees which may include: health, disability, life and dental insurance plans. In larger companies and corporations, there are occasionally profit-sharing and stock option plans, day care facilities or child-care subsidies, although these benefits are rare for most lower to middle management positions.

Job descriptions: Just as a contract serves as a clear understanding between a client and a free-lance artist, a written job description can give an artist a clear indication of what is expected of him/her during the term of employment. The Guild recommends that a written job description for all artists seeking a salaried position, since it helps both employer and employee to avoid expectations and assumptions that are not shared by the other party. A written job description is also useful in the event that a job changes significantly during the term of employment. When substantial changes are made in a job, an employee may approach the employer to have the description re-written and discuss title changes and salary adjustments.

Job review: A regular job review (semi-annual or annual) is a helpful practice for both employer and employee. A review allows the employee to get valuable feedback on how they are performing, and to bring up questions about job expectations.

The employer has, at review times, the opportunity to discuss changes in job descriptions and performance critiques. Formal job reviews also provide opportunities for both employer and employee to suggest ways to improve the "product" or the role being considered. When handled well, the job review can head off problems that might arise and help maintain good and productive relationships between employer and employee. It is recommended that the results of the job review be kept on file and that employees have access to their reviews.

While many of the above conditions of employment are not mandatory, they are recommended to help insure that both employer and employee develop and maintain good relations during the term of employment.

The broadcast designer

The demands of the one-eyed television medium that sits in 98 percent of the living rooms in the United States present a unique challenge to broadcast designers. The challenge demands knowledge and creativity in every aspect of design.

For on-air duties, broadcast designers are required to be illustrators, cartoonists, and type designers. It is necessary to know, prepare, and sometimes shoot animations, on both film and tape. Knowledge of stand and remote still photography is essential. For print media broadcast designers devise everything from small-space program-listing ads to full-page newspaper ads as well as trade publication ads, booklets, brochures, invitations, and similar material.

Broadcast designers double as corporate designers who coordinate everything from the on-air look, to the stationery, memo pads, and sales promotion materials. cast designers even design news vehicle Broad-markings and occasionally design helicopter markings.

In addition to the preceding fields, scenic design is another area of responsibility. Here the understanding of construction techniques, materials, and paints is of primary importance, not to mention the awareness of staging, furnishing, lighting, spatial relationships, and camera angles.

As an art director it is necessary to be proficient in managerial skills of organization, budgeting, purchasing, directing a

*This section on the broadcast designer was written by Gil Cowley, art director at WCBS-TV; Chairman of the advisory board and former president of the Broadcast Designer's Association.

staff, and working with upper management.

Obviously, not all of these skills apply to every individual or situation, and each design staff is built around personal strengths; nevertheless, a broad spectrum of design possibilities does exist. The broadcast designer is called upon to meet these requirements and others.

The textile designer

The following trade practices are relevant to the salaried textile design artist.

1. Physical working conditions It is strongly recommended that the textile designer survey prospective work space and evaluate such aspects as lighting, ventilation, cleanliness, equipment, supplies, and other conditions necessary for effective work.

2. Free-lance Out-of-company free-lance work is a common practice in the industry. It is forbidden only if the converter requires the textile designer to sign a form stating that the textile designer will not work for other companies while employed by the converter. In-company free-lance work should be competitively priced according to current market guidelines. It is to the converter's advantage to have the textile designer at hand to complete work quickly and in the way wished. The textile designer should therefore not be penalized for helping the converter.

3. Mill work Long-standing, unfair practices have existed concerning mill work by staff employees. Extended travel time, 24-hour shifts with sleep deprivation, working weekends and weekdays, and enduring poor physical conditions at mills are common practices that are rarely given appropriate compensation. These extra duties are expected for the usual in-studio salary and benefits. Trends are changing, however, by providing compensation such as days off, overtime pay, and by increasing personnel to limit shift hours. These goals require that the textile designer firmly negotiate from his or her own point of view.

4. Work practices The New York State Labor Board forbids working without at least one-half hour for lunch in a 9 a.m. to 5 p.m. workday. Contact the board for other information on rest periods and working conditions. It is important for every textile designer to know his or her rights as an employee. The Guild discourages working extra hours consistently without overtime pay.

5. Salary reviews Most converters evaluate work quality and salary advancement on an annual basis. Each staff artist should be acquainted with the policies of the company. Most converters are stringent about the limited amounts and numbers of raises given. Each textile designer should know what to expect and negotiate or act accordingly.

6. *Artists on per diem* Per diem rates are usually not beneficial to textile designers because rates are lower than prevailing free-lance prices. In addition, the textile designer does not receive medical or life insurance and pension benefits. However, hiring a per diem textile designer for even one day requires the company to pay taxes, social security, and unemployment insurance to the government for that textile designer. Also, according to government regulation, consistent per diem can make a worker automatically eligible for benefits. With respect to wages for per diem work, the Guild strongly recommends that the textile designer review the ability level required and the work assigned. The work day should be priced accordingly.

7. *Knock-offs* Ethically, a textile designer should not be forced to knock-off or copy a design for an employer unless that converter is willing to sign a release that the converter alone accepts full responsibility in the event of any potential infringement. Knocking off designs is a common practice, but the textile designer must be aware that it is improper to infringe on anyone else's designs and that any infringement can lead to serious legal liabilities.

8. *Changing jobs* Textile staff artists change jobs frequently in order to improve salaries, achieve promotions or better working conditions. The Guild advises giving your present employer a standard two-week notice when leaving a job. Anything less can jeopardize severance or vacation pay due you.

Note: Some companies request test coloring samples as part of the interview process. The Guild recommends against this process unless the test colorings are paid for or remain the property of the artist.

Converters

Staff at converters may include:

Stylists: creative & managerial heads of departments, sometimes referred to as style directors or art buyers.

Assistant stylists: managerial and creative assistants to stylists; may or may not work at drawing board; may or may not buy art.

Studio head: directly in charge of non-management studio personnel; answers to stylist; usually works at drawing board.

Designer: executes original art work.

Colorist: executes color combinations, usually painted but occasionally "chipped."

Repeat artist: executes precise continuous repeat patterns, imitating original artist's "hand."

Mill worker: can be any of the above employees trained to shade fabric at the mills.

Studios

Staff at studios may include:

Studio director: creative and managerial head, in some cases the studio owner.

Rep: sells original artwork or seeks clients who need colorings, repeats, etc. A few also solicit mill work.

Artists: usually work at the studio; may execute original artwork, colorings, repeats.

Earnings gap still a problem

The textile design field has historically been composed of many more women designers than men. While this fact is well-known in the industry, the corollary that men and women are not paid equally for the same job is less well publicized. According to 1983 U.S. Census Bureau statistics, "women working year round at full-time jobs still earn only about 62% of what men make." The commissioner of labor statistics cites clothing and textile industries as areas where "most women continue to work in the country's lowest paying industries."

The 1983 Graphic Artists Guild survey found that the situation for textile designers is at least in keeping with the general Census Bureau statistics. For example, the majority of members surveyed report that their annual gross salaries are $20,000 and under. Only 1% of the respondents report gross incomes of $40,000 or more. Since the survey includes free-lance as well as salaried designers, the net figures for income are significantly lower.

In once case, a man with 11 years of design experience was being paid $4,000 more per year in a salaried position than a woman with 17 years of experience in a comparable job.

The issue of equal pay for equal work has received a great deal of attention from women's groups and labor organizations. The Guild believes that equal pay standards should be promoted and supported. It encourages members with information on problems in this area to contact the Guild.

Comparative salaries of advertising agency staff* ☆

	Small Agency	Large Agency
Art director	$16,000–30,000	$35,000–50,000
Assistant art director	10,000–12,000	10,000–14,000
Executive art director	15,000–25,000	40,000–60,000
Creative group head or director	40,000–65,000	150,000+
Associate creative director or supervisor	—	60,000–80,000
Comp illustrator	16,000–25,000	25,000–30,000
Graphic designer	16,000–30,000	30,000–40,000

*A small agency has between $5 and 10 million in annual billings; a large agency has more than $75 million.

Comparative salaries of corporate art department staff* ☆

	Medium	Large
Art director	$20,000–35,000	$30,000–40,000
Graphic designer	20,000–30,000	30,000–35,000
Packaging designer	30,000–35,000	35,000–40,000
Packaging art director	20,000–28,000	20,000–30,000
Production artist	15,000–18,000	18,000–22,000

*A medium corporation has less than $300 million in annual sales revenues; a large corporation has $300 million or more.

Comparative salaries of design studio staff* ☆

	Small Studio	Large Studio
Graphic designer	$14,000–18,000	$20,000–25,000
Production artist	12,000–16,000	18,000–22,000

*A small design studio has less than $250,000 in annual sales revenue; a large design studio has $750,000 or more.

Comparative salaries of book publishing art department staff*☆

	Small Publisher	Large Publisher
Book designer	$18,000–20,000	$20,000–25,000
Art director	20,000–25,000	30,000–35,000
Production artist	14,000–16,000	18,000–22,000

Comparative salaries of textile studio or converter art department staff

	Weekly	Yearly
Beginning artist (colorist, designer)	$210-300	$10,920-15,600
Colorist, junior designer, sample weaver	250-350	13,000-18,200
Repeat artist	250-400	13,000-20,800
Senior designer (with & without millwork)	400-550	20,000--28,600
Studio head	400-600	20,000-31,200
Assistant stylist	400-700	20,000-36,400
Stylist	550-1100	28,600-57,200
Student trainee		MINIMUM WAGE

Note: In most cases woven design personnel are not paid as much as print design personnel.

Comparative salaries of broadcast station art department staff*☆

	Smallest Markets, 51–100*	Largest Markets, 1–10*
Art director or design manager	$14,000–18,000	$28,000–33,000
Graphic designer	–	17,000-20,000
Specialized art staff	–	–
Comp and finished hand letterer	–	18,000-23,000
Black and white retoucher	–	18,000-23,000
Black and white plus color retoucher	–	28,000-33,000

*Market sizes are ranked according to population in the broadcast area. The most populous market (i.e., New York metropolitan area) is ranked number 1.

Comparative salaries of animation staff*

	Hourly	Weekly		Hourly	Weekly
Director	$24.00	$840.00	Apprentice background, third 3 months	10.83	379.05
Story, story sketch	17.25	603.75			
Layout	17.25	603.75	Preplanner/checker (animation)	11.25	393.75
Assistant layout	11.25	393.75	Apprentice preplanner, first 3 months	9.00	315.00
Apprentice layout (8 months)	9.45	330.75			
Animator I†	18.00	630.00	Apprentice preplanner, second 3 months	10.05	351.75
Animator II	12.75	446.25	Junior checker (ink and paint only)	8.85	309.75
Assistant animator	11.25	393.75			
Apprentice assistant animator, first 6 months	9.00	315.00	Junior checker apprentice, first 3 months	6.45	225.75
Apprentice assistant animator, second 6 months	10.05	351.75	Junior checker apprentice, second 3 months	7.50	262.50
Inbetweener	9.75	341.25	Inker	8.85	309.75
Apprentice inbetweener, first 3 months	7.50	262.50	Apprentice inker, first 3 months	6.45	225.75
Apprentice inbetweener, second 3 months	8.55	299.25	Apprentice inker, second 3 months	7.50	262.50
Production coordinator	12.39	433.65	Graphic film artist I	13.50	472.50
Background	14.79	517.65	Graphic film artist II	12.33	431.55
Assistant background	11.25	393.75	Apprentice graphic film artist, 0-6 months	5.25	183.75
Apprentice background, first 3 months	7.55	278.25	Apprentice graphic film artist, 7-9 months	6.30	220.50
Apprentice background, second 3 months	9.45	330.75			

†Benefits: medical plan, annuity, 10 day sick time, 13 paid holidays, 2 week vacation (under 5 years), 3 weeks vacation (5-10 years), 4 weeks vacation (over 10 years).

*The above salaries are based on union rates.

Comparative salaries of animation staff (continued)*

	Hourly	Weekly
Apprentice graphic film artist, 10-12 months	7.35	257.25
General apprentice, 0-6 months	5.25	183.75
General apprentice, 7-9 months	6.30	220.50
General apprentice, 10-12 months	7.35	257.25

STANDARD
CONTRACT FORMS

Introduction

The Guild has created a number of standard contracts for use by its members and other professionals. The purpose of these standard forms is to aid both creator and art buyer in reaching a clear understanding of their rights and obligations. Too often contracts are merely oral and consequently vague, which places both parties at a disadvantage if some disagreement later arises. Also, the Guild's contracts conform to the Code of Fair Practice and provide a basis for fair dealing between the parties.

What is a contract? It is simply a binding agreement between two or more parties. Normally each party gains certain benefits and must fulfill certain obligations. To be valid a contract must include the important terms of an assignment—such as the fee and the job description. Other terms, such as a time when payment must be made, will be presumed to be reasonable (such as within thirty days of submitting an invoice or completing the assignment) if the parties have not actually specified that particular item. Although it is wise to always have written contracts, oral contracts are also binding in many cases and can be the basis of a legal suit. Thus contracts can take many forms—oral, a purchase order, a confirmation form, a letter, an exchange of letters, or a formal document. Both parties need not sign a contract to make it binding, although it is wise to have both parties sign. For example, if a buyer receives a confirmation form from an artist and does not object to the terms of the form, the artist is justified in starting work in reliance on the form as a binding contract. And even if purchase orders or invoices are not complete enough to be called a contract, they can be used as evidence of the terms of the unwritten contract on which the artist relied to start work.

A common way of entering into a contract is to have one party send a letter to the other party. If the party receiving the letter agrees with the terms set forth in the letter, he or she signs at the bottom of the letter beneath the words "Agreed to" (and returns a signed copy of the letter to the party that sent it). While informal, such a letter of agreement is a binding contract. It may make both artist and art buyer feel more comfortable in some situations if the letter-of-agreement format is used. In the event that one party is signing a contract on behalf of a corporation, that person should give the corporate name, their own name, and their title that authorizes them to sign for the corporation, such as "xyz Corp. By Alice Buyer, Art Director."

In creating a contract, there must be an offer and an acceptance. In this way the parties reach a mutually acceptable understanding. If one party makes an offer and the other party makes a counteroffer, the original offer is automatically terminated. For a contract to be binding, each party must give something of value to the other party. This giving of value is called consideration. The most common form of consideration is a promise to do something or refrain from doing something. So a promise to work or a promise to pay could be consideration, although doing the work or making the payment would also be consideration. A valid contract requires parties that are competent adults (otherwise no understanding can be reached). And for the contract to be enforceable, its purpose must be both legal and not against public policy (as might occur, for example if a contract provided that the public be misinformed as to some aspect of a product).

One common problem that arises in contracts is the battle of the forms. Each party sends its own forms to the other party, but the terms are never the same. The question then arises: whose forms will govern if a dispute arises? If work has commenced on the basis of one form, that form should take precedence over forms sent after completion of the work (such as an invoice or a check with a condition on its back). However, the best way to resolve a battle of the forms is to deal with it directly. As soon as either party realizes that agreement has not been reached as to one or more points, the other party should be notified. The points of disagreement should then be discussed and worked out to the understanding and satisfaction of both parties. Only in this way can the ambiguities that usually arise in a battle of the forms be avoided.

Each of the Guild's contracts is a model that can be used, but each is also a model that can be modified to suit individual needs and circumstances. No contract is sacrosanct. It is merely the method by which both parties seek to achieve their goals in a mutually beneficial relationship.

The purchase orders will be given by a client to an artist prior to commencement of an assignment. If the purchase order is merely an assignment description, the artist will want to use a confirmation form or order-acknowledgement form detailing rights, payments, and other terms. An estimate would normally be given before a purchase order is issued. And a holding form would be used when work is left for consideration by a client. An invoice is normally presented to a client with the finished work. The contracts with agents, of course, apply when the artist seeks representation.

Most of the forms have been discussed in detail in various parts of the text (and the Textile Designer-Agent Agreement is accompanied by its own introduction). However, one important point should be explained about all these forms. They seek to impose limits on rights that are granted, whether rights to use art or rights to represent artwork. Usage rights are limited because most clients do not want to pay for all conceivable uses. Representation rights are limited because agents can only represent certain types of work successfully.

The usage limitations take the following format:

Title or product This specifies by name which book or other product is going to use the art, so that the art cannot be used in addition to this.

Category of use This specifies whether the use is for advertising, promotion, editorial, corporate, or other indicated types of use, so that, for example, artwork purchased for editorial use may not be used in advertising without further agreement or consideration.

Medium of use This specifies the form in which the art will reach the public, such as trade magazine, brochure, annual report, album cover, etc.

Edition This can be used for publishing to limit usage to a given edition, such as a hardcover, quality paperback, or other edition.

Geographic area This can be used to limit the territory in which the art can be distributed.

Time period This can limit the length of time during which the art can be used.

All of these concepts can be refined to fit the exact needs of artist and client. It is the client who establishes usage, since the client knows its needs with respect to the art. In response to the requested usage, the artist sets an appropriate fee. If the client later wishes to make uses not contemplated originally, an appropriate reuse fee is established without difficulty in most cases.

All-Purpose Purchase Order

F R O N T : A R T B U Y E R ' S L E T T E R H E A D

TO	COMMISSIONED BY
	DATE
	PURCHASE ORDER NUMBER

ASSIGNMENT DESCRIPTION

(remove all italics before using this form)

(indicate any preliminary presentations required by the buyer)

DELIVERY DATE	FEE

BUYER SHALL REIMBURSE ARTIST FOR THE FOLLOWING EXPENSES

RIGHTS TRANSFERRED. BUYER PURCHASES THE FOLLOWING EXCLUSIVE RIGHTS OF USAGE

TITLE OR PRODUCT	*(name)*
CATEGORY OF USE	*(advertising, corporate, promotional, editorial, etc.)*
MEDIUM OF USE	*(consumer or trade magazine, annual report, TV, book, etc.)*
EDITION (IF BOOK)	*(hardcover, mass market paperback, quality paperback, etc.)*
GEOGRAPHIC AREA	*(if applicable)*
TIME PERIOD	*(if applicable)*

ARTIST RESERVES ANY USAGE RIGHTS NOT EXPRESSLY TRANSFERRED. ANY USAGE BEYOND THAT GRANTED TO BUYER HEREIN SHALL REQUIRE THE PAYMENT OF A MUTUALLY AGREED UPON ADDITIONAL FEE. SUBJECT TO ALL TERMS ON REVERSE SIDE OF FORM.

Terms:

1. Time for Payment. All invoices shall be paid within thirty (30) days of receipt.

2. Changes. Buyer shall make additional payments for changes requested in original assignment. However, no additional payment shall be made for changes required to conform to the original assignment description. The Buyer shall offer the Artist first opportunity to make any changes.

3. Expenses. Buyer shall reimburse Artist for all expenses arising from this assignment, including the payment of any sales taxes due on this assignment. Buyer's approval shall be obtained for any increases in fees or expenses that exceed the original estimate by 10% or more.

4. Cancellation. In the event of cancellation of this assignment, ownership of all copyrights and the original artwork shall be retained by the Artist, and a cancellation fee for work completed, based on the contract price and expenses already incurred, shall be paid by the Buyer.

5. Ownership of Artwork. The Artist retains ownership of all original artwork, whether preliminary or final, and the Buyer shall return such artwork within thirty (30) days of use.

6. Credit Lines. The Buyer shall give Artist and any other creators a credit line with any editorial usage. If similar credit lines are to be given with other types of usage, it must be so indicated here:

_____

_____

_____

_____

☐ If this box is checked, the credit line shall be in the form:

© _____ 198___

7. Releases. Buyer shall indemnify Artist against all claims and expenses, including reasonable attorney's fees, due to uses for which no release was requested in writing or for uses which exceed authority granted by a release.

8. Modifications. Modification of the Agreement must be written, except that the invoice may include, and Buyer shall pay, fees or expenses that were orally authorized in order to progress promptly with the work.

9. Arbitration. Any disputes in excess of $_____ (maximum limit for small claims court) arising out of this Agreement shall be submitted to binding arbitration before the Joint Ethics Committee or a mutually agreed upon arbitrator pursuant to the rules of the American Arbitration Association. The Arbitrator's award shall be final, and judgment may be entered upon it in any court having jurisdiction thereof. The Buyer shall pay all arbitration and court costs, reasonable attorney's fees, and legal interest on any award or judgment in favor of the Artist.

CONSENTED AND AGREED TO
_____

DATE
_____

ARTIST'S SIGNATURE
_____

COMPANY NAME
_____

AUTHORIZED SIGNATURE
_____

NAME AND TITLE

MEMBER

Artist-Agent Agreement

Agreement, this_____day of
_____, 19_____, between

_____

(hereinafter referred to as the
"Artist"), residing at

_____ ,

and_____ ,
(hereinafter referred to as the
"Agent" residing at

_____ .

Whereas, the Artist is an established artist of proven talents; and

Whereas, the Artist wishes to have an agent represent him or her in marketing certain rights enumerated herein; and

Whereas, the Agent is capable of marketing the artwork produced by the Artist; and

Whereas, the Agent wishes to represent the Artist;

Now, therefore, in consideration of the foregoing premises and the mutual covenants hereinafter set forth and other valuable consideration, the parties hereto agree as follows:

1. Agency. The Artist appoints the Agent to act as his or her exclusive representative: (A) in the following geographical area:

_____

_____

(B) for the markets listed here (specify publishing, advertising,etc.):

_____

_____

The Agent agrees to use his or her best efforts in submitting the Artist's work for the purpose of securing assignment for the Artist. The Agent shall negotiate the terms of any assignment that is offered, but the Artist shall have the right to reject any assignment if he or she finds the terms thereof unacceptable.

2. Promotion. The Artist shall provide the Agent with such samples of work as are from time to time necessary for the purpose of securing assignments. These samples shall remain the property of the Artist and be returned on Termination of this Agreement. The Agent shall take reasonable efforts to protect the work from loss or damage, but shall be liable for

such loss or damage only if caused by the Agent's negligence. Promotional expenses, including but not limited to promotional mailings and paid advertising, shall be paid _____% by the Agent and _____% by the Artist. The Agent shall bear the expenses of shipping, insurance, and similar marketing expenses.

3. Term. This Agreement shall take effect on the_____day of _____, 19_____, and remain in full force and effect for a term of one year, unless terminated as provided in Paragraph 9.

4. Commissions. The Agent shall be entitled to the following commissions: (A) On assignments incurred by the Agent during the term of this Agreement, twenty-five (25%) percent of the billing. (B) On house accounts, ten (10%) percent of the billing. For purposes of this Agreement, *house accounts* are defined as accounts obtained by the Artist at any time or obtained by another agent representing the Artist prior to the commencement of this Agreement and are listed in Schedule A attached to this Agreement.

It is understood by both parties that no commissions shall be paid on assignments rejected by the Artist or for which the Artist fails to receive payment, regardless of the reason payment is not made. Further, no commissions shall be payable in either (A) or (B) above for any part of the billing that is due to expenses incurred by the Artist in performing the assignment, whether or not such expenses are reimbursed by the client. In the event that a flat fee is paid by the client, it shall be reduced by the amount of expenses incurred by the Artist in performing the assignment, and the Agent's commission shall be payable only on the fee as reduced for expenses.

5. Billing. The ☐Artist ☐Agent shall be responsible for all billings.

6., Payments The Party responsible for billing shall make all payments due within ten (10) days of receipt of any fees covered by this Agreement. Late payments shall be accompanied by interest calcu-

lated at the rate of_____% per month thereafter.

7. Accountings. The party responsible for billing shall send copies of invoices to the other party when rendered. If requested, that party shall also provide the other party with semi-annual accountings showing all assignments for the period, the clients' names, the fees paid, expenses incurred by the Artist, the dates of payment, the amounts on which the Agent's commissions are to be calculated, and the sums due less those amounts already paid.

8. Inspection of the books and records. The party responsible for the billing shall keep the books and records with repect to commissions due at his or her place of business and permit the other party to inspect these books and records during normal business hours on the giving of reasonable notice.

9. Termination. This Agreement may be terminated by either party by giving thirty (30) days written notice to the other party. If the Artist receives assignments after the termination date from clients originally obtained by the Agent during the term of this Agreement, the commission specified in Paragraph 4(A) shall be payable to the Agent under the following circumstances. If the Agent has represented the Artist for six months or less, the Agent shall receive a commission on such assignments received by the Artist within ninety (90) days of the date of termination. This period shall increase by thirty (30) days for each additional six months that the Agent has represented the Artist, but in no event shall such period exceed one hundred eighty (180) days.

10.Assignment. This Agreement shall not be assigned by either of the parties hereto. It shall be binding on and inure to the benefit of the successors, administrators, executors, or heirs of the Agent and Artist.

11. Arbitration. Any disputes arising under this Agreement shall be settled by arbitration under the rules of the American Arbitration

Association in the City of

_____

Any award rendered by the arbitrator may be entered in any court having jurisdiction thereof.

12. Notices. All notices shall be given to the parties at their respective addresses set forth above.

13. Independent Contractor Status. Both parties agree that the Agent is acting as an independent contractor. This Agreement is not an employment agreement, nor does it constitute a joint venture or partnership between the Artist and Agent.

14. Amendments and merger. All amendments to this Agreement must be written. This Agreement incorporates the entire understanding of the parties.

15. Governing Law. This Agreement shall be governed by the laws of the State of

_____

In witness whereof, the parties have signed this Agreement as of the date set forth above.

SCHEDULE A: HOUSE ACCOUNTS	
DATE	*(remove all italics before using this form)*
1.	*(name and address of client)*
2.	
3.	
4.	
5.	
6.	
7.	
8.	
9.	

ARTIST _____

AGENT _____

MEMBER

Needleart Designer's Confirmation/Invoice Form

FRONT: DESIGNER'S LETTERHEAD

PRIMARY CLIENT	DATE
	COMMISSIONED BY
	TITLE

CONTRIBUTING CLIENT	COMMISSIONED BY
	TITLE

DELIVERY DATE	
THIS DELIVERY DATE IS PREDICATED UPON RECEIPT OF ALL MATERIALS TO BE SUPPLIED BY CLIENT(S)	
MATERIALS SUPPLIED BY	
PUBLICATION DATE	

ASSIGNMENT DESCRIPTION

(remove all italics before using this form)

(Describe each item in terms of

technique, design, size, material, coloration, complexity

and instructions required for duplication)

B A C K

FEES	PRIMARY CLIENT	CONTRIBUTING CLIENT
FIRST NORTH AMERICAN REPRODUCTION RIGHTS	*(list figures in column)*	*(list figures in column)*
OTHER REPRODUCTION RIGHTS		
	(remove all italics before using this form)	
OTHER USES OR RIGHTS	*(list figures in column)*	*(list figures in column)*
CLIENT RETENTION OF COMPLETED PROJECTS	*(list figures in column)*	*(list figures in column)*
MATERIALS AND SUPPLIES	*(list figures in column)*	*(list figures in column)*
ADDITIONAL EXPENSES	*(list figures in column)*	*(list figures in column)*
	(toll telephones, transportation and travel, shipping and insurance)	
SUBTOTAL		
SALES TAX		
TOTAL		

ARTIST RESERVES ANY USAGE RIGHTS NOT EXPRESSLY TRANSFERRED. ANY USAGE BEYOND THAT GRANTED TO BUYER HEREIN REQUIRES THE PAYMENT OF A MUTUALLY AGREED UPON ADDITIONAL FEE. SUBJECT TO ALL TERMS ON SECOND SHEET OF FORM.

Terms:

1. Publication rights. The negotiated fee (unless specified otherwise below) is for first North
American reproduction rights only
for photographs of each project
and instructions for their execution. All other rights, including
copyright, are retained by the Artist. If publication does not take
place within one year of delivery of
the design, all rights granted hereunder revert to the Artist.
Other rights:

_____

_____

2. Name credit. On any contribution for magazine or book use, the
Artist shall receive name credit in
print. If name credit is to be given
with other types of use, it must be
specified here:

_____

_____

*3. Return of projects and borrowing
privileges.* The negotiated fee
assumes that the project(s) remains the property of the Artist
and is to be returned to the Artist
within_____months following
photography. If the Client desires
to retain the project(s), an additional fee of_____dollars will
be charged.

The Client has the right to bor-
row a project on a short-term
basis, for dislay promotion purposes only, for a period of
_____months from the pro-
ject's date of publication, and for a
fee of_____dollars each
time. The Artist shall receive
name credit as the designer on all
promotional displays of the project. All transportation costs for
the pickup and return of the project to the Artist will be borne by
the borrower.

The Artist shall be reimbursed
by the Client for the replacement
value of the artwork if the Client
loses, damages, or fails to return a
project. This reimbursement payment is in addition to the nego-

tiated project fee(s) and will be
_____dollars.

4. Materials purchase. Should the
Artist be required to purchase
materials for a project, unless specified otherwise, the Artist will
submit these bills to the Client for
reimbursement. These charges are
subject to the same payment
terms as the negotiated fee.

5. Proof of publication. When a project is published, the Artist shall
receive_____tearsheets and/or
_____ copies of the magazine as
proof of publication.

6. Project cancellation. Work cancelled by the Client while in progress shall be compensated for on
the basis of work completed at the
time of cancellation and assumes
that the Artist retains the project,
whatever its stage of completion.
Upon cancellation, all rights,
publication and other, revert to the
Artist. If the negotiated fee is to be
paid by both Client and "Secondary Source," the Client is obligated to pay the Artist's total cancellation fee.

7. Project revisions. Any changes in
a project that require additional
work on the part of the Artist, and
are not the result of an error by
the Artist, require supplementary
confirmation in writing and additional compensation to the Artist,
to be specified at the time.

Any changes in a project, due to
an error on the part of Artist, require no additional compensation to
the Artist.

*8. Projects used for publication
covers.* Should the photograph
of a project be used as a publication cover, an additional fee of
_____dollars will be
charged. This fee will be billed at
the time of the cover decision and
is subject to the same payment
terms as the original fee.

9. Right to timely publication. Since

most design projects are subject to
trends within the marketplace, the
Artist is guaranteed the right of
timely publication. If a project is
not photographed within six
months of its delivery, it is assumed that the project is cancelled,
and that all rights to the project revert to the Artist, with no cost or
penalty to the Artist. Further,
should the design not be published
within one year of its date of delivery, it is assumed that the project
is cancelled and all rights to the
design revert to the Artist, with no
cost or penalty to the Artist.

10. Multiple billing. If the Artist's
Client is a publication, but the Artist's fee is to be paid by both the
publication and a contributing
manufacturer, it is the responsibility of the publication, unless the
Artist chooses to assume this responsibility, to negotiate the Artist's fee with the manufacturer and
arrange for prompt payment of
this fee in accordance with the
Artist's payment terms for the
publication.
☐ If this box is checked, the Artist
shall receive copyright notice adjacent to the work in the form:

© _____ 198____.

11. Unauthorized use. Client will indemnify Artist against all claims
and expenses, including reasonable attorney's fees, due to uses
for which no release was requested in writing or for uses which
exceed authority granted by a
release.

12. Modifications. Modification of
the Agreement must be written,except that the invoice
may include, and Client shall be
obligated to pay, fees or expenses
that were orally authorized in order
to progress promptly with the work.

13. Arbitration. Any disputes in
excess of $_____(maximum
small claims court limit) arising

out of this Agreement shall be submitted to binding arbitration before the Joint Ethics Committee or a mutually agreed upon arbitrator pursuant to the rules of the American Arbitration Associaton. The Arbitrator's award shall be final and judgment may be entered upon it in any court having jurisdiction thereof. The Client shall pay all arbitration and court costs, reasonable attorney's fees, and legal interest on any award or judgment in favor of the Artist.

14. The above terms incorporate Article 2 of the Uniform Commercial Code. If not objected to within ten (10) days, these terms shall be deemed accepted.

15. The Client and Artist agree to comply with all the provisions of the Joint Code of Ethics, a copy of which may be obtained from the Joint Ethics Committee, P.O. Box 179, Grand Central Station, New York, New York 10017.

_____

CONSENTED AND AGREED TO

_____

DATE

_____

ARTIST'S SIGNATURE

_____

COMPANY NAME

_____

AUTHORIZED SIGNATURE

_____

NAME AND TITLE

MEMBER

Illustrator's Confirmation of Engagement

TO	DATE
	AUTHORIZED ART BUYER
	ILLUSTRATOR'S JOB NUMBER
	CLIENT'S JOB NUMBER

ASSIGNMENT DESCRIPTION

DELIVERY SCHEDULE

FEE (PAYMENT SCHEDULE)

ADDITIONAL ESTIMATED EXPENSES

CANCELLATION FEE (PERCENTAGE OF FEE)

BEFORE SKETCHES	
AFTER SKETCHES	
AFTER FINISH	

B A C K

RIGHTS TRANSFERRED (ALL OTHER RIGHTS RESERVED BY THE ILLUSTRATOR)	
FOR USE IN MAGAZINES AND NEWSPAPERS, FIRST NORTH AMERICAN REPRODUCTION RIGHTS UNLESS SPECIFIED OTHERWISE HERE	
(remove all italics before using this form)	
FOR ALL OTHER USES, THE CLIENT ACQUIRES ONLY THE FOLLOWING RIGHTS	
TITLE OR PRODUCT	*(name)*
CATEGORY OF USE	*(advertising, corporate, promotional, editorial, etc.)*
MEDIUM OF USE	*(consumer or trade magazine, annual report, TV, book, etc.)*
GEOGRAPHIC AREA	*(if applicable)*
TIME PERIOD	*(if applicable)*
NUMBER OF USES	*(if applicable)*
OTHER	*(if applicable)*

ORIGINAL ARTWORK, INCLUDING SKETCHES AND ANY OTHER PRELIMINARY MATERIAL, REMAINS THE PROPERTY OF THE ILLUSTRATOR UNLESS PURCHASED BY A PAYMENT OF A SEPARATE FEE.

Terms:

1. Time for Payment. Payment is due within thirty (30) days of receipt of invoice. A 1½% monthly service charge will be billed for late payment. Any advances or partial payments shall be indicated under Payment Schedule on front.

2. Default in Payment. The Client shall assume responsibility for all collection and legal fees necessitated by default in payment.

3. Grant of Rights. The grant of reproduction rights is conditioned on receipt of payment.

4. Expenses. The Client shall reimburse the Illustrator for all expenses arising from the assignment.

5. Sales Tax. The client shall be responsible for the payment of sales tax, if any such tax is due.

6. Cancellation. In the event of cancellation or breach by the Client, the Illustrator shall retain ownership of all rights of copyright and the original artwork, including sketches and any other preliminary materials.

7. Revisions. Revisions not due to the fault of the Illustrator shall be billed separately.

8. Credit Lines. On any contribution for magazine or book use, the Illustrator shall receive name credit in print. If name credit is to be given with other types of use, it must be specified here:

_____

_____

☐ If this box is checked by the Illustrator, the Illustrator shall receive copyright notice adjacent to the work in the form:
©_____198_____

9. Return of Artwork. Client assumes responsibility for the return of the artwork in undamaged condition within thirty (30) days of first reproduction.

10. Unauthorized Use. Client will indemnify Illustrator against all claims and expenses, including reasonable attorney's fees, arising from uses for which no release was requested in writing or for uses which exceed the authority granted by a release.

11. Arbitration. Any disputes in excess of $_____ (maximum limit for small claims court) arising out of this Agreement shall be submitted to binding arbitration before the Joint Ethics Committee as a mutually agreed upon arbitrator pursuant to the rules of the American Arbitration Association. The Arbitrator's award shall be final, and judgment may be entered upon it in any court having jursidiction thereof. The client shall pay all arbitration and court costs, reasonable attorney's fees and legal interest on any award or judgment in favor of the Illustrator.

12. Acceptance of Terms. If the terms of this confirmation are not objected to within ten (10) days of receipt, the terms shall be deemed accepted.

CONSENTED AND AGREED TO
_____

DATE
_____

ILLUSTRATOR'S SIGNATURE
_____

COMPANY NAME
_____

AUTHORIZED SIGNATURE
_____

NAME AND TITLE

MEMBER

Illustrator's Invoice

TO	DATE
	AUTHORIZED ART BUYER
	ILLUSTRATOR'S JOB NUMBER
	CLIENT'S JOB NUMBER

ASSIGNMENT DESCRIPTION

	FEE

ITEMIZED EXPENSES (OTHER BILLABLE ITEMS)

CLIENT'S ALTERATIONS	
SALE OF ORIGINAL ART	
MISCELLANEOUS	
	TOTAL
	SALES TAX
	PAYMENTS ON ACCOUNT
	BALANCE DUE

ORIGINAL ARTWORK, INCLUDING SKETCHES AND ANY OTHER PRELIMINARY MATERIALS, REMAIN THE PROPERTY OF THE ILLUSTRATOR UNLESS PURCHASED BY PAYMENT OF A SEPARATE FEE SUBJECT TO TERMS APPEARING ON REVERSE SIDE.

BACK

RIGHTS TRANSFERRED (ALL OTHER RIGHTS RESERVED BY THE ILLUSTRATOR)	
FOR USE IN MAGAZINES AND NEWSPAPERS, FIRST NORTH AMERICAN REPRODUCTION RIGHTS UNLESS SPECIFIED OTHERWISE HERE	
(remove all italics before using this form)	
FOR ALL OTHER USES, THE CLIENT ACQUIRES ONLY THE FOLLOWING RIGHTS	
TITLE OR PRODUCT	*(name)*
CATEGORY OF USE	*(advertising, corporate, promotional, editorial, etc.)*
MEDIUM OF USE	*(consumer or trade magazine, annual report, TV, book, etc.)*
GEOGRAPHIC AREA	*(if applicable)*
TIME PERIOD	*(if applicable)*
NUMBER OF USES	*(if applicable)*
OTHER	*(if applicable)*
ORIGINAL ARTWORK, INCLUDING SKETCHES AND ANY OTHER PRELIMINARY MATERIAL, REMAINS THE PROPERTY OF THE ILLUSTRATOR UNLESS PURCHASED BY A PAYMENT OF A SEPARATE FEE.	

Terms:

1. Time for Payment. Payment is due within thirty (30) days of receipt of invoice. A 1½ % monthly service charge will be billed for late payment.

2. Default in Payment. The client shall assume responsibility for all collection and legal fees necessitated by default in payment.

3. Grant of Rights. The grant of reproduction rights is conditioned on receipt of payment.

4. Credit Lines. On any contribution for magazine or book use, the Illustrator shall receive name credit in print. If name credit is to be given with other types of use, it must be specified here:

_____

☐ If this box is checked by the Illustrator, the Illustrator shall receive copyright notice adjacent to the work in the form
©_____ 198_____

5. Additional Limitations. If Illustrator and Client have agreed to additional limitations as to either the duration or geographical extent of the permitted use, specify here:

_____

6. Return of Artwork. Client assumes responsibility for the return of the artwork in undamaged condition within thirty (30) days of first reproduction.

7. Unauthorized Use. Client will indemnify Illustrator against all claims and expenses, including reasonable attorney's fees, arising from uses for which no release was requested in writing or for uses which exceed the authority granted by a release.

8. Arbitration. Any disputes in excess of $_____ (maximum limit for small claims court) arising out of this Agreement shall be submitted to bind-

ing arbitration before the Joint Ethics Committee or a mutually agreed upon arbitrator pursuant to the rules of the American Arbitration Association. The Arbitrator's award shall be final, and judgment upon it may be entered upon it in any court having jurisdiction thereof. The client shall pay all arbitration and court costs, reasonable attorney's fees, and legal interest on any award or judgment in favor of the Illustrator.

9. Acceptance of Terms. If the terms of this invoice are not objected to within ten (10) days of receipt, the terms shall be deemed accepted.

MEMBER

Magazine Purchase Order for Illustrators

This letter is to serve as our contract for you to create certain illustrations for us under the terms described herein.

1. Job Description. We, the Magazine, retain you, the Illustrator, to create_____Illustrations(s) described as follows (indicate if sketches are required):

_____
_____
_____

to be delivered to the Magazine by _____ 19__, for publication in our magazine titled _____ .

2. Grant of Rights. Illustrator hereby agrees to transfer to the Magazine first North American magazine rights in the illustrations. All rights not expressly transferred to the Magazine hereunder are reserved to the Illustrator.

3. Price. The Magazine agrees to pay Illustrator the following purchase price: $_____ in full consideration for Illustrator's grant of rights to Magazine.

4. Changes. The Illustrator shall be given the first option to make any changes in the work that the Magazine may deem necessary. However, no additional compensation shall be paid unless such changes are necessitated by error on the Magazine's part, in which case a new contract between us shall be entered into on mutually agreeable terms to cover changes to be done by the Illustrator.

5. Cancellation. If, prior to the Illustrator's completion of finishes, the Magazine cancels the assignment either because the illustrations are unsatisfactory to the Magazine or for any other reason, the Magazine agrees to pay the Illustrator a cancellation fee of 50% of the purchase price. If, after the Illustrator's completion of finishes, the Magazine cancels the assignment, the Magazine agrees to pay 50% of the purchase price if cancellation is due to the illustrations not being reasonably satisfactory and 100% of the purchase price if cancellation is due to any other cause. In the event of cancellation, the Illustrator shall retain ownership of all artwork and rights of copyright, but the Illustrator agrees to show the Magazine the artwork if the Magazine so requests so that the Magazine may make its own evaluation as to degree of completion of the artwork.

6. Copyright Notice and Authorship Credit. Copyright notice shall appear in the Illustrator's name with the contribution. The illustrator shall have the right to receive authorship credit for the illustration and to have such credit removed if the Illustrator so desires due to changes made by the Magazine that are unsatisfactory to the Illustrator.

7. Payments. Payment shall be made within thirty (30) days of the billing date.

8. Ownership of Artwork. The Illustrator shall retain ownership of all original artwork and the Magazine shall return such artwork within thirty (30) days of publication.

To constitute this a binding agreement between us, please sign both copies of this letter beneath the words "Consented and Agreed to" and return one copy to the Magazine for its files.

_____
CONSENTED AND AGREED TO

_____
DATE

_____
ARTIST'S SIGNATURE

_____
MAGAZINE

_____
AUTHORIZED SIGNATURE

_____
NAME AND TITLE

MEMBER

Textile Designer's Holding Form

TO	DATE

NUMBER OF DESIGNS HELD		
DESIGN I.D. NUMBER	SKETCH	PRICE
DESIGN I.D. NUMBER	SKETCH	PRICE
DESIGN I.D. NUMBER	SKETCH	PRICE
DESIGN I.D. NUMBER	SKETCH	PRICE
DESIGN I.D. NUMBER	SKETCH	PRICE
DESIGN I.D. NUMBER	SKETCH	PRICE
DESIGN I.D. NUMBER	SKETCH	PRICE

Terms:

The submitted designs are original and protected under the copyright laws of the United States, Title 17 United States Code. These designs are submitted to you in confidence and on the following terms:

1. Ownership and Copyrights. You agree not to copy, photograph, or modify directly or indirectly any of the materials held by you, nor will permit any third party to do any of the foregoing. All artwork, photographs, and photostats developed from these designs, including the copyrights therein, remain my property and must be returned to me unless the designs are purchased by you.

2. Responsibility for Artwork. You agree to assume responsibility for loss, theft, or any damage to the designs while they are being held by you. It is agreed that the fair market value of each design is the price specified above.

3. Holding of Artwork. You agree to hold these designs for a period not to exceed _____ working days from the above date. Any holding of artwork beyond that period shall constitute a binding sale at the price specified above. You further agree not to allow any third party to hold designs unless specifically approved by me.

4. Arbitration. All disputes in excess of $_____ (maximum limit for small claims court) arising out of this agreement shall be submitted to binding arbitration before the Joint Ethics Committee or a mutually agreed upon arbitrator pursuant to the rules of the American Arbitration Association. The Arbitrator's award shall be final, and judgment may be entered upon it in any court having jursidiction thereof. The party holding the designs shall pay all arbitration and court costs, reasonable attorney's fees, and legal interest on any award or judgment in favor of the Textile Designer.

5. The above terms incorporate Article 2 of the Uniform Commercial Code.

CONSENTED AND AGREED TO
_____

DATE
_____

DESIGNER'S SIGNATURE
_____

COMPANY NAME
_____

AUTHORIZED SIGNATURE
_____

NAME AND TITLE

MEMBER
TEXTILE DESIGNERS
GUILD

A DISCIPLINE OF
THE GRAPHIC ARTISTS
GUILD

Textile Designer's Confirmation Form

TO	DATE
	PATTERN NUMBER
	DUE DATE

ESTIMATED PRICES	
SKETCH	
REPEAT	
COLORINGS	
CORNERS	
TRACINGS	
OTHER	

DESCRIPTION OF ARTWORK		
REPEAT SIZE		
COLORS		
TYPE OF PRINTING		
½ DROP	☐ YES	☐ NO

SPECIAL COMMENTS

Terms:

1. Time for Payment. Because the major portion of the above work represents labor, all invoices are payable fifteen (15) days net. A 1½% monthly service charge is payable on all unpaid balances after this period. The grant of textile usage rights is conditioned on receipt of payment.

2. Estimated Prices. Prices shown above are minimum estimates only. Final prices shall be shown in invoice.

3. Payment for Changes. Client shall be responsible for making additional payments for changes requested by Client in original assignment.

4. Expenses. Client shall be responsible for payment of all extra expenses arising from assignment, including but not limited to photostats, mailings, messengers, shipping charges, and shipping insurance.

5. Sales Tax. Client shall assume responsibility for all sales taxes due on this assignment.

6. Cancellation Fees. Work cancelled by the client while in progress shall be compensated for on the basis of work completed at the time of cancellation and assumes that the Designer retains the project whatever its stage of completion. Upon cancellation, all rights, publication and other, revert to the Designer. Where Designer creates corners which are not developed into purchased sketches, a labor fee will be charged, and ownership of all copyrights and artwork is retained by the Designer.

7. Insuring Artwork. The client agrees when shipping artwork to provide insurance covering the fair market value of the artwork.

8. Arbitration. Any disputes in excess of $_____ (maximum limit for small claims court) arising out of this agreement shall be submitted to binding arbitration before the Joint Ethics Committee or a mutually agreed upon arbitrator pursuant to the rules of the American Arbitration Association. The Arbitrator's award shall be final, and judgment may be entered upon it in any court having jurisdiction thereof. The Client shall pay all arbitration and court costs, reasonable attorney's fees, and legal interest on any award or judgment in favor of the Designer.

9. The above terms incorporate Article 2 of the Uniform Commercial Code.

CONSENTED AND AGREED TO

DATE

DESIGNER'S SIGNATURE

COMPANY NAME

AUTHORIZED SIGNATURE

NAME AND TITLE

Textile Designer's Invoice

TO	DATE
	INVOICE NUMBER
	PURCHASE ORDER NUMBER
	STYLIST
	DESIGNER

PATTERN NUMBER	DESCRIPTION	PRICE
		SUBTOTAL

ITEMIZED EXPENSES	
	SUBTOTAL
	TOTAL
	SALES TAX
	TOTAL DUE

Terms:

1. Receipt of Artwork. Client acknowledges receipt of the artwork specified above.

2. Time for Payment. Because the major portion of the above work represents labor, all invoices are payable fifteen (15) days net. The grant of textile usage rights is conditioned on receipt of payment. A 1½% monthly service charge is payable on unpaid balance after expiration of period for payment.

3. Adjustments to Invoice. Client agrees to request any adjustments of accounts, terms, or other invoice data within ten (10) days of receipt of the invoice. These terms incorporate Article 2 of the Uniform Commercial Code.

4. Arbitration. All disputes in excess of $_____ (maximum limit for small claims court) arising out of this agreement shall be submitted to binding arbitration before the Joint Ethics Committee or a mutually agreed upon arbitrator pursuant to the rules of the American Arbitration Association. The Arbitrator's award shall be final, and judgment may be entered upon it in any court having jursidiction thereof. The Client shall pay all arbitration and court costs, reasonable attorney's fees, and legal interest on any award or judgment in favor of the Designer.

_____

CONSENTED AND AGREED TO

_____

DATE

_____

DESIGNER'S SIGNATURE

_____

COMPANY NAME

_____

AUTHORIZED SIGNATURE

_____

NAME AND TITLE

Introduction: Textile Designer-Agent Agreement

The Textile Designer-Agent Agreement has been drafted by the Steering Committee of the Textile Designers Guild in consultation with the Graphic Artists Guild's General Counsel. It seeks to clarify Designer-Agent relationships by providing a written understanding to which both parties can refer. Its terms are not immutable and can be modified to meet the special needs of either Designer or Agent. The Agreement has been drafted with a minimum of legal jargon, but this in no way changes its legal validity.

The Agreement balances the needs of both Designer and Agent. The agency in Paragraph 1 is limited to a particular market. In that market the Agent has exclusive rights to act as an agent, but the Designer remains free to sell in that market also (except to accounts secured by the Agent). Because both Agent and Designer will be selling in the same market, the Designer may want to provide the Agent with a list of clients previously obtained by the Designer and keep this list up to date.

If the Agent desires greater exclusivity—such as covering more markets—the Designer may want to require that the Agent exercise best efforts (although it is difficult to prove best efforts have not been exercised) and perhaps promise a minimum level of sales. If that level is not met, the Agreement would terminate.

Paragraph 2 seeks to protect the Designer against loss or damage to his or her artwork, in part by requiring the Agent to execute with the client contracts that protect the designs.

Paragraph 3 sets forth the duration of the Agreement. A short term is usually wise, since a Designer and Agent who are working well together can simply extend the term by mutual agreement in order to continue their relationship. Also, as time goes on, the Designer may be in a better position to negotiate with the Agent. The term of the Agreement has less importance, however, when either party can terminate the agency relationship on thirty days notice as Paragraph 10 provides.

The minimum base prices in Paragraph 4 ensure the Designer of a minimum remuneration. Flexibility in pricing requires that the Designer and Agent consult one another in those cases in which particular sale justifies a price higher than the base price. The Designer can suggest that the Agent follow the Graphic Artists Guild's *Pricing and Ethical Guidelines* to establish the minimum base price.

The Agent's rate of commission in Paragraph 5 is left blank so the parties can establish an acceptable rate. If the Designer is not paid for doing an assignment, the Agent will have no right to receive a commission. Nor are commissions payable on the amount of expenses incurred by the Designer for work done on assignment (as opposed to work done on speculation). Discounts given by the Agent on volume sales of the work of many designers shall be paid out of the Agent's commission.

Optional provisions

Additional provisions could be used to govern certain aspects of the Designer-Agent relationship. Such provisions might include:

The scope of the agency set forth in Paragraph 1 is limited to the following geographic area:_____
_____.

Despite any provisions of Paragraph 1 to the contrary, this agency shall be nonexclusive and the Designer shall have the right to use other Agents without any obligation to pay commissions under this Agreement.

The Agent agrees to represent no more than _____ designers.

The Agent agrees not to represent conflicting hands, such hands being designers who work in a similar style to that of the Designer.

The Agent agrees to have no designers as salaried employees.

The Agent agrees not to sell designs from his or her own collection of designs while representing the Designer.

The Agent agrees to employ _____ full time and _____ part time salespeople.

The Agent agrees that the Designer's name shall appear on all artwork by the Designer that is included in the Agent's portfolio.

The Agent agrees to seek royalties for the Designer in the following situations:
_____

The Agent agrees to hold all funds due to the Designer as trust funds in an account separate from funds of the Agent prior to making payment to the Designer pursuant to Paragraph 8 hereof.

Additional provisions

Or the additional provisions might be requirements for terms that the Agent must obtain from the client, such as:

The Agent agrees to enter into a written contract with each client that shall include the following provisions:

Credit line for designer The Designer shall have the right to receive authorship credit for his or her design and to have such credit removed in the event changes made by the client are unsatisfactory to the Designer. Such authorship credit shall appear as follows on the selvage of the fabric:

_____

☐ If this box is checked, such authorship credit shall also accompany any advertising for the fabric:_____

Copyright notice for designer Copyright notice shall appear in the Designer's name on the selvage of the fabric, the form of notice being as follows:

© _____ 19____ .

The placement and affixation of the notice shall comply with the regulations issued by the Register of Copyrights. The grant of rights in this design is expressly conditioned on copyright notice appearing in the Designer's name.

☐ If this box is checked, such copyright notice shall also accompany any advertising for the fabric.

Paragraph 6 covers the Agent's obligations when commissioned work is obtained for the Designer. Of particular importance are the terms of the order form secured by the Agent from the client. The Agent is required to use the order form developed by the Textile Designers Guild or a form incorporating similar terms.

Holding of designs by clients can present a problem which Paragraph 7 seeks to resolve by establishing a maximum holding time of five working days. Again, the Agent is required to use the holding form developed by the Textile Designers Guild or a form with similar terms.

In Paragraph 8 the Agent assumes responsibility for billing and pursuing payments which are not made promptly. The reason for keeping any single billing under the maximum allowed for suit in small claims court is to make it easier to collect if a lawsuit is necessary. The Agent is required to use the invoice form of the Textile Designers Guild or a form with similar provisions.

Paragraph 9 allows the Designer to inspect the Agent's books to ensure that proper payments are being made.

Termination is permitted on giving thirty days written notice to the other party. Paragraph 10 distinguishes between sales made or assignments obtained prior to termination (on which the Agent must be paid a commission, even if the work is executed and payment received after the termination date) and those after termination (on which no commission is payable). Within thirty days of notice of termination, all designs must be returned to the Designer.

Paragraph 11 provides that the Agreement cannot be assigned by either party since the relationship between Designer and Agent is a personal one.

In Paragraph 12, arbitration is provided for disputes in excess of the maximum limit for suits in small claims court. For amounts within the small claims court limit, it is probably easier to simply sue rather than seek arbitration.

The manner of giving notice to the parties is described in Paragraph 13.

Paragraph 14 affirms that both Designer and Agent are independent contractors, which avoids certain tax and liability issues that might arise from the other legal relationships mentioned.

This Agreement is the entire understanding of the parties and can only be amended in writing. In stating this, Paragraph 15 points out a general rule that a written contract should always be amended in a writing that is signed by both parties.

Paragraph 16 leaves room for the parties to add in any optional provisions that they consider necessary. Some of the optional provisions that might be agreed to appear under Optional Provisions below.

Finally, Paragraph 17 sets forth the state whose law will govern the Agreement. This is usually the law of the state in which both parties reside or, if one party is out of state, in which the bulk of the business will be transacted.

Textile Designer-Agent Agreement

Agreement, this_____day of
_____, 19_____, between
_____
(hereinafter referred to as the
"Designer"), residing at:
_____
_____ ,
and_____
(hereinafter referred to as the
"Agent"), residing at:
_____
_____ .

Whereas, the Designer is a professional textile designer; and

Whereas, the Designer wishes to have an Agent represent him or her in marketing certain rights enumerated herein; and

Whereas, the Agent is capable of marketing the artwork produced by the Designer, and

Whereas, the Agent wishes to represent the Designer;

Now, therefore, in consideration of the foregoing premises and the mutual covenants hereinafter set forth and other valuable consideration, the parties hereto agree as follows:

1. Agency. The Designer appoints the Agent to act as his or her representative for:
☐ Sale of textile designs in apparel market,
☐ Sale of textile designs in home furnishing market,
☐ Securing of service work in apparel market. Service work is defined to include repeats and colorings on designs originated by the Designer or other designers,
☐ Securing of service work in home furnishing market
☐ Other _____
_____
_____

The Agent agrees to use his or her best efforts in submitting the Designer's artwork for the purpose of making sales or securing assignments for the Designer. For the purposes of this Agreement, the term *artwork* shall be defined to include designs, repeats, colorings, and any other product of the Designer's effort. The Agent shall negotiate the terms of any assignment that is offered, but the Designer shall have the right to reject any assignment if he or she finds the terms unacceptable. Nothing

contained herein shall prevent the Designer from making sales or securing work for his or her own account without liability for commissions except for accounts which have been secured for the Designer by the Agent. This limitation extends only for the period of time that the Agent represents the Designer. Further, the Designer agrees, when selling his or her artwork or taking orders, not to accept a price which is under the price structure of his or her Agent.

After a period of _____ months, the Designer may remove his or her unsold artwork from the Agent's portfolio to do with as the Designer wishes.

2. Artwork and Risk of Loss, Theft or Damage. All artwork submitted to the Agent for sale or for the purpose of securing work shall remain the property of the Designer. The Agent shall issue a receipt to the Designer for all artwork which the Designer submits to the Agent. If artwork is lost, stolen, or damaged while in the Agent's possession due to the Agent's failure to exercise reasonable care, the Agent will be held liable for the value of the artwork. Proof of any loss, theft, or damage must be furnished by the Agent to the Designer upon request. When selling artwork, taking an order, or allowing a client to hold artwork for consideration, the Agent agrees to use invoice, order, or holding forms which provide that the client is responsible for loss, theft, or damage to artwork while being held by the client, and to require the client's signature on such forms. The Agent agrees to enforce these provisions, including taking legal action as necessary. If the Agent undertakes legal action, any recovery shall first be used to reimburse the amount of attorney's fees and other expenses incurred and the balance of the recovery shall be divided between Agent and Designer in the respective percentages set forth in Paragraph 5. If the Agent chooses not to require the client to be responsible as described herein, then the Agent agrees to assume these responsibilities. If the Agent receives in-

surance proceeds due to loss, theft, or damage of artwork while in the Agent's or a client's possession, the Designer shall receive no less than that portion of the proceeds that have been paid for the Designer's artwork.

3. Term. This Agreement shall take effect on the_____day of _____19_____, and remain in full force and effect for a term of one year, unless terminated as provided in Paragraph 10.

4. Prices. At this time the minimum base prices charged to clients by the Agent are as follows:
Sketch (apparel market):
_____
Repeat (apparel market):
_____
Colorings (apparel market):
_____
Sketch (home furnishing market):
_____
Repeat (home furnishing market):
_____
Colorings (home furnishing market):
_____
Other:
_____

The Agent agrees that these prices are minimum prices only and shall be increased whenever possible as the work become larger or more complicated than is usual. Higher prices shall also be charged for rush jobs, whenever possible. The Agent also agrees to try to raise the base price to keep pace with the rate of inflation. The Agent shall obtain the Designer's written consent prior to entering into any contracts for payment by royalty.

No discounts shall be offered to clients by the Agent without first consulting the Designer.

When leaving a design with the Agent for possible sale, the Designer shall agree with the Agent as to the price to be charged if the design should bring more than the Agent's base price.

5. Agent's Commissions. The rate of commission for all artwork shall be_____. It is mutually agreed by both parties that no commissions shall be paid on assignments rejected by the Designer or for which the Designer does not receive payment, regardless of the reasons payment is not made.

On commissioned originals and service work, expenses incurred in the execution of a job, such as photostats, shipping, etc. shall be billed to the client in addition to the fee. No Agent's commission shall be paid on these amounts. In the event that a flat fee is paid by the client, it shall be reduced by the amount of expenses incurred by the Designer in performing the assignment, and the Agent's commission shall be payable only on the fee as reduced for expenses. It is mutually agreed that if the Agent offers a client a discount on a large group of designs including work of other designers, then that discount will come out of the Agent's commission since the Agent is the party who benefits from this volume.

6. *Commissioned Work.* Commissioned work refers to all artwork done on a nonspeculative basis. The Agent shall provide the Designer with a copy of the completed order form which the client has signed. The order form shall set forth the responsibilities of the client in ordering and purchasing artwork. To this the Agent shall add the date by which the artwork must be completed and any additional instructions which the Agent feels are necessary to complete the job to the client's satisfaction. The Agent will sign these instructions. Any changes in the original instructions must be in writing, signed by the Agent, and contain a revised completion date.

It is mutually agreed that all commissioned work generated by the Designer's work shall be offered first to the Designer. The Designer has the right to refuse such work.

The Agent agrees to use the order confirmation form of the Textile Designers Guild, or a form that protects the interests of the Designer in the same manner as that form. The order form shall provide that the Designer will be paid for all changes of original instructions arising out of no fault of the Designer. The order form shall also provide that if a job is can-

celed through no fault of the Designer, a labor fee shall be paid by the client based on the amount of work already done and the artwork will remain the property of the Designer. In a case in which the job being cancelled is based on artwork which belongs to the client such as a repeat or coloring, a labor fee will be charged as outlined above and the artwork will be destroyed. If the artwork is already completed in a satisfactory manner at the time the job is canceled, the client must pay the full fee.

7. *Holding Policy.* In the event that a client wishes to hold the Designer's work for consideration, the Agent shall establish a maximum holding time with the client. This holding time shall not exceed five (5) working days. Any other arrangements must first be discussed with the Designer.

The Agent agrees to use the holding form of the Textile Designers Guild, or a form that protects the interests of the Designer in the same manner as that form. All holding forms shall be available for the Designer to see at any time.

8. *Billings and Payments.* The Agent shall be responsible for all billings. The Agent agrees to use the invoice form of the Textile Designers Guild, or a form that protects the interests of the Designer in the same manner as that form. The Agent agrees to provide the Designer with a copy of all bills to clients pertaining to the work of the Designer. The Designer will provide the Agent with a bill for his or her work for the particular job. The Designer's bill shall be paid by the Agent within one week after the delivery of artwork or, if the Agent finds it necessary, within ten (10) working days after receipt of payment from the client. The terms of all bills issued by the Agent shall require payment within thirty (30) calendar days or less. If the client does not pay within that time, the Agent must immediately pursue payment and, upon request, inform the Designer that this has

been done. The Agent agrees to take all necesary steps to collect payment, including taking legal action if necessary. If either the Agent or Designer undertakes legal action, any recovery shall first be used to reimburse the amount of attorney's fees and other expenses incurred and the balance of the recovery shall be divided between Agent and Designer in the respective percentages set forth in Paragraph 5. The Agent agrees, whenever possible, to bill in such a way that no single bill exceeds the maximum that can be sued in small claims court.

Under no circumstances shall the Agent withold payment to the Designer after the Agent has been paid. Late payments by the Agent to the Designer shall be accompanied by interest calculated at the rate of 1½ percent monthly.

9. *Inspection of Books.* The Designer shall have the right to inspect the Agent's books and records with respect to proceeds due to the Designer. The Agent shall keep the books and records at the Agent's place of business and the Designer may make such inspection during normal business hours on the giving of reasonable notice.

10. *Termination.* This Agreement may be terminated by either party by giving thirty (30) days written notice by registered mail to the other party. All artwork executed by the Designer not sold by the Agent must be returned to the Designer within these thirty (30) days. In the event of termination, the Agent shall receive commissions for all sales made or assignments obtained by the Agent prior to the termination date, regardless of when payment is received. No commissions shall be payable for sales made or assignments obtained by the Designer after the termination date.

11. *Assignment.* This Agreement shall not be assigned by either of the parties hereto. It shall be binding on and inure to the benefit of the successors, administrators, executors, or heirs of the Agent and Designer.

12. Arbitration. Any disputes in excess of $_____ (maximum limit for small claims court) arising out of this agreement shall be submitted to binding arbitration before the Joint Ethics Committee or a mutually agreed upon aribitrator pursuant to the rules of the American Arbitration Association. The Arbitrator's award shall be final, and judgement may be entered upon it in any court having jurisdiction thereof. The Agent shall pay all arbitration and court costs, reasonable attorney's fees, and legal interest on any award or judgment in favor of the Designer.

13. Notices. All notices shall be given to the parties at their respective addresses set forth above.

14. Independent Contractor Status. Both parties agree that the Agent is acting as an independent contractor. This Agreement is not an employment agreement, nor does it constitute a joint venture or partnership between the Designer and Agent.

15. Amendments and Merger. All amendments to this Agreement must be written. This Agreement incorporates the entire understanding of the parties.

16. Other Provisions

_____

_____

_____

17. Governing Law. This Agreement shall be governed by the laws of the State of

_____

In witness whereof, the parties have signed this Agreement as of the date set forth above.

_____
DESIGNER

_____
AGENT

Computer Illustration/Graphics Job Order Form

This job order form is a sample of a possible contract for computer-generated art. Since the field is so new, the artist should view this as a model and amend it to fit their situations and the needs of their clients, based on a negotiated agreement.

FRONT: DESIGNER'S LETTERHEAD

DATE		
AUTHORIZED BUYER		
CLIENT		
FOR USE IN	ISSUE	DATE
DEFINITION/TYPE OF ASSIGNMENT		
ADDITIONAL USES	*(promotional, packaging, etc.)*	
NUMBER OF SCREENS	*(single frame, multiple frame)*	
STILL FRAME		
*SECTOR LENGTH PER SCREEN: MAXIMUM	PREFERRED	MINIMUM

JOB DESCRIPTION/APPEAL   *(nature of market):*

COPY TO READ

*BE SURE COPY IS CORRECTLY SPELLED AND TITLED. ARTIST IS NOT RESPONSIBLE FOR ANY COPY OTHER THAN EXACTLY WHAT APPEARS ABOVE.

PRODUCTION SCHEDULE:	
FIRST SHOWING	
REVIEW	
FINAL ACCEPTANCE	
RIGHTS TRANSFERRED	*(one time use, etc.)*
TYPE OF USE	*(game program, advertising, etc.)*
MEDIUM OF USE	*(floppy, documentation, packaging, promotion, etc.)*
DISTRIBUTION/GEOGRAPHICAL AREA *(method of distribution, electronically downloaded, floppy disk, store distribution)*	
TIME/NUMBER OF PRINTINGS	

SYSTEM APPLICATIONS	*(for use on specific machine, or compiled into other operation languages)*

PURCHASE PRICE/PAYMENT SCHEDULE

Terms:

1. Time for Payment. All invoices are payable within thirty (30) days of receipt. A 1½% monthly service charge is payable on all overdue balances. The grant of any license or right of copyright is conditioned on receipt of full payment.

2. Estimates. If this form is used for an estimate or assignment confirmation, the fees and expenses shown are minimum estimates only. Final fees and expenses shall be shown when invoice is rendered. Client's approval shall be obtained for any increases in fees or expenses that exceed the original estimate by 10% or more.

3. Changes. Client shall be responsible for making additional payments for changes requested by Client in original assignment. However, no additional payment shall be made for changes required to conform to the original assignment description. The Client shall offer the Illustrator the first opportunity to make any changes.

4. Expenses. Client shall reimburse Illustrator for all expenses arising from this assignment, including the payment of any sales taxes due on this assignment, and shall advance $_____ to the Illustrator for payment of said expenses.

5. Cancellation. In the event of cancellation of this assignment, ownership of all copyrights and the original artwork is retained by the Illustrator and a cancellation fee for work completed, based on the contract price and expenses already incurred, shall be paid by the Client.

6. Ownership of Artwork. The Illustrator retains ownership of all original artwork, whether preliminary or final, and the Client shall return such artwork within thirty (30) days of use.

7. Credit Lines. The Illustrator shall be given credit in: (a) floppy disk, (b) documentation, (c) packaging, (d) illustrator's mark on art.

8. Any electronic alteration of original art (color shift, mirroring, flopping, combination cut and paste, deletion) creating additional art, shall constitute additional use and will be billed accordingly.

9. Other operating systems conversions. Illustrator shall be given first option at compiling the work for operating systems beyond the original use.

10. Unauthorized use and program licenses. Client will indemnify illustrator against all claims and expenses arising from uses for which client does not have rights to or authority to use. The Client will be responsible for payment of any special licensing or royalty fees resulting from the use of graphics programs that require such payments.

11. Illustrators guarantee for program use. Illustrator guarantees to notify Client of any licensing and/or permissions required for art generating/driving programs to be used.

12. Arbitration. Any disputes in excess of $_____ (maximum limit of small claims court) arising out of this agreement shall be submitted to binding arbitration before the Joint Ethics Committee or a mutually agreed to arbitrator pursuant to the rules of the American Arbitration Association. The arbitrator's award shall be final and judgement upon it may be entered upon it in any court having jurisdiction thereof. The Client shall pay all arbitration and court costs, attorney's fees and legal interest on any judgement or award in the favor of the Illustrator.

13. The Client must copy protect all final art which is the subject of this agreement against duplication or alteration.

14. The Client waives the right to challenge the validity of the Illustrator's ownership of the art, subject to this agreement because of any change or evolution of the law.

15. Acceptance of terms: If the terms of this agreement are not objected to within ten (10) days of receipt, the terms shall be deemed accepted.

Member

Graphic Designer's Estimate/Confirmation/Invoice Form

F R O N T :   D E S I G N E R ' S   L E T T E R H E A D

☐ ESTIMATE	☐ ENGAGEMENT CONFIRMATION	☐ INVOICE
TO		DATE
		COMMISSIONED BY
		ASSIGNMENT NUMBER
		INVOICE NUMBER
		CLIENT'S PURCHASE ORDER NUMBER

ASSIGNMENT DESCRIPTION	DELIVERY DATE
	(PREDICATED ON RECEIPT OF ALL MATERIALS TO BE SUPPLIED BY CLIENT)
	MATERIALS SUPPLIED BY
	FEE

ITEMIZED EXPENSES. CLIENT SHALL REIMBURSE DESIGNER FOR ALL EXPENSES. IF THIS IS AN ESTIMATE OR ASSIGNMENT CONFIR-MATION, ANY EXPENSE AMOUNTS ARE ESTIMATES ONLY. IF THIS IS AN INVOICE, EXPENSE AMOUNTS ARE FINAL.

ILLUSTRATION PHOTOGRAPHY	
MATERIALS AND SUPPLIES	
MECHANICALS	
MESSENGERS	
PHOTOGRAPHIC REPRODUCTION	
PRINTING	
TOLL TELEPHONES	
TRANSPORTATION AND TRAVEL	
MODELS AND PROPS	
SHIPPING AND INSURANCE	
TYPE	
STATS	
OTHER	
	EXPENSES SUBTOTAL
	TOTAL
	SALES TAX
	TOTAL DUE

ANY USAGE RIGHTS NOT EXCLUSIVELY TRANSFERRED ARE RESERVED TO DESIGNER. USAGE BEYOND THAT GRANTED TO CLIENT HEREIN SHALL REQUIRE PAYMENT OF A MUTUALLY AGREED UPON ADDITIONAL FEE SUBJECT TO ALL TERMS ON REVERSE.

RIGHTS TRANSFERRED. DESIGNER TRANSFERS TO THE CLIENT THE FOLLOWING EXCLUSIVE RIGHTS OF USAGE. *(remove all italics before using this form)*	
TITLE OR PRODUCT	*(name)*
CATEGORY OF USE	*(advertising, corporate, promotional, editorial, etc.)*
MEDIUM OF USE	*(consumer or trade magazine, annual report, TV, book, etc.)*
EDITION (IF BOOK)	*(hardcover, mass market paperbook, quality paperback, etc.)*
GEOGRAPHIC AREA	*(if applicable)*
TIME PERIOD	*(if applicable)*

ANY USAGE RIGHTS NOT EXCLUSIVELY TRANSFERRED ARE RESERVED TO DESIGNER. USAGE BEYOND THAT GRANTED TO CLIENT HEREIN SHALL REQUIRE PAYMENT OF A MUTUALLY AGREED UPON ADDITIONAL FEE SUBJECT TO ALL TERMS ON REVERSE.

Terms:

1. Time for Payment. All invoices are payable within thirty (30) days of receipt. A 1½% monthly service charge is payable on all overdue balances. The grant of any license or right of copyright is conditioned on receipt of full payment.

2. Estimates. If this form is used for an estimate or assignment confirmation, the fees and expenses shown are minimum estimates only. Final fees and expenses shall be shown when invoice is rendered. Client's approval shall be obtained for any increases in fees or expenses that exceed the original estimate by 10% or more.

3. Changes. Client shall be responsible for making additional payments for changes requested by Client in original assignment. However, no additional payment shall be made for changes required to conform to the original assignment description. The Client shall offer the Designer the first opportunity to make any changes.

4. Expenses. Client shall reimburse Designer for all expenses arising from this assignment, including the payment of any sales taxes due on this assignment, and shall advance $_____ to the Designer for payment of said expenses.

5. Cancellation. In the event of cancellation of this assignment, ownership of all copyrights and the original artwork is retained by the Designer and a cancellation fee for work completed, based on the contract price and expenses already incurred, shall be paid by the Client.

6. Ownership of Artwork. The Designer retains ownership of all original artwork, whether preliminary or final, and the Client shall return such artwork within thirty (30) days of use.

7. Credit Lines. The Designer and any other creators shall receive a credit line with any editorial usage. If similar credit lines are to be given with other types of usage, it must be so indicated here:

_____

_____

8. Releases. Client will indemnify Designer against all claims and expenses, including reasonable attorney's fees, due to uses for which no release was requested in writing or for uses which exceed authority granted by a release.

9. Modifications. Modification of the agreement must be written, except that the invoice may include, and Client shall be obligated to pay, fees or expenses that were orally authorized in order to progress promptly with work.

10. Arbitration. Any disputes in excess of $_____ (maximum limit for small claims court) arising out of this Agreement shall be submitted to binding arbitration before the Joint Ethics Committee or a mutually agreed upon arbitrator pursuant to the rules of the American Arbitration Association. The Arbitrator's award shall be final and judgment may be entered upon it in any court having jurisdiction thereof. The Client shall pay all arbitration and court costs, reasonable attorney's fees, and legal interest on any award or judgment in favor of the Designer.

11. Acceptance of Terms. The above terms incorporate Article 2 of the Uniform Commercial Code. If not objected to within ten (10) days, these terms shall be deemed acceptable.

12. Code of Fair Practice. The Client and Designer agree to comply with the provisions of the Code of Fair Practice, a copy of which may be obtained from the Joint Ethics Committee, P.O. Box 179 Grand Central Station, New York, New York 10017.

CONSENTED AND AGREED TO

_____

DATE

_____

DESIGNER'S SIGNATURE

_____

COMPANY NAME

_____

AUTHORIZED SIGNATURE

_____

NAME AND TITLE

MEMBER

BUSINESS
MANAGEMENT

Business Management

As creators of unique products, graphic artists have the ethical right to share in the economic proceeds that the uses of their products generate. Securing economic interests and rights is the responsibility of individual graphic artists.

In addition to producing quality artwork, artists must develop a competent business aptitude to market and protect the art successfully. This is the basic survival skill for the independent practitioner.

The commissions offered graphic artists must be able to be accurately evaluated, often at a moment's notice. Artists will need to pinpoint critical provisions and be able to take steps to avoid loss of economic control or legal problems down the road.

Negotiation skills must be learned and continuously honed. This "fine art" of negotiating with the buyer can often make the difference in effectuating the artist's business goals.

If problems should develop during or after the job, artists must also be prepared to act. Artists therefore should be aware of the resources available to minimize potential losses.

Also, looking a little closer to home, artists will need to manage the paperwork part of their profession efficiently. Records of jobs must be maintained, invoices sent and accurately stated, and outstanding fees tracked.

In short, the viability of the artist's professional life is dependent to a great degree on acquiring relevant business and legal knowledge. This new chapter of the *Handbook* will discuss the fundamental business management issues common to all graphic art professionals.

Negotiation

In the graphic arts industry a great deal depends on repeat business, and a professional and honorable reputation. In negotiations, a "winner-take-all" attitude can do more harm than good. Whenever possible, an atmosphere of mutual trust and collaboration should be established and encouraged by the parties involved. From there, both sides can go on to create an agreement that will satisfy their respective needs.

This cooperation is attained not merely by the exchange of concessions, but through the attitudes and professional manner of the persons negotiating. The terms of the agreement may not be those stated by either party at the outset. Rather, the participants must use their creative energies to manufacture solutions that meet the needs of all concerned.

It is important for artists to remember that art buyers are not "the enemy." During the years the Guild has handled grievance procedures between artists and clients, a common source of the majority of complaints has been a failure on the part of both sides to communicate effectively prior to the commencement of work. Both sides must take responsibility for knowing their own needs, articulating them, and taking the other party's needs into account. Even if only one of the negotiators is making a conscientious effort to understand and elicit both the other party's point of view as well as their own, chances of a misunderstanding and/or conflict are greatly reduced. Many artists are reluctant to ask questions or raise objections to clients' demands for fear of appearing difficult to work with. The Guild's experience shows, however, that as long as the discussion is carried out in an appropriate professional manner, clients appreciate artists who can be specific in their dealings, since it prevents misunderstandings later.

Attitude

Relaxation is very important in negotiation. By preparing properly, and making the situation as comfortable as possible, it is possible to relax. Focusing on breathing and concentrating on relaxing muscles in the head, neck and shoulders can be surprisingly useful in a stressful situation. Even though at the moment, the deal at hand may seem like a "make it or break it" proposition, that is usually not the case. In fact, most careers in the graphic arts are built upon hundreds of projects, not one. It is important to create a mental distance from the desperation and anxiety that can come into play in the middle of a negotiation. This relaxation will help with concentration, maneuverability and the ability to respond quickly so that the opportunity to get the right job at the right price won't slip away.

When faced with a negotiation, both sides begin by implying or stating a set of demands based on their needs. The demands should not be confused with underlying needs. These needs are what a skilled negotiator attempts to discern. Where the problem stated is, "My company is looking for a first class brochure that we can produce for under $10,000," there may be several underlying needs that are not articulated directly. The art buyer may be asking, "Do you want this project? Are you excited about it?" and "Are you going to mess up and cost me my job?" In attempting to determine what kind of brochure is required, what degree of work is involved, and the amount of money the client will have to pay for it, a skilled negotiator is communicating other messages as well. "I'm just the right person for this job, I know what I'm doing, and I'm going to make you look good."

Convey positive expectations about the job. Instead of "What is the deadline?" use a phrase like, "When would you want me to deliver the art?" From the outset, contact with a client can show a personal interest and attachment to the project—that's contagious.

The answer to a stated problem will not always be obvious. It is critical to be able to relax and to perceive the other person's position. By understanding that, there can be a positive response to the "sub-text" of what's being said, and the negotiation can proceed with harmony.

Moving forward in a patient, quiet, unemotional and methodical way helps give the peace of mind necessary to read clues and information available. In addition, that mood is picked up by others.

Know when to quit. Getting greedy when things start to go well, or pushing too far can lead the other party to abandon the whole deal out of spite. A show of generosity may pay off in future negotiations.

Preparation and research

Adequate preparation is a key ingredient to successful negotiation. Artists should attempt to know everything possible about a client prior to a meeting. Business libraries contain valuable information about the marketplace: directories for corporations and advertising agencies show amounts of billing, circulation, officers, media, etc. In addition, publication directories list magazines with circulation, advertising rates, names of staff, etc. Subscriptions for all appropriate major trade magazines should be maintained. Active membership in arts organizations such as the Guild helps to give artists the extra "edge" that may be needed in a job situation. Magazine stands, mass transit posters, billboards, retail stores, supermarkets, bookstores all contain valuable information about clients that artists may need to know.

Agendas and contracts

When a negotiation begins, it is important to ask the right questions and formulate an *agenda* for meetings or phone calls that outlines topics that need to be covered. Additionally, artists should establish a "position paper" that will help answer the most important question of all, "What do I want from this job?" and, "What will I do *instead* if I turn it down or am not right for it?"

Whether a project is interesting purely for the money, because it is a valuable showcase, or will help establish a working relationship with a new client, whatever the reason, an agenda will affect what the artist will agree to in negotiations (consult checklist in this section for suggestions on an agenda and checklist).

Prior to commencing work, agreements should be put in writing whenever possible. This protects the client as well as the artist by confirming terms before a misunderstanding can occur. The document can be as simple or complicated as the situation requires, from an informal "letter of agreement," to a complicated contract requiring signatures of all parties. In order to be able to formulate such letters and contracts or to analyze contracts offered, it is absolutely necessary to have a thorough working knowledge of copyright law and its phraseology. By careful review of model contracts and supplementary sections of this book and other publications from the Guild, artists will be able to re-phrase contractual terms on the spur of the moment.

The majority of art directors and creative services personnel who commission art have little or no expertise in the area of copyright and contracts. Like artists, most of them would prefer not to have to deal with the subject. They are attempting to conduct business in what are usually hectic, high pressure surroundings. Having a clear understanding of how to suggest, phrase and put contract amendments into writing, can help solve any problems that might appear. When clients use work-for-hire clauses in contracts or demand all rights to artwork, every effort should be made to determine what the client *really* needs. Often such a term in a contract was put in by a lawyer trying to cover all bases. But such terms are usually excessive and, if priced accordingly, make work too expensive to afford.

Keep thorough written records of a job's progress, including the initial checklist containing job description, deadlines, money, notes on the person representing the client, records of follow-up meetings and phone calls, hours and expenses on the job, layouts, memos, sketches, contracts, invoices and business letters. This should form a "job packet" that is a "paper trail" in the event that a disagreement or misunderstanding gets in the way of completion of a project and payment.

The meeting

As far as possible, create an environment for meeting that will allow as comfortable a situation as possible. If negotiating "on your own turf" is impossible, bring your own turf with you. Clothing should always be professional and neat, but make sure it is also *comfortable*. Any presentation or portfolio should be of the very best work. An unusual and creative presentation that shows thought and is well designed goes a long way in establishing the expertise of an artist—and making a sale. Negotiation should be avoided if the artist lacks sleep, is overtired, is taking medication, under the influence of alcohol, or has recently eaten a heavy meal. Very expensive errors can occur when the artist is not as sharp as he or she should be. If the situation is uncomfortable or potentially disruptive, arrange to conduct the negotiation another time. There is a right and wrong time for negotiation. Recognize an opportunity and make use of it, but recognize also when there is *no* opportunity and wait until another day.

The golden rules during a meeting are:

stop, look and listen. Stop—quiet down breathing, relax and get "centered." Refrain from lots of "small talk" unless what's being said is to a purpose. A well-placed word here and there does more to establish professional credibility. In addition, giving out information also can give clues about the artist's situation and weakness inadvertently. Conducting presentations can also distract clients from carefully reviewing the work.

Look—a great deal can be learned by close attention to physical clues and behavior of others. Office environments (wallpaper, furniture, desktops, artwork and photographs) can give clues as to the personality of the client. Notice if a seat is offered, if someone consults a watch constantly, or is interrupting and is not focused on the discussion. If understood, behavioral clues can give a substantial advantage of knowing how to deal with someone during the negotiation.

Listen—people appreciate someone who is alert, attentive and indicates that he or she understands what is being said. It is important to indicate that *understanding*, even if the listener doesn't agree with the point made. Listen *actively*, with nods of agreement, encouraging the other party to express themselves. It is very useful to repeat what was heard, such as, "Let me see if I'm understanding correctly, you're saying that, etc., etc..." This indicates a good listener who is eager to understand. Listening effectively helps to determine and address the other party's needs and expectations.

Power

Negotiation itself cannot turn every situation into a golden opportunity. There are some relationships where the balance of power is out of alignment such that one party must either yield to unfavorable conditions or give up the negotiation. However, it is possible to maximize assets and protect from an agreement that may be detrimental.

Remembering that not every negotiation is destined to end in a *deal* is important. Two parties can "agree to disagree" most amicably and part ways hoping for another try at a later date. It is this ability to regard a negotiation with a level-headed objectivity, keeping it in perspective, that provides a skilled negotiator with the relaxation and attitude necessary to effect the most favorable agreement.

Parties in a discussion should bear in mind what their course of action will be if the negotiation should end. "What other jobs do I have?" or "What else will I do with my professional time if I don't take this assignment?" are questions the artist should ask, just as the client is asking, "What else can I do, or who else can I hire to make this project work?" These questions provide negotiators with a realistic assessment of how much power they actually have in a negotiation. Power can be regarded as the ability to say *no*, and assessing alternatives clarifies a position.

Often parties will establish an arbitrary limit from which they will not bend, such as "I won't pay more than $25,000," or "I won't accept less than $3,000." Since the figure or condition is often arbitrarily selected in the first place, it is important to be able to *ignore* such a limit if necessary. A bottom line may become a focal point and inhibit the imagination necessary to establish terms that meet both parties' needs.

When entering into negotiations, it's important to decide what to do if negotiations break off. It's much easier to say no when there is a favorable alternative to pursue. As the saying goes, a bank will lend money if you prove you don't need it. In the same way, it's much easier to get a job if you already have one. If an artist is not busy with other jobs, the best alternative is to create a mental "priority" list of important and valuable projects to pursue. This helps alleviate the often ill-founded notion that a deal must be made "at any cost."

Tactics

Tactics are used throughout every negotiation, whether intentional or not. By separating emotional responses from calm and detached observation of tactics, the ability of the tactic to work is defused. It is important in all phases of negotiation not to take things personally. Performance and ability to maneuver are seriously hampered when egos take charge.

Consider a few examples: 1) limited authority: a person claims to have no final say on the terms of a deal. This enables one negotiator to make rigid demands, leaving the other to offer concessions in order that some headway is made. One possible solution is to treat the project under discussion as a joint venture, recruiting the other person as your new found "partner". By emphasizing terms that create partnership and sharing a stake in decisions, that person is encouraged to "go to bat" with the higher

ups to defend the artist's needs and goals. 2) phony legitimacy: it is stated that a contract is a "standard contract" and cannot be changed. Contracts are working documents that serve to protect two or more parties in an agreement. Don't agree to sign standardized contracts if they don't protect you. Don't be reluctant to strike out unfavorable sections or terms. If necessary, the defense "my attorney has instructed me not to sign contracts with these conditions" may be used to suggest alterations (see GAG sample contracts for guidelines). 3) emotions: anger, threats, derisive laughter, tears or insults may be convincing and may, in fact be genuine, but should be regarded as tactical maneuvers. Listen carefully to the *point* of the message and separate it from the style of delivery. Never escalate an emotional situation. Any attempt to "roll up the sleeves and jump in" is very risky.

Phone

Use of the telephone has distinct advantages over in-person meetings. It provides ample opportunity to refer to written materials for reference and support. Often, when calling from the office or home, being surrounded by one's own environment can bolster confidence. Telephones seem to be very easy for some to work with and much harder for others. Like personal contact, it has its good and bad parts. Skill in the use of the phone is very important to a good negotiator: some individuals go as far as to write "scripts" for particularly difficult situations where performing under pressure can cause confusion. A simpler negotiation "agenda" or checklist can be used to outline all the points that need to be covered. This prevents the problem of forgetting important details, and helps keep the conversation centered on the important matters at hand. Note taking during phone conversations is highly recommended. Artists are often attempting to understand the aesthetic requirements of a project, all the details of a business arrangement, and build up a personal understanding of the individual on the phone. These are complicated details and should be written down. Such notes can also be valuable references should a misunderstanding occur during the project.

Use of the phone has disadvantages as well. It's easier to refuse someone over the phone. If a difficult demand has to be made, it might be preferable to arrange a meeting. Being unable to see a person's face, it is also difficult to judge reactions to what is being said. A person's attention to what is being said may not be focused, this can make it more difficult to establish the rapport and "partnership" that is so important to many successful negotiations. Should a discussion become difficult, it is easy to put the caller on hold, or get off the telephone and call back when it is more advantageous. This allows time for consultation of research materials, other phone calls for research, cooling off if emotions are in play, or just time to make a difficult decision.

Money

Money should be the last item in a discussion for several reasons. It is the one area where the majority of disagreements can occur, and it is important in the earlier stages of a negotiation to focus on areas where there is accord. In this way the partnership stressed earlier is given time to bloom. Also, money should only be a reflection of all the factors that lead up to it.

The job description, deadline, expenses, usage and reproduction rights, difficulty of execution, etc. all tell the story of how much a job should cost. So negotiating money before this information has been clearly agreed to is premature and can be a costly error.

When discussing money, insofar as is possible, outline expectations, then attempt to get the other side to make the first offer. The old game of "I say 10, you say 6, I say 9, you say 7, we agree on 8" is still played out, but is not always necessary. Depending on how it is stated, though, a first offer is rarely a final offer, and should almost always be tested. Once again, the artist must weigh the risk of losing a possible working relationship by refusing to budge past a certain price. It always depends on the situation. Don't feel obligated to respond right away if someone starts out a negotiation with "I only have $500 but I think you'd be great for the job." One can show acknowledgement of the figure and still bring it up *later* when there is more of a foundation of a working relationship on which to base requests for more money.

Often, artists are asked to bid on jobs. It is important to clarify the nature of the bid. Is the client looking for a sealed bid that will be used to compete against other artists? Is this bid an attempt to help structure a budget? Is it only a "ballpark" estimate? Do they wish to negotiate directly? Since a

sealed bid encourages negotiation against yourself, it should be clarified if the bid is final and binding. It is unfair to ask an artist to develop a competitive sealed bid and then use that figure as the starting point for future negotiations. In a "ballpark" estimate, the client will often hear only the low figure, so use care in offering a set of figures that brackets your price in the middle.

It is not only practical, it's actually good business to ask for a price slightly higher than what you would expect. Like it or not, people in business often like to feel that they've gotten you to bend somewhat, and in that sense it is an obligation to manufacture a few concessions without harming your own interests.

Hourly rate formula

Another way to figure pricing, as opposed to "the going rate" or supply and demand, is the *hourly rate formula*. This formula takes into consideration factors that make up an artist's overhead such as rent, utilities, salaries, benefits, promotion, outside professional services, equipment, transportation, office and art supplies, business taxes and entertainment. In order to come up with an hourly rate, divide the annual total for "overhead" figures by 1800, which is the number of hours worked in an average year. The resulting figure would be an hourly rate (based on a 35 hour week) that could be expected to cover all of your costs *including* your salary.

However, most artists, especially those who are self-employed, bill at some smaller number, for example dividing the yearly overhead figure by 900 hours. This may give a more practical rate since it allows for the fact that self-employed artists rarely work on a full-time continuing basis for one or two clients.

When a project is being considered, it is important to figure a close estimate of hours of work. This estimate multiplied by your hourly rate will demonstrate whether the client's fee for the project will mean profit, loss or a "break-even" amount. At that point, the artist has the option of figuring out a solution to the project that will mean fewer hours of work to make the job more profitable, or rejecting the job because the fee is too small.

Many large jobs, such as corporate design projects, require that the hours involved be used as a gauge to see if the project is on budget.

FORM VA
UNITED STATES COPYRIGHT OFFICE

REGISTRATION NUMBER

VA   VAU

EFFECTIVE DATE OF REGISTRATION

Month   Day   Year

DO NOT WRITE ABOVE THIS LINE. IF YOU NEED MORE SPACE, USE A SEPARATE CONTINUATION SHEET.

1 TITLE OF THIS WORK ▼   NATURE OF THIS WORK ▼ See instructions

THE PIRATE CORFRESEE   2 BRUSH DRAWINGS

PREVIOUS OR ALTERNATIVE TITLES ▼

PUBLICATION AS A CONTRIBUTION If this work was published as a contribution to a periodical, serial, or collection, give information about the collective work in which the contribution appeared. **Title of Collective Work ▼**

THE SKULL-AND-BONES OVER THE CARIBBEAN

If published in a periodical or serial give: Volume ▼   Number ▼   Issue Date ▼   On Pages ▼

2 NAME OF AUTHOR ▼   DATES OF BIRTH AND DEATH
                                                        Year Born ▼   Year Died ▼
a BERNICE M. LUGO   1956

Was this contribution to the work a   AUTHOR'S NATIONALITY OR DOMICILE   WAS THIS AUTHOR'S CONTRIBUTION TO
"work made for hire"?   Name of Country   THE WORK   If the answer to either
☐ Yes   OR { Citizen of ▶ USA   Anonymous?   ☐ Yes ☑ No   of these questions is
☑ No   Domiciled in ▶   Pseudonymous? ☐ Yes ☑ No   "Yes," see detailed
                                                                                                              instructions.

NOTE

Under the law, the "author" of a "work made for hire" is generally the employer, not the employee (see instructions). For any part of this work that was "made for hire" check "Yes" in the space provided, give the employer (or other person for whom the work was prepared) as "Author" of that part, and leave the space for dates of birth and death blank.

NATURE OF AUTHORSHIP Briefly describe nature of the material created by this author in which copyright is claimed. ▼

ARTWORK

NAME OF AUTHOR ▼   DATES OF BIRTH AND DEATH
                                                        Year Born ▼   Year Died ▼
b

Was this contribution to the work a   AUTHOR'S NATIONALITY OR DOMICILE   WAS THIS AUTHOR'S CONTRIBUTION TO
"work made for hire"?   Name of country   THE WORK   If the answer to either
☐ Yes   OR { Citizen of ▶   Anonymous?   ☐ Yes ☐ No   of these questions is
☐ No   Domiciled in ▶   Pseudonymous? ☐ Yes ☐ No   "Yes," see detailed
                                                                                                              instructions.

NATURE OF AUTHORSHIP Briefly describe nature of the material created by this author in which copyright is claimed. ▼

NAME OF AUTHOR ▼   DATES OF BIRTH AND DEATH
                                                        Year Born ▼   Year Died ▼
c

Was this contribution to the work a   AUTHOR'S NATIONALITY OR DOMICILE   WAS THIS AUTHOR'S CONTRIBUTION TO
"work made for hire"?   Name of Country   THE WORK   If the answer to either
☐ Yes   OR { Citizen of ▶   Anonymous?   ☐ Yes ☐ No   of these questions is
☐ No   Domiciled in ▶   Pseudonymous? ☐ Yes ☐ No   "Yes," see detailed
                                                                                                              instructions.

NATURE OF AUTHORSHIP Briefly describe nature of the material created by this author in which copyright is claimed. ▼

3 YEAR IN WHICH CREATION OF THIS   DATE AND NATION OF FIRST PUBLICATION OF THIS PARTICULAR WORK
WORK WAS COMPLETED This information   Complete this information Month ▶ _____ Day ▶ _____ Year ▶ _____
                   must be given   ONLY if this work
                   in all cases.   has been published.
◀ Year   ◀ Nation

4 COPYRIGHT CLAIMANT(S) Name and address must be given even if the claimant is the   APPLICATION RECEIVED
same as the author given in space 2.▼
                                                                                          ONE DEPOSIT RECEIVED
See instructions   BERNICE M. LUGO
before completing 6 CLAREMONT PARK   TWO DEPOSITS RECEIVED
this space.   BOSTON MA 02118
                   TRANSFER If the claimant(s) named here in space 4 are different from the author(s) named   REMITTANCE NUMBER AND DATE
                   in space 2, give a brief statement of how the claimant(s) obtained ownership of the copyright.▼

DO NOT WRITE HERE OFFICE USE ONLY

MORE ON BACK ▶   • Complete all applicable spaces (numbers 5-9) on the reverse side of this page.   DO NOT WRITE HERE
                 • See detailed instructions.   • Sign the form at line 8.
                                                                                          Page 1 of _____ pages

Copyright Registration

Although the copyright law automatically protects artwork of original authorship from the moment it is created, there are advantages to be gained in registering the art with the Copyright Office formally. Registration establishes a public record of the artist's copyright claim in the artwork. Thus if someone infringes or copies the art to the artist's detriment, the artist possesses presumptive evidence of ownership, leaving the burden to prove differently on the other party. With registration the artist also gains a broader range of legal remedies in the event of infringement.

The registration procedure is not at all complex or lengthy. Form VA is generally used by graphic artists to register pictorial, graphic or sculptural artwork. Along with the properly completed form, the artist must enclose one or two copies of the entire artwork, depending on whether the art is unpublished or published, and a $10 fee. The accompanying example of a completed Form VA is for a published illustration appearing in a book.

At other times registration forms may

EXAMINED BY _____

CHECKED BY _____

☐ CORRESPONDENCE
  Yes

☐ DEPOSIT ACCOUNT
  FUNDS USED

FORM VA

FOR
COPYRIGHT
OFFICE
USE
ONLY

DO NOT WRITE ABOVE THIS LINE. IF YOU NEED MORE SPACE, USE A SEPARATE CONTINUATION SHEET.

PREVIOUS REGISTRATION Has registration for this work, or for an earlier version of this work, already been made in the Copyright Office?
☐ Yes ☒ No If your answer is "Yes," why is another registration being sought? (Check appropriate box) ▼
☐ This is the first published edition of a work previously registered in unpublished form.
☐ This is the first application submitted by this author as copyright claimant.
☐ This is a changed version of the work, as shown by space 6 on this application.
If your answer is "Yes," give: **Previous Registration Number** ▼   **Year of Registration** ▼

5

DERIVATIVE WORK OR COMPILATION Complete both space 6a & 6b for a derivative work; complete only 6b for a compilation.
a. Preexisting Material Identify any preexisting work or works that this work is based on or incorporates. ▼

b. Material Added to This Work Give a brief, general statement of the material that has been added to this work and in which copyright is claimed. ▼

6

See instructions
before completing
this space.

DEPOSIT ACCOUNT If the registration fee is to be charged to a Deposit Account established in the Copyright Office, give name and number of Account.
Name ▼   **Account Number** ▼

7

CORRESPONDENCE Give name and address to which correspondence about this application should be sent. Name/Address/Apt/City/State/Zip ▼
BERNICE M. LUGO
6 CLAREMONT PARK
BOSTON, MA. 02118

Be sure to
give your
daytime phone
number

Area Code & Telephone Number ▶ (617) 653-8800

CERTIFICATION* I, the undersigned, hereby certify that I am the
Check only one ▼
☒ author
☐ other copyright claimant
☐ owner of exclusive right(s)
☐ authorized agent of _____
   Name of author or other copyright claimant, or owner of exclusive right(s) ▲

8

of the work identified in this application and that the statements made
by me in this application are correct to the best of my knowledge.

Typed or printed name and date ▼ If this is a published work, this date must be the same as or later than the date of publication given in space 3.
BERNICE M. LUGO   date ▶ 6/9/84

Handwritten signature (X) ▼
Bernice M. Lugo

MAIL CERTIFICATE TO
Name ▼
BERNICE M. LUGO
Number/Street/Apartment Number ▼
6 CLAREMONT PARK
City/State/ZIP ▼
BOSTON, MA. 02118

Certificate
will be
mailed in
window
envelope

Have you:
• Completed all necessary spaces?
• Signed your application in space 8?
• Enclosed check or money order for $10 payable to Register of Copyrights?
• Enclosed your deposit material with the application and fee?
MAIL TO: Register of Copyrights, Library of Congress, Washington, D.C. 20559.

9

* 17 U.S.C. § 506(e): Any person who knowingly makes a false representation of a material fact in the application for copyright registration provided for by section 409, or in any written statement filed in connection with the application, shall be fined not more than $2,500.
☆ U.S. GOVERNMENT PRINTING OFFICE: 1981: 355-312

Nov. 1981-600,000

need to be used by graphic artists. If audio-visual work is created, including motion pictures, then Form PA is the appropriate registration form. Where both art and text in a work are to be registered by the artist and the text predominates, then Form TX should be used. For computer software Form TX is used, and for computer graphics, Form VA. All forms are accompanied by line-by-line instructions.

The protection of the copyright law may be lost easily if a proper *copyright notice* does not accompany a public distribution or publication of any art. Refer to page 28 for the elements that make up a copyright notice. Rather than having the art enter the public domain and thus losing esthetic and economic control over it, a notice should accompany *all* publications of the art. The form and placement of the notice should be covered by written agreements with the client. Where use of the art has been temporarily granted to a client, the name in the notice should preferably be the artist's, but may be the client's for the duration of the usage.

A means for cutting costs on repeated registration fees for *unpublished* artwork, is to register a group of artworks under a single title. For example, the artist may collect 75 drawings, put them into an orderly unit and then register them under a single identifying title. A similar inexpensive means of group registration is possible for *published* artwork having appeared in periodicals. Such contributions to periodicals must have been made within a one-year period and must have included the individual artist's copyright notice. In this latter instance, Form GR/CP must be completed in addition to any of the other forms noted above.

In submitting copies of the artwork along with the registration form, original art need not be submitted. The artist can submit tearsheets, photocopies or transparencies.

Whatever type of copies are submitted, they should show all copyrightable contents of the artwork.

A basic discussion of the copyright law is provided on pages 27-29. The graphic artist requiring a more detailed analysis may wish to refer to the Guild publication entitled *The Visual Artist's Guide to the New Copyright Law.*

The Copyright Office also serves the artist as a resource. Information on the copyright law and the registration procedure can be obtained at 202/287-8700 and forms can be requested at 202/287-9100. Additionally, literature about the various elements of registration are available for free. A list of these publications may be found in *Publications on Copyright* (Circular 2). The forms and literature may also be obtained by writing:

Copyright Office
Information & Publications Section
Library of Congress
Washington, DC 20559

Invasions and infringements

Any illustration or design could involve problems of invasion of privacy and copyright infringement. The "advertising or trade" use of a living person's name or likeness without permission is an invasion of privacy. It is a field in which claims may be in the hundreds of thousands of dollars. "Advertising or trade" means virtually all uses outside of the factually correct editorial contents of magazines, newspapers, books, television pro-

grams, etc. Thus, "advertising or trade" includes print and TV ads, company brochures, packaging, etc. Public and private figures are protected equally in this connection. The test of "likeness" is whether an ordinary person would recognize the complainant as the person in the illustration in question. It needn't be a perfect likeness. The best protection is a signed release and any contract should provide for this if a problem is likely to arise.

In addition, if the artist copied another work (say a photograph) in making the illustration, then someone might sue for copyright infringement. The copyright holder would be either the photographer or the publisher of the photograph, depending on the relationship between them. The test of an infringement is whether an ordinary person would say that one work is copied from the other; the copying need not be exact. Given the substantial amount of photography used in reference files for illustration as well as the frequent incorporation of photographs into designs, it is likely that everyone should be exercising extreme caution in this area. Of course, common themes and images (such as squares or triangles) are in the public domain and may be freely used in a different way by another artist. Infringement requires the copying of a substantial portion of a work, so a mere similarity of style or concept will not be an infringement. The Guild is currently developing a form to prevent "knock-offs" in the textile design field.

Because of the privacy and infringement risks, many firms carry "advertisers (or 'publishers') liability" insurance to cover claims pertaining to these subjects. That, however, is not the ultimate salvation. Claims and lawsuits mean increased insurance premiums, or loss of coverage altogether. For that reason, caution in the use of artwork is always necessary.

Checks with conditions

It is not uncommon for an artist to receive payment in the form of a check with several conditions stated on the back. Most commonly these will be conditions to the effect that endorsement of the check constitutes a transfer of all reproduction rights and/or ownership of the original art to the payer. Although legal opinion is divided on this matter, it is doubtful that endorsement of such a check would constitute a legal contract, especially if it conflicts with a previous contract. The artist has at least three options to consider when handling checks with conditions.

First, a safe procedure is simply to return the check and request a new check be issued without conditions. If the conditions on the check violate a prior contract, a refusal to issue a check without conditions will be a breach of contract.

Second, if an artist has previously signed a contract or sent an invoice that restricts the client's rights of use, the artist should strike out the conditions on the check and deposit it if the artwork has already been used. In making the deposit, the artist should probably not sign the back of the check, but instead use an endorsement stamp after striking out all the conditions. If the artwork has not been used, the artist should notify the client in writing that he or she is striking out the conditions on the check. If the artist does not hear from the client within two weeks, the check can safely be deposited.

Finally, if the artist has neither signed a contract with the client nor sent any prior invoice restricting the rights of use, the check should be returned in order to protect all rights. Along with the check the artist should include an appropriate invoice restricting the rights of use. Of course, the best procedure is to pin down in writing from the beginning of an assignment what rights are going to be transferred.

Records, billing and bill-tracking

G etting paid on time and in the full amount is the just entitlement of any artist. Proper planning and preparation at the right time—and in writing—can do much towards having this expectation met. These preparations may, at times, require an extra effort on the artist's part, but they will certainly *pay off* in the long run.

At the start of each job, artists should secure a complete understanding of the negotiated terms and obtain a final agreement in writing to help insure timely and proper payment of fees.

To encourage timely payment, artists may include additional terms providing penalties for accounts that become past-due and the retention of rights until payment is made.

Since job changes often alter the original terms, it becomes particularly important to confirm in writing any additional fees due to the artist as a result of such changes.

Model business forms prepared by the Guild (refer to page 130) incorporate a number of these measures and can aid members in securing their agreements and rights.

To facilitate accurate billing, artists should maintain proper records through job files, job ledgers, or similar means. Tracking invoices provides the means to remind buyers of outstanding obligations and to take such follow-up steps as necessary to obtain payment.

When a buyer refuses to make payment, written agreements and invoices can serve as a basis to protect the artist's rights, either through negotiation, arbitration or a law suit.

Keeping Records

The artist should have a system for record-keeping. Such a system facilitates billing, bill-tracking, and fees collection, as well as providing a basis for claiming and verifying tax deductions.

Job File: One common method of record-keeping is the use of a folder or envelope for each job. As a new job is received the job file is prepared to retain all information and documents, such as agreements, receipts, letters, invoices, and so on. The job file then provides a single and complete record.

Identifying information is usually placed on the cover. This may include the artist's job number, the title of the project, the buyer's name, and the delivery date. If the job is complex, the job file should be subdivided into sections to permit easy access to information.

Job Ledger: A job ledger contains standard columns for information such as the *job description* (Job Number, Client, Description of Artwork, Delivery Date), *rights granted* (Usage Rights, Status of Original Artwork), *fees and expenses* (Fee, Reimbursable Expenses, Sales Tax, Advance, etc.), and *billing information* (Balance Due, Invoice Date, Payment Due Date, and Payment Received Date).

The artist could then, at a glance, determine the status of each aspect of the job. The ledger's format can vary from a form specifically created by the artist to a printed journal readily available in stationery stores.

Billing procedure

Most art assignments, whether written or verbal, are contractual arrangements. Essentially, the buyer promises to make a specific payment in return for the artist's grant of usage rights to the buyer. Invoices serve as formal communications to the buyer of monies that have or will become due.

The manner and time of payment are normally established in the written agreement. Where the parties have not specified a payment due-date, the generally accepted practice is payment within 30 days of delivery of the art.

An invoice should be presented whenever a payment becomes due. In many instances, invoices should accompany delivery of the finished art. Where a partial-payment is due or costs are to be billed during the job, the invoice(s) should be delivered accordingly. If cancellation or rejection occurs the buyer should be billed immediately according to the agreement or, if such a provision is absent, according to Guild policy discussed on page 48.

Verbal requests for payment should not be substituted for invoices but, rather, regarded as additional means in the collection process. In many businesses an invoice is mandatory for the buyer or others to authorize and issue a check. A copy should also be sent to the accounting department, if the business is large enough to have one, to facilitate prompt processing.

The wording of invoices should be accurate and complete to avoid delaying the payment. Copies of receipts for reimbursable costs are usually attached to document expenditures. At least one copy of the invoice should be retained by the artist.

Tracking outstanding payments

Once the invoice has been given to the buyer, the artist will need to track or monitor the outstanding debt until paid. A tracking method should be established that ties into the artist's record-keeping.

One simple method is to set up a separate folder marked as "Accounts Receivable." Copies of all invoices forwarded to buyers, in an order based upon payment due dates, the artist's job numbers, or the billing

dates should be kept in this folder.

To track fees, the invoices should be periodically reviewed as to their status. When payments are received, the invoice is pulled and placed into the individual job file.

Where the job ledger is used, the artist can determine at a glance which payments remain outstanding by referring to the "Payment Due Date" column. When payment is received, the appropriate date is entered under "Payment Received Date."

Continual tracking of outstanding payments also keeps the artist current on cash flow and allows him or her to take timely follow-up steps to collect past-due fees or other outstanding obligations.

Collecting

Having completed and delivered artwork that met the buyer's specifications, it's quite natural to anticipate that payment will be made as agreed. Graphic artists who are not paid in a reasonable time, will need to undertake additional efforts to collect outstanding fees, or to absorb losses of income and productive time personally.

Artists can often prevent payment problems in the first place by taking certain steps beforehand. (The principal safeguard for artists is to outline clearly payment and related terms in a written and signed agreement right at the start of a job.) Once the job is begun the artist's subsequent use of certain protective practices (to deal with job changes and to provide proper billing) will further encourage timely and full payment. This advance preparation will give artists something to fall back on and facilitate the collection of fees should non-payment occur.

Whether or not there's been early preparation, artists who are not paid will want to implement an appropriate and efficient collection strategy. This section will look at some of the collection resources available—how they work, what they entail and when they may be incorporated into an artist's strategy. Background information will be presented to guide graphic artists in their individual collection efforts.

Formulating a collection strategy

At the time payment becomes due but

is not received in full, the artist should put a collection process into effect that has been planned well in advance. Not taking such action immediately will only work to the artist's disadvantage. Artists' invoices tend to get more difficult to collect as they get older. Both artist and buyer may lose or misplace important documents or experience memory lapses, or new events may complicate matters.

Any initial effort in a collection strategy requires the artist to communicate directly with the buyer. In so doing, the artist may gain an insight into the nature of the problem and the buyer's attitude, which serves as the basis for determining subsequent action.

If a misunderstanding or error is involved, then further discussion between artist and buyer may be appropriate. If this direct discussion between artist and client is not sufficient, then artist and buyer could take advantage of arbitration, mediation, or the support services of a local Guild grievance committee.

If the artist encounters an unreasonable or evasive buyer, more forceful measures may be required to collect outstanding fees. Artists may have to sue in small claims court, or engage a collection agency or lawyer.

Direct negotiation

As noted, the first step in the collection process involves direct communication with the buyer to determine why payment has not been made. Unless complex legal matters or large amounts of money are at issue, direct negotiation is usually the most appropriate and simplest approach. The other resources to be discussed should be used only when direct negotiation proves unsuccessful.

A discussion by phone or a visit on a one-to-one basis may be most effective in resolving a payment problem. Alternately, the artist could write a brief business-like letter and attach a copy of the original invoice clearly marked "Second Notice." The buyer should be reminded of and requested to provide the overdue payment immediately.

At this stage the artist usually can presume, until facts indicate otherwise, that human error or "red tape" was involved and that the call or letter will clear things up. These reminders often prove sufficient. There is, therefore, no need to alienate anyone, at least until it is clear that the non-payment is deliberate.

It is of course in the artist's best interest to act professionally at all times in dealing with the buyer or anyone else that may be contacted. The artist should be objective and realistic while conducting collection efforts.

Where payment problems occur (or are anticipated), letters and invoices should be sent by "Certified Mail—Return Receipt Requested." At all times copies of correspondence between the parties should be retained. Documentation may prove to be crucial at a later stage.

Causes of non-payment

The artist can usually learn why the payment has not been made from initial contacts with the buyer. The following is a look at some of the more common causes of non-payment and suggested strategy for responding to them. These basic negotiating concepts can be applied to other types of non-payment situations as well.

Buyer's Error: Once the artwork is delivered, it's on to the next project for the buyer. Buyers or others may lose interest in processing the check. One purpose for providing an invoice is that it serves as a physical reminder. The buyer should not be expected to send the check automatically; nor are verbal requests for payment sufficient.

If oversight proves to be the cause of non-payment, a new immediate due-date should be established and the buyer requested to follow-up personally. The artist should send a letter confirming when payment will be made.

Artist's Error: The artist may be the cause of the buyer's delaying payment. Perhaps the invoice was not provided or was forwarded to the wrong person, was incomplete or illegible, or, possibly, reimbursable expenses were not documented. In this situation the artist must take timely remedial steps to expedite the payment process.

Disputes under the agreement or professional standards

Not all disputes between artist and buyer are the result of deliberate abuse; some are unintentional or the result of failing to act. For example, buyers may have made a wrong assumption or not have been aware of what constitutes appropriate professional conduct in a particular situation.

Once the artist finds out why payment has not been made or other rights not respected, and the reason is contrary to the agreement or to professional standards, then the buyer should be informed that his or her position is incorrect.

When contacting the buyer, reference should first be made to the written (or verbal) agreement. Well-negotiated agreements will usually cover the disputed issue and therefore specify either the obligations of the buyer or the rights of the artist.

Other provisions in the agreement providing for alternatives or penalties in the event that the buyer does not act as originally agreed, should also be brought to the buyer's attention. These provisions may provide additional negotiating leverage.

If necessary, the buyer's attention should be directed to appropriate professional standards. Such relevant sources for citing include the industry's "Code of Fair Practice" and the Guild's *Pricing & Ethical Guidelines*.

The buyer should be asked to comply with the artist's request or to respond to the issue if further discussion appears appropriate.

Extension of payment time

A buyer may claim to be experiencing a "cash-flow problem," not having sufficient funds on hand to pay. It is difficult to verify whether this is a legitimate reason or an evasive maneuver.

Nor is it unusual for the buyer to blame the late-payment on the company's computer. Long intervals between programmed payments are unreasonable. Exceptions to automatic payments can and are made all the time. The artist should insist that the buyer authorize a handwritten check within a specified number of days.

If the cause of the delay appears legitimate and future payment clearly will be made, the artist may wish to accommodate the buyer and grant a reasonable extension. If an extension is granted, the new payment deadline should be put in writing.

Granting extensions should be viewed as a professional courtesy on the part of the artist. It is not a right to be exercised by the buyer. To compensate the artist fairly for the delay, the buyer should be willing to pay a stated percentage on the balance due as a service fee. This practice should be used particularly when longer periods are granted.

Refusal to negotiate

After direct negotiating attempts, a buyer may still refuse to make payment. The buyer may not respond to the artist's letters and calls, provide unreasonable explanations, not address the issue at hand, or not make payment as promised according to newly negotiated terms.

Faced with this situation, and as a last effort before turning to other alternatives, the artist should send a "demand letter." This can be done either directly or through a lawyer. The basis of the artist's claim should be briefly restated with a demand for immediate payment of outstanding monies.

The artist should also state in this demand letter that a legal proceeding will be commenced unless payment is received. The artist may also note that the Graphic Artist Guild would be notified to alert other artists about what the artist considers to be unprofessional practices. The buyer will then have to reconsider his position in view of the artist's determination to pursue his or her legal rights.

Planning ahead

Up to this point in the collection strategy a number of reasonable efforts have been made and sufficient time allowed the buyer to respond or pay the debt. The artist has also accumulated several documents to verify the continued indebtedness and the attempts made to collect, which may later prove helpful.

If the buyer does not make the payment as agreed, or requested, or fails to respond or acts evasively, the artist may reasonably presume that the buyer is intentionally avoiding payment or has excessively slipshod accounting procedures.

The artist must now select alternative recourses as a logical follow-up action. Various recourses are discussed individually in the following sections.

The Guild's grievance committee

As a professional association, the Guild has from its formative years included the support services of the Grievance Committee to provide guidance and assistance to members in resolving their differences with their clients. An overview of the Committee, its various functions and objectives, is provided on pages 39 to 40. Guild members requesting this service can contact the Grievance Committee of their Guild chapter.

To facilitate the Committee's ability to make an objective assessment of a grievance and to be able to enter a dialogue with the client based on fact, specific information is requested. The following elements need to be incorporated within the submitted grievance:

1. The member's full personal name and business name (if any), address(es) and phone number(s).

2. The member's current membership category and dues status.

3. The full name of the client, the name and title of the art buyer and the relevant address(es) and phone number(s).

4. The exact job description.

5. The nature of the grievance, including a chronological narration of facts and the respective positions of the parties.

6. The names of other agencies and persons contacted in regard to the grievance, and the result of such contacts.

7. Copies, not originals, of relevant documents substantiating the grievance should accompany the grievance, i.e. agreement forms or purchase orders, invoices, correspondence, receipts, and so on.

The Committee's support cannot be claimed until the member is notified of such a decision formally. The Committee cannot communicate with the buyer if steps have been taken in the course of litigation.

Submitted grievances are reviewed by the Committee at its first opportunity. If it is determined that the grievance is justified, the Committee will contact the member. A plan of action will be recommended and such support or direct assistance provided as possible. It is crucial that the member participate fully and keep the Committee advised of subsequent developments.

The Grievance Committee cannot offer assistance in a dispute involving questionable professional conduct on the member's part. Such issues involve misrepresentation of talent, accepting work on speculation, plagiarism, or any violation of the Code of Fair Practice.

Arbitration & mediation

Arbitration and mediation are long-established processes for settling disputes privately and professionally. They involve the services of an impartial outside person to bring about a resolution.

In arbitration a person is asked to act as a judge, reviewing the facts presented by both sides—and then making a legally binding decision. In mediation the outside person is asked to act as an umpire—to guide artist and buyer in working out their own resolution. The mediator cannot make a legally binding decision. (If the parties do not reach an agreement they must then proceed to arbitration or court if they wish to obtain a binding determination.)

Both parties must agree in order to use these services. Arbitrators and mediators cannot summon the parties. Where the artist has an arbitration provision in the signed agreement, the buyer's consent, having thus already been given, is not necessary again. Should the buyer not appear for arbitration, a binding decision may be reached in the buyer's absence.

Arbitration and mediation are speedier and far less expensive than suing in formal court. Their conciliatory and private atmosphere may be more conducive to the artist who has had or anticipates a long business relationship with the buyer. These services may also be relevant where the artist's monetary claim is in excess of the small claims court's limit. Fees are usually moderate, consisting of a flat fee or a percentage of the monies claimed.

The Joint Ethics Committee, comprised of professional associations representing artists, art buyers and agents, including the Guild, has provided these services to the metropolitan New York City area for over 20 years. The JEC is not a collection agency; it deals with ethical issues only. This independent organization is unique to the industry as it's arbitrators and mediators are for the most part graphic art practitioners. A similar ethics committee is currently being organized in Los Angeles by local professional associations, including the Los Angeles Guild Chapter. A full discussion of the JEC appears on pages 36-39.

The American Arbitration Association is available in 24 cities around the country and services may be arranged for in other localities. Arbitration and mediation may also be sponsored by some of the volunteer arts-lawyer groups, including Volunteer Lawyers for the Arts in New York City and Bay Area Lawyers for the Arts in San Francisco.

Small claims court

Small claims courts give artists access

to the legal system, while avoiding the usual encumbrance, costs and lengthy duration of formal courts. The small claims procedure is streamlined, speedy and available for a very minimal fee.

Artists can handle their own cases with a little preparation. Information can be obtained from flyers prepared by the court, "how-to" publications and, best, from local rules books. The court clerk, or a legal advisor in some localities, is often available to help with preparation.

The artist can bring claims in which a monetary judgment is sought before the court. Such claims would include non-payment for completed or cancelled artwork (as well as non-payment for the original art, subsequent re-uses, or for unreturned or damaged art.)

Each court has a dollar limit for what it considers a "small claim." Amounts in excess of the limit would normally have to be brought to a formal court. However if the monies owed are only slightly in excess of the court's limit, a reduced amount that fits within the limit can be sued for. It must be made with the understanding that the balance is permanently forfeited. It may also be possible to split up larger amounts of owed monies into several smaller claims to be sued for individually. This can be done for distinctly separate legal claims.

Collection services

Collection alternatives, authorized by law, may be used by the artist who remains empty-handed despite a favorable arbitration or court decision. The failure to pay after the court has affirmed an arbitration award or rendered it's decision makes the buyer liable to further legal action not previously available to the artist.

When the buyer fails to pay, the artist gains the right, within limitations, to place a lien on the buyer's funds and assets. Available funds, such as bank accounts or a portion of an individual's salary, can then be seized by a sheriff or marshal and turned over to the artist. Similarly the proceeds of property or cars sold at a public auction may be used to settle the debt.

Commercial collection agencies are available to seek payment on the artist's behalf before an arbitration decision or judgment is obtained. Their efforts involve escalated demands on the buyer with letters and phone calls, possibly even visiting the buyer or using a lawyer.

Fees of collection agencies, in addition to their routine expenses, range from 20 percent to 50 percent of the monies actually recovered. If the artist has the agency engage a lawyer, an additional fee would most likely be required.

A signed agreement between the artist and the agency will be involved and should be reviewed carefully for actions the agency will take and the attendant costs. Particular care should be taken in dealing with a commercial agency that may use practices that could be deemed unprofessional since they may reflect unfavorably on the artist.

Consulting or hiring a lawyer

The services of a lawyer can assist in a number of ways and at different stages in the artist's collection strategy. Consulting with a lawyer about a problem at hand may provide the artist with sufficient information to continue his or her own efforts. The lawyer may be able to advise about available resources, chances for successful resolution, and legal matters to consider.

For simple payment-due problems a general practitioner or collection lawyer could be engaged. The lawyer's efforts would be similar to that of a collection agency. The psychological effect of receiving a lawyer's letter or call often produces a quick payment or brings other disputes to a conclusion.

If the nature of the dispute involves the artist's legal rights in and economic control over artwork, then a lawyer specializing in art matters should be selected. It is important that the lawyer be familiar with the applicable laws as well as the business aspects of the artist's profession.

When a dispute must be cleared up before payment can be made, engaging a lawyer to negotiate with the buyer might be helpful. The lawyer may be able to take a more forceful role on the artist's behalf and may bring about a fairer and quicker settlement. A lawyer's presence and negotiating skills may also result in avoiding a lawsuit. Where the problem is resolved, and it proves advisable, the lawyer could provide a written agreement to bring complex issues to a final and binding close.

Whether the problem relates to the nature of the rights involved or the amounts owed, the artist should, at the very least, arrange for an initial consultation. In this manner the artist can obtain a determination as to what the relevant law is and whether the artist's position is supportable under the law.

Lawyer's fees vary, and different arrangements exist from flat fees to a percentage of the monies recovered. Initial one-time consultation fees are often lower. Artists with specified limited income may well be able to take advantage of volunteer art-lawyer groups for their collection (as well as other legal) needs. These exist in or near the cities where there are Guild chapters, as well as in other cities around the country:

Georgia Volunteer Lawyers
     for the Arts
     32 Peachtree Street, N.W.
     Atlanta, GA 30303
     404/577-7378

Lawyers for the Creative Arts
     220 South State Street
     Chicago, IL 60604
     312/987-0198

Lawyers Committee for the Arts
     2700 Q Street, N.W., Suite 204
     Washington, DC 20007
     202/483-6777

Volunteer Lawyers and Accountants
     for the Arts
     1540 Sul Ross
     Houston, TX 77006
     713/526-4876

Los Angeles Lawyers for the Arts
     617 South Olive Street
     Los Angeles, CA 90014
     213/688-7404

Volunteer Lawyers for the Arts
     1560 Broadway, Suite 711
     New York, NY 10036
     212/575-1150

Philadelphia Volunteer Lawyers
     for the Arts
     260 South Broad Street
     Broad & Spruce Streets
     Philadelphia, PA 19102
     215/545-3385

San Diego Lawyers for the Arts
     7730 Herschel Avenue, Suite A
     La Jolla, CA 92037
     714/454-9696

Bay Area Lawyers for the Arts
     Fort Mason Center, Bldg. 310
     San Francisco, CA 94123
     415/775-7200

Suing in formal court

Bringing a suit in formal court is not normally necessary to resolve a payment or other dispute. Various alternatives, as already noted, are available to the artist and buyer for providing workable means for resolving most disputes.

Formal court should only be considered as a last resort when the buyer refuses to negotiate or does so unrealisticallly, leaving the artist with no other choice.

Claims in excess of the small claims court limit must be brought to formal court. Similarly non-monetary issues, such as copyright disputes or action required of the buyer, must also be taken to formal court.

The artist does not necessarily have to hire a lawyer in order to sue in formal court. The law provides for a person to appear as his or her own lawyer.

In disputes where the issue is clear, artists will usually not be prejudiced by representing themselves in court. In disputes not involving large sums of money, some lawyers will provide legal consultation to the artist on how to prepare the case. This alternative can benefit the artist by reducing legal costs.

Of course, where a great deal of money or complex legal issues are involved, it is prudent to hire a lawyer to handle the entire matter. In such event, the fees and expenses should be discussed with the lawyer at the outset. The artist will therefore be aware of what the monetary commitment will be before using a formal court.

Putting it into perspective

Preparation for the possibility of non-payment of fees is best made right at the beginning of the job. Written agreements should establish clearly the buyer's payment obligations as well as the conditions that would go into effect when payment is not made as agreed.

As the first step in the collection of fees the buyer should be contacted directly to ascertain the nature of the problem. This communication will also enable the artist, should it prove necessary, to determine which alternative recourses to pursue.

The services of an outside party, such as an arbitrator, (which should be provided for in the original agreement) or mediator, or the Guild's Grievance Committee, may assist the parties in achieving a resolution.

Should arbitration not be available or

the buyer prove uncooperative, the artist
may be required to use more forceful
alternatives.

The small claims court can provide an
inexpensive and speedy legal determination
for claims within its jurisdiction.

When payment is refused despite a
favorable arbitration decision or court judgment, the artist can use the services of a
sheriff or marshal.

Lawyers may be engaged at any stage
of the collection process, depending upon
the issues involved, to provide advice or full
representation.

Commercial collection agencies may
also be used to seek payment of fees in the
artist's behalf.

Establishing written safeguards early
can prevent payment problems as well as
provide the artist with practical alternatives.
These alternatives protect the artist's rights
and facilitate the collection of outstanding
fees; and *getting paid* is, of course, the just
entitlement of professional artists.

REFERENCE

On the Guild

The Graphic Artists Guild was formed as a union 15 years ago by a dozen professional illustrators to affect industry standards, practices and pricing. Today, most graphics professionals come together through the Guild to act in unison: sharing information, discussing problems in the industry and acting to improve the profession. This activity exists on both regional and national levels.

The Graphic Artists Guild brings a broad variety of artists together to work on contractual standards, pricing, artists rights legislation; and to communicate with their professional peers, allowing each member of the union to take advantage of the experiences of the group.

Member benefits established over the years range from lobbying on state and federal levels, publications on business standards and practices; pricing guidelines, educational seminars and workshops, and group health, life and disability insurance plans.

From its beginning among a small group of professional artists in the Detroit area, the Guild has grown to include 5,000 artists from all over the country, in every professional discipline. Regional chapters now exist in New York, Atlanta, Baltimore, Boston, Buffalo, Colorado, Indianapolis, Los Angeles, and Burlington, Vermont.

Each chapter meets frequently to develop and run programs for its members, discuss industry issues, establish regional goals, and keep up membership contact. The National meets monthly to establish national goals, assess programs and projects that affect all members, and to update board members on regional activities. Twice a year the full National board, including regional representatives, meets for updates on activities, review of national programs, and to decide on future projects for the Guild. It's this constant communication on local and national levels that keeps the Guild close to its membership and aware of what's happening in the industry.

From the start, the Guild has reached out to other creative professionals and their organizations to form coalitions on issues of mutual concern. The first creator's coalition was formed in 1976 around an issue of copyright control. That coalition has since grown to include 42 creators' organizations that represent fine artists, photographers, journalists, and freelance writers, among others. In the past three years the coalition has been active lobbying for an amendment to the copyright law that will eliminate instances in which work for hire can be used. The "work-for-hire" coalition is the first time that creators from all areas of the arts have joined together on a legislative issue.

As we heard more from our members about problems of artwork that had been altered by clients, retention of originals by clients when only reproduction rights had been sold, and the problems of the work-for-hire clause, the Guild's lobbying efforts began to grow.

On a state level, the Guild began working in New York and California on the Moral Rights and Fair Practices bills. Moral Rights allows an artist legal recourse when a creative work has been defaced, altered or mutilated by a client, to the detriment of the creator's reputation or work. The act also allows creators to claim or disclaim authorship for the work in those instances. A version of this law was passed in California in 1982, and the Moral Rights Act was signed into law by New York's Governor Mario Cuomo in August 1983.

The Fair Practices act, signed into law in N.Y. in 1983, was the result of four years of lobbying by the Guild. It provides that the original artwork remains the property of the artist unless it is specifically sold in writing. Further, any ambiguity in the language of a contract results in the presumption of ownership rights remaining with the artist. Since most graphic artists make at least part of their livelihoods on the resale of reproduction rights and additionally, by the sale of the original art, this law is critical to the economic survival of our members.

The Guild went to Washington in 1979 to give an indepth presentation on graphic design for the Copyright Office. Our representatives presented an extensive visual and verbal analysis that showed how most graphic design is a form of creative expression worthy of copyright protection. As a result, the Copyright Office reassessed its interpretation of graphic design for the purposes of copyright law. Graphic designers are now vested with the same status that is applied to illustrators, photographers and fine artists.

Other national lobbying activity includes the effort to amend the work-for-hire provision of the copyright law. The provision allows a client, in certain specific instances, to become the creator of the work he/she commissions for the purposes of the copyright law. Through work for hire, a client can buy a piece of art, claim authorship, alter or reuse it in any way without the approval of the original creator of the piece. In October 1982, the U.S. Senate, urged by the Graphic Artists Guild, held a hearing on the issue. Legislation to amend the work-for-hire provision is expected to be introduced in Congress in the near future.

The Guild offers an educational program available to members and non-members alike, including business schools active in each regional chapter. Seminars and workshops are held on subjects such as: negotiating, self-promotion techniques, running a freelance business, new technologies and other business-related issues. Additionally, the Guild publishes model contracts and forms, and books on pricing and ethical issues.

Most rewarding for the Guild and its members is our activity on a more philosophical level. As a guild, we work together to cultivate the *respect, support* and *dignity* that we all deserve as professionals. And as professionals, we all understand our responsibilities to promote the highest level of professionalism in our industry.

The Guild is totally egalitarian. Our constitution states that we will accept any working professional graphic artist as a voting member, "regardless of race, gender or belief." We found that we attract the most gifted artists, since they are the ones who recognize most readily the need to protect their professional integrity and their art.

Good Works

Good Works is the job referral service of the Graphic Artists Guild. Formed in response to members' needs, Good Works operates on several levels; its functions include matching client job needs with a number of artists whose skills and styles are appropriate; providing artists with help in portfolio presentation; interview techniques, pricing, and resources for self-promotion; and tracking market trends and seasonal changes in industry conditions, as well as providing overviews of pricing and contract standard fluctuations.

When a client calls Good Works, the job is registered with a clear description of skills and styles desired, budget, deadline and contract provisions. Good Works then searches its files to find three to ten artists who meet the client's criteria. The artists are contacted and referred to the client with all the job specifications. This provides both client and artist with enough information to hold a productive first negotiation. At this point, both parties are able to establish a working professional relationship based on a value-for-value exchange. In fact, many of Good Works' one-time referrals develop into long-term associations between satisfied client and artist.

Good Works remains available to work with both parties in facilitating the best working situation if necessary; however, once the referral is made, the continued relationship is between client and artist.

As a program of the Guild, Good Works operates within and supports ethical standards and practices and the Code of Fair Practice of the Joint Ethics Committee (refer to page 36).

For the client, Good Works' pre-screening allows for portfolio review prior to interviewing an artist, saves time in searching through inappropriate books, and saves money, since the service is *free* to clients.

For artists, Good Works offers entry into the market for beginning professionals, an additional source of clients for established professionals, and help in structuring portfolios, interview techniques, resumes, pricing and self-promotion. An artist may come to Good Works for a portfolio review, register for the job service, and discuss contractual terms. Because Good Works does initial screening on clients, artists who are referred have the best information on the job and the client. Good Works also encourages clients to adhere to standard business practices and pricing according to Graphic Artists Guild guidelines.

Further information about Good Works' services is available through the Graphic Artists Guild, or you may call Good Works directly at (212) 677-6607. Deborah Kaufman, Executive Director.

More Guild resources

Protecting Your Heirs & Creative Works, edited by Tad Crawford

An estate planning guide for artists, authors, composers, and other creators of artistic works written in clear, easy-to-understand language.

Focusing on estate planning, wills, charitable bequests, and the role of a legal advisor, this book includes many interesting case histories to provide a wealth of information. One copy is free with Guild membership. Additional copies are available to members at $4.50 each. Non-members may purchase this book at $6.95 per copy, or $4.50 per copy for orders of 10 or more.

The Visual Artists Guide to the New Copyright Law, by Tad Crawford

Written expressly for the Guild, this book explains the benefits for artists under the generally favorable provisions of the federal copyright law, which took effect on January 1, 1978. It carefully explains the law's pitfalls, especially the "work-for-hire" provision, which leaves the artist without any rights to his/her work. You can find out what is copyrightable, what the benefits of copyright work are, how to display copyright notice, advantages of group registration, special rules for selling to magazines, and the meaning of "fair use." Also included are sample forms with helpful directions. All members of the Graphic Artists Guild receive one free copy with membership. Additional copies are available to members at $3.50 each. Non-members may purchase the book at $5.95 per copy, or $3.50 per copy for orders of ten or more.

To Order:

Please specify the publications and number of copies you wish to order. All orders must be pre-paid. Add $1.50 per book for postage and handling. New York residents add applicable sales tax. Allow 4-6 weeks for delivery. Address your order to:

Graphic Artists Guild
30 East 20th Street
New York, NY 10003
Attn: Publications

Graphic Artists Guild Foundation

The Graphic Artists Guild Foundation was formed in 1983 to "foster, promote and advance greater knowledge, appreciation and understanding of the graphic arts. . . (by) the presentation and creation of the graphic arts, activities designed to promote, aid and advance the study of existing work, and to promote the creation, presentation and dissemination of new works; to sponsor workshops, training sessions, symposia, lectures and other educational endeavors."

Further, the Foundation's constitution states among its goals, "to help monitor and establish rules governing industry practices and to contribute to modifying these when necessary."

The Foundation receives grants and donations to conduct studies whose information will benefit the industry, the public and the arts in general. It is presently involved in a two-year study of art contests and competitions in the United States in order to assess the nature of contests and competitions and to develop a set of ethical guidelines and standards for those activities. This study is funded in part by a matching grant from the National Endowment for the Arts. Please refer to page 47 for more information.

The Graphic Artists Guild Foundation is a 501 (c) 3 organization. The Board of Directors includes: Simms Taback, president; Jeff Seaver, treasurer; Elizabeth Cook, vice-president; and Joel Hecker, Esq.

The arts professions: what we know, what we don't know.

According to the Bureau of Labor Statistics (BLS), 1,055,000 artists were employed in 1982, out of a total artists labor force of 1,129,000. The artist population increased by 9,000 in 1982, indicating a drop in growth compared with the last decade when the number of persons in the arts professions nearly double (there were 697,000 artists in 1971).

Unemployment was up for artists and reached 6.6 percent, a figure comparable to the peak unemployment figures for the 1973-75 recession years. Unemployment among *all* professional and technical workers (including artists) was only 3.3 percent, so artists as a group had doubled the average unemployment rate.

Who are "artists"?

The U.S. Bureau of Census uses the term *artist* to include the following occupations: actors; architects; dancers; designers; musicians and composers; painters and sculptors; photographers; radio and television announcers; teachers of art, drama and music in higher education; other artists not elsewhere classified.

There are 223,000 designers and 219,000 painters and sculptors according to the government figures. These are the two largest occupational groups. 106,000 photographers make up the fourth largest group.

Who are "designers"?

In the classified index of the Census, more specific occupations are listed under "designers": art director; graphic designer; layout artist; textile designer; display designer; package designer; interior designer. It also includes fashion designer, jewelry designer, industrial designer and set designer in this list.

Who are "painters & sculptors"?

Under the sub-occupation category for "painters and sculptors" are listed the following: cartoonist; catalogue illustrator; commercial artist; editorial cartoonist; fashion illustrator; free-lance artist; graphic artist; historical illustrator; illustrator; layout and paste-up artist; layout artist; layout man; medical artist; medical illustrator; newspaper illustrator; pattern illustrator; scientific artist; scientific illustrator; sports cartoonist; visualizer.

The classified census index also lists painters, sculptor, stained-glass artist and necktie painter!

We have met the artists and they are us

Surprisingly enough, specialty occupations listed under Painters/Sculptors, though at first confusing, are mostly graphic and commercial art specialties, not fine artists as the title would suggest. Furthermore, almost *all* the specialties under "Designers" are commercial art or commercial art-related occupations. These two groups comprise a very large number of commercial artists, and with photographers, total about 36 percent of the total artist labor force.

Women artists

The percent of women in the total artist labor force increased noticeably to 1/3 female, resulting from a great number of women entering the arts professions in the 70's and women artists now outnumber men in the Painters/Sculptors category according to the 1980 Census. The proportion of female photographers is about 25 percent, a growth of about 10 percent over the decade preceding this census.

Employment and unemployment

According to the BLS, the unemployment rate for the three groups of commercial artists (Designers, painters/sculptors, photographers) averaged about 5.3 percent in 1982. But while the number of employed photographers and painters/sculptors has declined, the number of employed designers has steadily increased.

The largest unemployed group are actors—reaching nearly 40 percent during this same period.

The questions are the problem

Data collected on artists' occupations have some important limitations. Most important for us is that no specific figures are available for the number of people employed and unemployed in the graphic arts and related communications field.

Survey questions, for example, identify only the primary occupation of an individual. We are all aware that artists often work simultaneously in other occupations to support their income and are, therefore, not counted in the statistical studies as artists unless more time was devoted to art than the second occupation. Generally the figures do not reflect this high degree of self-employment.

Sometimes no occupational code exists for a certain discipline (i.e., photo-retoucher), therefore, no estimate for this population group can be ascertained.

The data does not include people with art skills who work for little or no pay in order to gain experience and it also does not include those *not* seeking active employment because of poor training or job market factors. Many artists get stuck at the entry level since getting the first job can be a real hurdle.

How many artists work?

The 1984/85 edition of the Occupational Outlook Handbook (published by the Bureau of Labor Statistics) estimates that graphic artists held 132,000 permanent and free-lance jobs in 1982. However, this is not consistent with other figures published by the BLS which would suggest that more like 210,000 are employed at various graphic art and graphic art-related jobs. There are, perhaps, as many as 40,000 other artists seeking employment, or who are "discouraged workers" (i.e. have stopped looking for employment because of the lack of jobs).

What's ahead

The projection of growth by BLS is "about as fast as average for all occupations" as the communications field continues to expand into the 1990's. The supply of applicants seeking to enter the field, however, will continue to exceed the need.

Sources:
Report #16, Artist Employment and Unemployment, 1971-1980,
National Endowment for the Arts, Washington, D.C.

Research Division Note, January 24, 1983, Artist
Employment in 1982, National Endowment for the Arts, Washington, D.C.
Professional Specialty Occupations, 1980 Classified Index,
U.S. Department of Labor.

U.S. Census, 1980

U.S. Census 1970

© 1983 Simms Taback

Glossary

accessories, clothing: Hat, gloves, shoes or slippers, jewelry, socks, belt, suspenders, necktie, collar, cuffs, scarf, umbrella, hair decorations, apron, handbag, tote, etc.

accessories, home furnishings: Floral arrangement, basket, lamp, coat hanger, storage box, garment bag, shoe organizer, drying towel, pot holder, shower curtain, tissue cover, toilet lid cover, bolster, pillow, cushion, door stop, book ends, frame, appliance cover, laundry bag, etc. (*Note:* Some home accessories can overlap as novelties.)

account executive: A representative of an advertising agency who handles specific accounts and acts as a client liaison to the art director, creative director, and others creating advertising for the account. Pejorative synonym: *a suit.*

adult clothing: Clothing in sizes for teengirls, teenboys, misses', miss petite, junior, junior petite, women's, half-sizes, and men's.

advance: An amount paid prior to the commencement of work or in the course of work. It may be to cover expenses or it may be partial payment of the total fee. An advance as partial payment is common for a time-consuming project.

advance on royalties *or* **advance payment against royalties:** An amount paid prior to actual sales of the commissioned item or work; sometimes paid in installments. Advances are generally not expected to be returned, even if unearned in sales. Both the terms and the size of the advance are negotiable.

afghan: A small blanket, sometimes called a nap blanket, designed for use by one person. It can be formed in a variety of techniques, such as crochet, knitting, weaving, etc.

agreement: See *contract.*

all rights: The purchase of all rights of usage for reproduction of an art work forever.

animator: An artist who is responsible for articulation of characters' movements.

applique *or* **applied work:** To apply or stitch one layer of fabric over another so that the applied pieces form a motif. See also *reverse applique.*

art director: One whose responsibilities include the selection of talent, purchase of visual work, and the supervision of the quality and character of visual work. Usually an employee of the advertising agency, publishing house, magazine, or other user of the graphic artist's work, although some organizations hire freelance art directors to perform these duties.

art staff: A group of artists working for a company such as an advertising agency, publisher, magazine, or large design studio and under art director supervision.

artwork: Any finished work of a graphic artist.

assistant animator: Cleans up the animator's drawings according to a model sheet and does in-betweens. In some larger studios the assistants solely do the clean-up work.

author's alterations (AAs) *or* **author's corrections (ACs):** Alterations or corrections of type that has been set due to the client's errors, additions, or deletions. The typographer's or printer's charges for making AAs are usually passed on to the client. See also *printer's error.*

background: One who paints backgrounds which have already been designed.

bailment: An obligation on the part of the individual(s) with whom art is left to take reasonable care of it. This is a legal requirement and applies to situations such as leaving a portfolio for review.

basketry: The art of forming baskets from wood, reeds, yarns, etc., by weaving, braiding, coiling, or other techniques.

bedspread: The final or top cover for a bed of any size, primarily used for decorative purposes. See also *quilt.*

blanket: A layer of bedclothing placed over the top sheet and under the bedspread, used primarily for warmth. See also *quilt.*

bleed: A small extra area on the exterior dimensions of a page to allow for trimming. Also called "trim" area; the printing that runs into this area.

braiding: To plait together strands of yarn or strips of fabric to form a larger ply to be coiled and sewn together flat or dimensionally to make rugs, mats, baskets, etc.

buy-out (*n*) buy o Payment of such a large fee that sale of a   s, and sometimes the original art, is agreed to by the artist. Usu ly used in advertising.

camera-ready art *or* **camera copy:** Usually a mechanical or pasteup accompanied with finished art that is prepared for photographing for platemaking.

cancellation fee: When a project is terminated or not used by the client, this fee is paid as compensation for the artist's or studio's effort in developing the illustration or design.

cartoonist: A professional artist who creates art in a humorous and satirical style and/or as political commentary.

castoff: To provide a breakdown or estimate of length. In knitting, to put stitches on a knitting needle. In publishing, to estimate the typeset length or number of pages from manuscript or galley proof. In textiles, sometimes used as a synonym for knock-off; refers to a pattern or design that a company wishes to alter for a new pattern while retaining similarity to the original.

cel: Short for celluloid. A transparent sheet of celluloid on which the finished drawings are inked.

center truck: The center page spread in a magazine or newspaper which is a premium space for the placement of advertisements.

children's clothing: Sizes pertaining to boys and girls from toddlers to teens.

Chromalin proofs: A proprietary term for a color proof process employing a photosensitized clear plastic. Color separation film negatives are exposed to the plastic in such a way that process color will adhere to dots on the plastic. Four sheets (one for each process color) are exposed, treated with the separate process colors, placed in register, and then laminated. Such proofs are used for presentations and for checking register, obvious blemishes, and size. The color may be very accurate but is subject to variation due to exposure and the application of the process color. Also *transfer key.* See also *Color Key* and *progressive proofs.*

chrome: See *transparency.*

Cibachrome: A proprietary term for a full-color positive photographic print made from a transparency.

client accommodation: To work at fees below the normal rate in order to accommodate budgetary restrictions and to preserve a long-term working relationship.

Color Key: A proprietary term of the 3M Company; sometimes referred to as "3Ms." A method for obtaining separate film positives showing progressive color breakdown of the color separation negatives. Such proofs are useful for presentations and for checking register, obvious blemishes, and size; they are not a true indication of final printed color. *Chromalin* proofs are preferred for more accurate (though still not exact) color representation. *Progressive proofs* using process inks on press are the most accurate method for checking color. See also *Chromalin proofs* and *progressive proofs.*

color proofs: The first full-color printed pieces pulled off the press for approval before the press is considered ready to roll for the entire press run. Sometimes called *simple color proofs,* these proofs are useful for making corrections in color on press, particularly for those problems resulting from improper registration and the effects of overprinting. *Progressive proofs* are the preferred methods for accurately checking color.

commission (*n*) commission (*v*): Percentage of a fee paid by an artist to the artist's agent or gallery for service provided or business transacted. The act of giving an artist an assignment to create a work of art.

comprehensive *or* comp: A visualization of the idea for an illustration or design usually created for the client and artist to use as a guide for the finished art. *Tight comp* or *loose comp* refers to the degree of detail, rendering, and general accuracy used in the comprehensive. art direction, illustrations and book, book jacket, and

confirmation form: A contract form that is used by an artist when no purchase order has been given or when the purchase order is incomplete with respect to important terms of the

contract, such as amount of fee, rights transferred, etc.

contract: An agreement whether oral or written, whereby two parties bind themselves to perform certain obligations. Synonyms: *agreement* or *letter of agreement* (if the contract takes the form of a letter).

converter: A company that transfers designs onto printed or woven fabric.

copy: The text of an advertisement, editorial content of a magazine or a newspaper, or the text of a book.

copyright: The right to copy or authorize the copying of creative work. Any free-lance artist creating artwork automatically owns the right of that work unless provisions have been made prior to the commencement of the project to transfer the copyright to the buyer.

corners: A type of layout for specific textile designs in which a single layout of a complete corner is used for the repeated design on all four corners. Commonly used in home furnishings (e.g., the design for the corners of a tablecloth, napkin, or scarf).

C print *or* inter neg: A full-color positive print from a negative transparency.

creative director: Usually an employee or officer of an advertising agency whose responsibilities may include overall supervision of all aspects of the character and quality of the agency's work for its clients. The creative director's background may be art, copy, or client contact.

crochet: A method of making a lace or a textile structure from any yarn, fabric strip, or stringy material with a hook, using the chain stitch or variations on the chain to form the textile.

croques: Rough sketches made by an artist, particularly by fashion illustrators.

design brief: An analysis of a project prepared either by the publisher or the designer. When the designer assumes this responsibility it should be reflected in the design fee. The design brief may include: (1) a copy of the manuscript, with a selection of representative copy for sample pages and a summary of all typographical problems, copy areas, code marks, etc; (2) an outline of the publisher's manufacturing program for the book: compositor and composition method, printer and paper stock, binder and method of binding; (3) a description of the proposed physical characteristics of the book, such as trim size, page length, list price, quantity of first printing, and whether the book will print in one color or more than one. The publisher should so indicate whether any particular visual style is expected.

director: One who oversees the complete picture from conception to finish. Has complete control over all phases: character design (which is usually supplied by an agency), layout, sound, etc.

dummy: A book, brochure, or catalog idea in a roughly drawn form usually made up to contain the proper number of pages and used as a reference for positioning, pagination, and imposition.

dye transfer: Similar in appearance to a color photograph but different in the important respect that it is produced from a transparency by printing continuous tones of color dyes.

embroidery: A general term referring to decorating the surface of any fabric with free-formed stitches that are based on plain sewing. For example: embroidery with wool or a wool-like yarn on fabric is called *crewel embroidery;* embroidery with cotton yarn is called *cotton* or *floss embroidery.* Stitches and fabric vary according to the will of the designer. Also *counted embroidery:* the formation of regimented stitches on even-weave fabrics or on needlepoint canvas known by various names which denote their style of stitches (e.g., hardanger, black work, drawn thread work). *Cross stitch embroidery:* can be either free-formed embroidery over Xs printed on the fabric or counted embroidery worked on an even-weave fabric or canvas.

employee, free-lance: Terms of free-lance employment include: work hours determined by assignment using one's own workspace and materials; free-lancers generally provide their own benefits. The free-lancer often collects state sales tax from clients and pays his or her own income taxes.

employee, regular: Terms of regular employment include: the imposition of normal working hours; workspace on the employer's premises using the employer's equipment and materials under the employer's supervision. The employer generally provides the regular employee with health insurance, workman's and unemployment compensation and pays one-half of his or her social security and withholding taxes. Other compensations such as vacation pay, sick pay, pensions, and educational benefits, are negotiated with the employer.

engineered design: A pattern specifically designed to fit certain size factors and to be repeated in a particular fashion (e.g., panel print to fit a Tressi blouse or dress design).

engraver *or* **photoengraver:** One who makes plates or film negatives by the photoengraving process in preparation for printing the finished artwork.

finished art: Usually an illustration, photograph, or mechanical that is prepared and ready for the engraver or printer.

first North American serial rights: The right to be the first magazine to publish art for use in one specific issue to be distributed in North America.

first rights: The right to be the first user of art for one-time use; frequently used to describe the right to publish art in a magazine serial or drawn from a book in which the art will appear.

floor covering: Any textile structure or painting technique that is used to cover a floor partially or completely for either decorative or functional purposes.

format: An arrangement of type and illustration that is used for many layouts; an arrangement used in a series.

Fortune double-500 company: The *Fortune* magazine's annual listing based on sales revenues of the 1000 largest corporations in the United States.

general apprentice: One who does a little of everything except camera work.

graphic artist: Any visual artist working in a commercial area.

graphic designer: A professional graphic artist who works with the elements of typography, illustration, photography, and printing to create commercial communications tools such as brochures, advertising, signage, posters, slide shows, book jackets, and other forms of printed or graphic communications. A visual problem solver.

graphic film artist: One who is skilled in creating special effects on film by use of computerized stands, mattes, and/or adding computerized movement to artwork (e.g., television logos with glows, set movement).

graphics: Visual communications.

group head: Some advertising agencies divide their clients into groups under a group head who supervises the work of art directors on the various accounts.

guild: An association of like-minded professionals seeking to protect and better their status and/or skills. When employees are members in equal proportion to free-lancers, such a guild qualifies with the United States government as a union. In this capacity, a guild may represent employees who are its members in collective bargaining.

gutter: The area in a magazine, newspaper, or book, where the left (verso) and right (recto) pages meet. Important elements are often not placed in this area because of the fold.

half-body garments: A garment that is worn either from the waist up or from the waist down, such as a vest, sweater, poncho, pants, skirt, etc.

hand letterer: A professional artist who creates letterforms for use in logotypes, alphabets, and specific titles or captions.

hard furniture: Any furniture that requires the designer to use a hard substance such as wood, metal, etc. for structural support or decorative purposes. It may also incorporate padding and a textile surface.

illustrator: A professional graphic artist who communicates a pictorial idea by creating a visual image using paint, pencil, pen, collage, or any other graphic technique except photography for a specific purpose.

image: A pictorial idea.

inbetweener: One who does the drawings in between the drawings that have been cleaned up by the assistant.

infant clothing: Refers to newborn and baby sizes up to toddler sizes. needleart design

inker: One who inks in onto cels the lines of finished drawings.

invoice: A statement given to a client showing the amount due on an assignment. Usually submitted after work has been completed unless advance payments are to be made. When advance payments are made, the invoice should reflect these and show the balance due.

jacquard sketches: A sketch usually done on graph paper to be used on jacquard woven fabrics such as tablecloths, upholstery, and towels.

junior checker (paint and ink only): One who inspects cels for the proper and thorough application of the correct paint colors.

key line artist: A sometimes pejorative term for a mechanical or pasteup artist.

kickback: A sum of money or a large gift that is given to an artist by a supplier for the artist's part in passing on work such as printing. Kickbacks are illegal. Quite often the supplier's kickback costs are hidden in its invoices submitted to the client for work completed.

knitting: The method of forming a lace or a textile structure from any yarn, fabric strip, or stingy material with two or more eyeless needles, pegged tools, or sticks, etc. using various looped stitches to form the structure.

knock-off (*n*) **knock off** (*v*): A term most often used in the textile design industry to identify a design that at the request of the client or stylist has been copied by a different artist than the one who created it. Broadly used to mean the copying of an artist's style or artwork when no creative input and/or significant changes are made by the artist in creating the knock-off. Knock-offs are unethical and often illegal.

lace: A general term for any openwork or sheer fabric with holes formed by any technique, including knitting, crochet, bobbin lace, netting, hairpin lace, tatting, eyelet, needle lace, etc.

latch hook: A method of knotting short or long lengths of yarn over crosswise threads of a rug canvas with a latch hook tool. The technique is generally used for rug making, pillows, and wall hangings.

layette: A coordinated ensemble for the newborn consisting of a receiving blanket, cap, jacket, and booties.

layout: The design, usually in sketch form, of the elements of an advertisement, magazine or book page, or any other graphic work (e.g., brochures, catalogs, etc.) intended for reproduction. Used as a guide and usually executed by an art director or illustration graphic designer.

layout: An artist who lays out and arranges backgrounds.

letterforms: Any forms that are made out of letters, numerals, or ampersands.

letter of agreement: See *contract.*

live area: The area on the camera copy of a page or a publication beyond which essential elements should not be positioned.

logo: A mark or symbol created for an individual, company, or product that translates the impression of the body it is representing into a graphic image.

logotype: Any alphabetical configuration that is designed to identify by name a product, company, publication, or individual.

lucey: One of several optical devices used to enlarge or reduce images.

macrame: A method of ornamental knotting for cords and yarns, generally used to form fringes, hammocks, wall hangings, plant holders, etc.

markup (*n*) **mark up** (*v*): A service charge added to expense account items to reimburse the artist for the time to process the billing of such items to the client and the cost of advancing the money to pay such expenses; the process of adding such a charge.

markers: Felt-tipped pens used in a technique for illustrating comprehensives or for sketching a rough in black and white or color. Proprietary synonyms: *Magic Markers, Stabilo.*

mechanical: Ruled and pasted flats or boards composed by a production artist for the printer to use in the printing and engraving process.

moonlighting: A free-lance commission taken on by a salaried person to be completed in the person's spare time.

needlepoint *or* **canvas work:** The formation of regimented stitches over the meshes or threads of a special open-weave fabric called canvas.

novelties: A general term for gift or boutique-type items or for clever decorative or functional items such as eyeglass, comb, or mirror case; Christmas decorations (stockings, tree skirt, ornaments, etc.); calendar; clock; cosmetic bag; jewelry bag; typewriter cover; golf bag and club covers; exercise or beach mat, etc. Also, wax transfer patterns for embroidery or applique motifs. (*Note:* some novelties can overlap as home accessories.)

opaque projector: A projector that uses reflected light to project the image of a nontransparent object onto a canvas, board, or screen; the image is then used by an artist to copy or show work.

overhead: Nonbillable expenses such as rent, phone, insurance, secretarial and accounting services, and salaries.

page makeup: Assembling in sequence the typographic and/or illustrative elements of a brochure, catalog, book, or similar item.

pasteup (*n*): Usually reproduction copy of galley type fastened in position with wax or glue by a production artist for the use of the engraver in the platemaking process. Also, *paste-up (adj.)* and *paste up (v)*.

patchwork: Piecing, sewing, or joining together pieces of fabric to form motifs or a complete fabric structure. Generally, the pieces are cut in planned shapes. When shapes are unplanned or take on a helter-skelter appearnce, it is called *crazy patchwork* or *crazy quilt.*

per diem: A day rate given to a professional by a client to complete a day's assignment.

portfolio *or* **artist's book:** Reproductions and/or originals that represent the body of an artist's work.

preplanner/checker: One who checks that the animation is in sync and flows correctly (before camera).

printer's error (PE): A mistake made in the film negatives, platemaking, or printing that is not due to the client's error, addition, or deletion. These alterations are normally absorbed by the printer or typographer. See also *author's alterations.*

production artist: A professional artist who works with a designer in taking a layout through to mechanicals, pasteups, and often on through the printing process.

production coordinator: One who is responsible for making sure that everything is in order before it goes under the camera.

professional: One who strives for excellence in busines and follows fair practices in every professional endeavor.

profit: The difference remaining (i.e., net income) after overhead, expenses, and taxes are subtracted from income received (gross income).

progressive proofs *or* **progs:** Proofs of color separation negatives that have been exposed to offset plates and printed using process inks. Presented in the sequence of printing, i.e., (1) yellow plate alone, (2) red alone, (3) yellow and red, (4) blue alone, (5) yellow, red, and blue, (6) black alone, and (7) yellow, red, blue, and black. The preferred way for checking the color of the separation negatives using the same inks, paper, ink densities, and color sequence as intended for the production run. See also *color proofs.*

proposal *or* **estimate:** A graphic designer's detailed analysis of the cost and components of a project. Used to firm up an agreement before commencing work on a project for a client.

punch needle: Refers to both a fine, delicate embroidery technique (fine yarns or threads and fine fabrics and needles) and to a heavy rug technique (using heavy yarns and coarse fabrics and needles) where loops of varying lengths are formed on the surface of the fabric by pushing a handled-needle through the fabric from the wrong side. Fine versions are generally used for decorations on clothing or home accesories; coarser versions for chair cushions, mats, rugs, and wall hangings.

purchase order: A form given by a client to an artist describing the details of an assignment and when signed by an authorized person, authorizing work to commence.

quilt: A bedcovering that functions as both a blanket and/or a bedspread that consists of two fabric layers, one placed above and the other below a filling layer. The filling can be a non-woven layer of cotton or polyester batting or a woven fabric such as flannel. Small hand running stitches, machine stitches, or yarn tufts formed through all layers over the item produce the quilted structure and design. Also, the quilted structure can be used as a technique to produce clothing and other decorative or functional items.

readers: Copies with type prepared for the author or client to proofread and mark corrections on. They are nonreproduction quality and their value is only in checking corrections.

ready-made: Refers to clothing or fabric that was purchased in a store or available to the designer at the stage when it could have been purchased at retail.

reel: A film or number of films spliced together.

reference file: File compiled by an illustrator or designer made up of clippings from newspapers, magazines, and other printed pieces that are referred to for ideas and inspiration as well as technical information.

repeat: The textile design process by which consecutive press impressions may be made to but together imperceptibly so that the textile will appear as one consecutive image and the press run may be continued indefinitely.

representative *or* **rep:** A professional agent who promotes specific talent in illustration, photography, or textile design and negotiates contracts for fees and commissions. Usually receives a percentage of the negotiated fee as payment for the services provided to the talent.

reprint rights: The right to print something that has been published elsewhere.

reproduction copy *or* **repro:** Proofs printed in the best possible quality for use as camera copy for reproduction. Also *reproduction proof.*

residuals: Payments received in addition to the original fee, usually for extended usage of a work. See also *royalty.*

retoucher: A professional artist who alters a photograph to improve or change it for reproduction. Usually working on transparencies, or color or black-and-white prints.

reverse applique *or* **cut-through applique:** When two or more layers of fabric are handled together, with the upper layer(s) cut away and stitched separately in order to reveal the under layer(s) and thus form a motif.

roughs: Loosely drawn ideas, often done in pencil on tracing paper, by an illustrator or designer. Usually several roughs are sketched out before a comprehensive is developed from them.

royalty: Payments to the artist that are based on a percentage of the revenue generated through the quantity of items sold (e.g., books, cards, calendars). See also *advance on royalties.*

sales tax: Each state government establishes the rate of taxation of items sold. It varies between 4 and 8 percent of the amount billed the client, which the free-lance graphic artist is often required to be licensed to charge, collect, and remit to the state on a quarterly basis.

second rights: The right to use art that has appeared elsewhere. Frequently applied to use by magazines of art that has appeared previously in a book or another magazine.

shoot (*v*)**:** In advertising, a day's filming or a day's shooting of still photography.

simultaneous rights: The right to publish art at the same time as another publication. Normally used when the two publications have markets that do not overlap.

sizing: The process of marking an original with a percentage or a multiplier for reduction or enlargement on camera.

sketch: design for textiles not done in repeat. See also *roughs.*

soft furniture: Any furniture that uses *only* a soft filling such as batting, foam pellets, etc. to form the inner structure.

soft sculpture: A decorative dimensional item formed from fabrics or in one of the many textile structures which is stuffed with a soft filling.

speculation: Accepting assignments without any guarantee of payment after work has been completed. Payment upon publication is also speculation.

spine: The area between the front and back book bindings and on which the author, title, and publisher are indicated.

spot: A small drawing or illustration used as an adjunct to other elements in an advertisement, editorial, or book page.

spot: A television commercial.

stenciling: A method of painting on a surface using a template and a stiff bristle brush with a blunt end.

storyboards: A series of sketches drawn by artists in small scale to a television screen and indicating camera angles, type of shot (e.g., close-up-, extreme close-up), backgrounds, etc. Essentially a plan for shooting a commercial for television; often accompanied by announcer's script and actor's lines.

storyboards: Sketches of action for animation. Synonyms: *story* or *story sketches.*

studio: The place where an artist works. Also an organization offering a complete graphic service. In textile design, an agency representing designs by more than one textile designer.

style: A particular artist's unique form of expression; also referred to as "a look." In textile design referred to as "hand."

subsidiary rights: In publishing, those rights not granted to the publisher but which the publisher has the right to sell to third parties in which case the proceeds are shared with the artist.

tablewear: Functional items that are used at the dining room or kitchen table, such as placemat, napkin, napkin ring, runner, tea cozy, hot pad, tablecloth, coaster, etc.

talent: A group of artists represented by an agent or gallery.

technique: Refers to the particular media used by a graphic artist.

textbook: In book publishing, applies to any book that is to be sold through schools and used for educational purposes.

textile designer: A professional artist who creates art usually to be used in repeat on surfaces such as fabric, wallpaper, wovens, or ceramics.

thumbnail: *or* **thumbnail sketch:** A very small, often sketchy visualization of an illustration or design. Usually several thumbnails are created together to show different approaches to the visual problem being solved.

trade book: In book publishing, applies to any book that is to be sold in bookstores to the general public.

transparency *or* **chrome:** A full-color translucent photographic film positive. Color slides are also referred to as transparencies.

union: The correct legal term for a group of people in the same profession and working to monitor and upgrade the business standards of their industry.

weaving: A method of interlacing yarns or any stringy material in both a lengthwise and crosswise manner simultaneously. A traditional loom is generally used to control the interlacing technique, but other devices may also be used.

whole-body garments: Any one-piece garment worn from the neck and stopping anywhere below mid-thigh, such as dresses, coats, capes, etc.

workbook: In book publishing, applies to any book accompanying a textbook, usually in the elementary school level, for students to complete exercises in by following written and pictorial instructions.

work-for-hire: For copyright purposes, "work-for-hire" or similar expressions such as "done-for-hire" or "for hire" signify that the commissioning party is the owner of the copyright in the artwork as if the commissioning party had, in fact, been the artist.

Index